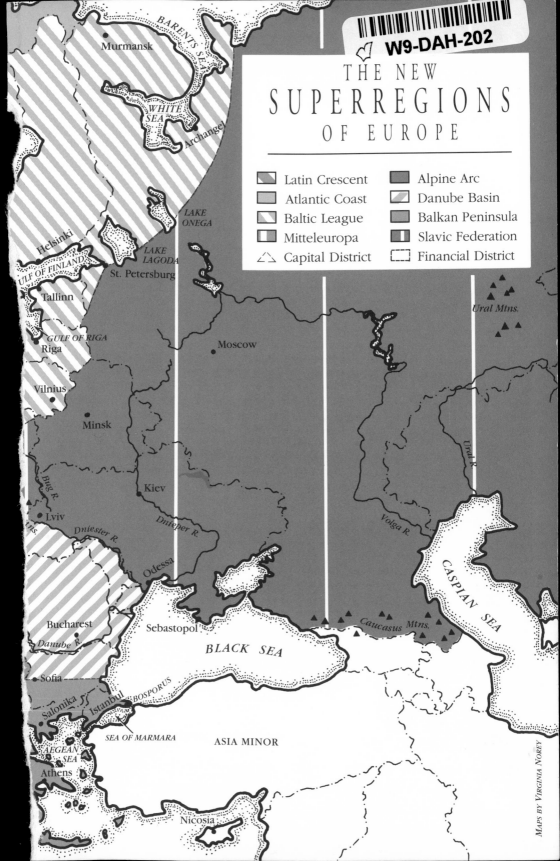

THE NEW
SUPERREGIONS
OF EUROPE

W9-DAH-202

Latin Crescent   Alpine Arc
Atlantic Coast   Danube Basin
Baltic League   Balkan Peninsula
Mitteleuropa   Slavic Federation
△ Capital District   Financial District

Murmansk

BARENTS SEA

*WHITE
SEA*

Archangel

*LAKE
ONEGA*

Helsinki

GULF OF FINLAND

*LAKE
LAGODA*

St. Petersburg

Tallinn

Ural Mtns.

GULF OF RIGA
Riga

Moscow

Vilnius

Minsk

Ural R.

Kiev

Bug R.

Lviv

Dniester R.

Dnieper R.

Odessa

Volga R.

CASPIAN SEA

Bucharest

Sebastopol

Caucasus Mtns.

Danube R.

BLACK SEA

Sofia

Salonika

Istanbul

BOSPORUS

SEA OF MARMARA

ASIA MINOR

*AEGEAN
SEA*

Athens

Nicosia

MAPS BY VIRGINIA NOREY

THE NEW
SUPERREGIONS
OF EUROPE

ALSO BY DARRELL DELAMAIDE

Debt Shock: The Full Story of the World Credit Crisis
(1984)

Gold, A Novel
(1989)

THE NEW
SUPERREGIONS
OF EUROPE

DARRELL DELAMAIDE

A DUTTON BOOK

In memory of
James Collins and Louis G. Cowan,
and to John Padberg, S.J.,
three wise men
who taught me what learning is.

DUTTON
Published by the Penguin Group
Penguin Books USA Inc., 375 Hudson Street,
New York, New York 10014, U.S.A.
Penguin Books Ltd, 27 Wrights Lane,
London W8 5TZ, England
Penguin Books Australia Ltd, Ringwood,
Victoria, Australia
Penguin Books Canada Ltd, 10 Alcorn Avenue,
Toronto, Ontario, Canada M4V 3B2
Penguin Books (N.Z.) Ltd, 182-190 Wairau Road,
Auckland 10, New Zealand

Penguin Books Ltd, Registered Offices:
Harmondsworth, Middlesex, England

First published by Dutton, an imprint of Dutton Signet, a
division of Penguin Books USA Inc.
Distributed in Canada by McClelland & Stewart Inc.

First Printing, March, 1994
10 9 8 7 6 5 4 3 2 1

 REGISTERED TRADEMARK—MARCA REGISTRADA

LIBRARY OF CONGRESS CATALOGING-IN-PUBLICATION DATA
Delamaide, Darrell.
     The new superregions of Europe / by Darrell Delamaide.
         p.   cm.
     ISBN 0-525-93651-3
     1. Europe—Economic conditions—Regional disparities.
     2. Regionalism—Europe. I. Title.
     HC240.D413   1994
     330.94—dc20   93-34333
                                              CIP

Printed in the United States of America
Set in Garamond Book
Designed by Leonard Telesca

CONTENTS

INTRODUCTION

Just when Europe seemed to be uniting, it started falling apart again. Apparent triumphs—like the overthrow of communism, the reunification of Germany, the Maastricht agreement—seem to have had adverse consequences: war and economic distress, right-wing extremism, and reactionary chauvinism. Instead of the promised United States of Europe, we have a dozen new smaller countries in a continent seemingly more fractious than ever. The kaleidoscope of European peoples and territories has been twisted again, as so often in the past, and a new pattern has emerged. Pieces hidden in the previous configuration feature prominently in the new one. The shift confuses not only those looking on from outside but the Europeans themselves.

History has a strong hold on Europe. Invisible frontiers crisscross the continent, marking divisions in language, wealth, customs, values. More than ever before, Europeans are looking into their past, beyond the rubble of recent history, for building blocks to use in constructing their future. This is where superregions come in: large territories reflecting historical patterns of migration and trade, ethnic and linguistic heritage, and social customs. They are emerging now because of the tremendous challenge Europe faces in building its future. Superregions reflect the dual trend so paradoxical at first sight—toward economic, and even political, integration of countries, on the one hand, and simultaneously toward greater autonomy at a smaller, regional level, where social and cultural cohesion is greater.

Superregions are the units arising from the tension between these two forces. The eight areas described here, spanning national borders, are emerging as the focus for many of the economic and social developments in Europe. These new superregions offer a better framework for analyzing and anticipating trends in the continent than the two score or more nations making up Europe. Other larger divisions of Europe—western Europe and eastern Europe, European Community and non-EC—will remain relevant, but the most significant trends will follow the lines of the superregions.

The gap between western and eastern Europe, for instance, predates the Iron Curtain. For four decades, the fortified border between capitalist Western Europe and communist Eastern Europe split the continent into two camps. Often the division seemed arbitrary, a whim of history and the vagaries of three old men meeting at Yalta. And yet, as Hungarian historian Jeno Szucs notes, the Iron Curtain more or less exactly followed the eastern frontier of Charlemagne's empire in the ninth century![1] Coincidence? Not likely. Already in the fifteenth century, the Hungarian scholar observes, that same line, following the rivers Elbe and Leitha, cut Europe into two economic blocs. The larger eastern bloc fell back into feudalism and trailed the more liberal western bloc in economic development.

The ideological divide five centuries later exacerbated an existing gap between the two halves of Europe. It was the entire history of this economic gap, and not just the collapse of communist regimes in the east, that prompted Jacques Attali, chief adviser to French President Francois Mitterrand, to lobby in 1989 for the creation of a European Bank for Reconstruction and Development. Attali, a scholar and writer, saw an urgent need for a new institution to lead the way in bridging this historic economic gap. For him, the gulf between a prosperous west and a backward east has been the cause of so many European wars, including the two world wars of this century.

There is an east-west divide among the proposed superregions themselves. Those emerging in the west—Latin Crescent, Atlantic Coast, Alpine Arc—are more advanced, more cohesive, because the integration of western Europe itself is more advanced, through the efforts of the European Community and the European Free Trade Association. Objectively speaking, then, the western superregions have more to show in the way of cross-border cooperation. The chapters describing these superregions contain more examples of recent collaboration in economic development. Because it lies mostly in the west, Mitteleuropa, based on the core union between Germany and France, has also achieved a high degree of integration. Even the Baltic League, because of its sharp geographic focus and the tradition of cooperation in northern Europe, has progressed rapidly in developing a regional cohesiveness, despite the depressed economic state of the former communist territories in Poland, Russia, and the Baltic republics.

The superregions in the east have much weaker cohesion. Like the EC, the Council for Mutual Economic Assistance (Comecon) also fostered a certain amount of economic and political integration, but much of that has been jettisoned in the eagerness of the newly liberated countries to reassert their sovereign rights. As a consequence, the superregions across the former ideological divide— Danube Basin, Balkan Peninsula, and Slavic Federation—are less advanced. In fact, it is far from certain that the Danube Basin superregion will actually take shape, despite the historical and geographical factors in its favor. The war in the former Yugoslavia and the tensions in the former Soviet Union show how bad things can become if cross-border collaboration cannot be realized. The chapters describing these superregions delve more into their history and geography to show the *potential* lines of future cooperation. Also, in more subjective terms, these territories and their history are for the most part less familiar to Western readers; the historical background in these chapters tries to fill that lacuna.

This book has two objectives. One is to describe the emergence of the superregions as a new terrain of economic and social development in a Europe currently experiencing an epochal change. The other is to use this new perspective to rediscover Europe, in all its diversity, and to identify some of the changes. To the extent it attains these goals, this book should change the way you look at Europe.

While most of us know where to locate the principal European countries on the map, the nuances of European geography often escape us. It's a rare newspaper reader who can readily distinguish between Slavonia, which is a region in Croatia, one of the newly independent nations emerging from the breakup of Yugoslavia, and Slovenia, another new country neighboring Croatia (Slavonia itself borders directly on Slovenia). How many avoid confusion between Galicia, a Slavic province now straddling the border between Poland and Ukraine, and Galicia, an ancient Germanic kingdom which is now an autonomous region in the northwestern corner of Spain? If those examples seem obscure, how about the difference between the Dniester and the Dnieper rivers? Both are in Ukraine and the latter is the third longest river in Europe. And yet, understanding these distinctions will provide us with the clues both to where opportunities are most promising in Europe and where the risks are the greatest.

Other models need to be kept in mind. Obviously, individual nation-states will continue to be the principal locus of political, diplomatic, and military power. But in many other areas—economic, social, cultural—the map of the superregions provides a new paradigm for sorting out many of the changes taking place on the continent. In describing the individual superregions, I have used mostly examples from economics and business as illustrations; this seems to be the sphere providing the strongest links within superregions. But there are myriad instances of other types of endeavors—literary, artistic, dramatic, athletic, social, and so on—that also demonstrate the coherence of the superregions. There are less tangible shared attributes, like attitudes or customs, that are also important in unifying these territories.

The superregions can help preserve peace in Europe by diffusing and channeling economic and political power. Shifting the orientation to a superregion level can ease the frictions between regions and nations, while avoiding the dangers of a centralized bureaucracy. Superregions can become the key component in restructuring Europe in a way that allows its countervailing forces of integration and decentralization to work together productively. Drawing on historic models of cooperation and federation like the Hanseatic League and the duchy of Burgundy, the new superregions of Europe can enable the continent to achieve its promise of prosperity in the vastly changed economic and political environment of the late twentieth century. If this book can help in some small way to realize that goal, it will have achieved its purpose.

A Note on Style

Geographical references throughout the book conform to the preferred spellings in *Webster's New Geographical Dictionary*. The only exceptions are some of the newly formed countries, like Belarus, where I have followed newspaper style.

The names of foreign places and persons that have no other English equivalent have been "anglicized" to the extent of omitting the diacritical markings—acute and grave accents, circumflexes, cedillas, umlauts, tildes, and so on—that they would have in their own languages. For example, Dusseldorf and Zurich are rendered without the umlaut over the *u,* and former French prime minister Pierre Beregovoy does not have the appropriate acute accents over the *e*'s in his last name. This may irritate some readers familiar with these languages, who will argue, rightly, that the names are misspelled without these signs. But the markings are meaningless for most readers of English, and distracting in an English text; please regard the spellings here as "translations."

Also, I have rendered the titles of the foreign-language books cited in the text into English, but this does not mean that these works are available in English. The original titles and publishing details can be found in the endnotes. There is a "Suggested Reading" list of English titles at the end of the book.

CHAPTER ONE

EUROPE'S NEW SUPERREGIONS

The map of Europe is changing.

In some places, borders are disappearing. The ideological divide between eastern and western Europe is gone. In western Europe, national borders are fading as the European Community evolves into a single market and strives for closer political union. In other places, new borders are being drawn. The breakup of the Soviet Union and Yugoslavia has produced a dozen new European nations—some of them independent for the first time in their history. The changes in Europe's geography mark a new epoch, as they did in 1815, when the defeat of Napoleon divided the continent into imperial Great Powers, and in 1918, when World War I put an end to these empires and carved the continent into nation-states.

In this play of countervailing forces of integration and disintegration, new blocs of economic and cultural cohesion are emerging. As the continent grows closer together economically and politically, the traditional nation-states are breaking into their component parts, regions with a history that long predates that of the nation-state itself. These historic territories, pursuing their own interests in a more integrated Europe, are recombining across old national borders to form new entities—Europe's superregions.

In other words, the more Europe becomes a single unit, the greater is the leeway for its interior borders to shift around. As part of this shift, superregions are emerging as a new terrain for economic and social interaction. The nation-states composing Europe continue to exist, of course, and preserve some of their "sovereignty." But as European integration progresses, many of the main social and economic trends will follow the boundaries of the new superregions.

These groupings are those large areas in Europe where geography has greatly influenced the interplay between people over centuries, creating cultural and social affinity. These transnational regions often have ties of trade, migration, conquest, or dynasty dating back centuries or even millennia. Such links have never completely disappeared, but they have been obscured or blocked for decades by the preeminence of strongly centralized nation-states. The evolution of a larger political structure in contemporary Europe is removing artificial barriers within these superregions so that they can realize their full potential once again.

The Paradox of Europe

Europe has a variety of supranational institutions, most of them related to the European Community, pulling the continent together. There are other forces of integration as well, ranging from business strategies in production and marketing to new technologies in communications and transportation, from satellite television to high-speed trains.

The EC's decision in 1985 to finally fulfill the dream of a common market in labor, capital, goods, and services by the end of 1992 forced many West Europeans, particularly businessmen, to discard old, nationalist ways of thinking, and to adopt a European perspective. The twelve member nations of the EC signed the Treaty of Maastricht in February 1992, outlining an ambitious political and economic union that they hoped to attain by the end of the century. At the same time, the collapse of communist rule in eastern Europe and the Soviet Union so changed the geopolitical landscape that the Twelve were compelled to consider expansion of the EC sooner than planned. Countries like Sweden and Finland, which had shunned the EC for fear of their huge Soviet neighbor, rushed to file applications for membership. East European countries struggled to transform their Soviet-style planned economies into free-market, capitalist systems, and their situation demanded some form of association with the EC, with the promise of full participation to follow.

The EC measures to eliminate national borders as barriers to economic activity had immediate, often unexpected, political effects. Cities and regions in the member countries began to assert themselves as the role of the national capital waned. The Alsace region in northeastern France found more common ground with the neighboring region of Baden-Wurttemberg in southwestern Germany and the canton of Basel in Switzerland than with national ministries in the French capital. Regional economic centers in southwestern France, like Toulouse and Montpellier, began to look across the Spanish border to Barcelona rather than northward to distant Paris. Many cities and regions set up their own offices in Brussels to lobby EC decision-makers directly.

During the watershed year 1992, the paradox that mystified people outside Europe, and many within, was that western Europe was becoming one while eastern Europe, finally free from communist dictatorship, was breaking up into numerous smaller countries. The two halves of Europe seemed to be going in opposite directions. In fact, though, each trend had a mirror image. West European nation-states were growing closer together, but regions within these nation-states were seeking and getting more power and autonomy. East European minorities were declaring their independence as sovereign nations but also their intentions of integrating as soon as possible into the European Community.

The paradox is partly in the eye of the beholder. *Nation* does not have the same meaning now as in the heyday of the nation-states at the end of the nineteenth century. Nations then had armies, navies, colonial empires, merchant fleets; they were viable economic entities in their own right. Recently, not even the superpowers have had empires, while European nations have been increasingly pooling their economic resources to keep up with the growing scale of business in a global economy. Slovenia or Estonia, even with their own flags and foreign ministers, have less autonomy than Catalonia, the resurgent region of Spain. Estonia looks to Finland for succor, while Slovenia looks to Austria, and *these* two countries, in turn, look to membership in the European Community. The newly independent countries in the former East Bloc are not really so different in their goals from Catalonia, Flanders, and other regions in western Europe.

This is the true paradox of contemporary Europe. Throughout the continent, in east and west, there is a resurgence of nationalism, a strongly felt attachment to ethnic and cultural roots. At the same time, global trends are forcing economic integration on a continental scale. As a consequence, Europe is experiencing a fundamental reshaping of the political structure to reduce the nation-states' monopoly on power, and to distribute it over several levels of decision-making. The simultaneous pull of these two forces—the one toward smaller, culturally homogenous units, and the other toward greater integration and cooperation—creates the tension that is driving development in Europe today. Cities, regions, networks, superregions—all these emerging players, along with the supranational institutions of the EC, are claiming their share of the power formerly concentrated in the nation-state alone.

The Rise of Superregions

As the consequences of European integration grew clearer, the contours of the superregions began to appear. *Newsweek* signaled their emergence in November 1990, coining the term *superregion* and taking the Baltic Sea region as an example of the phenomenon. The American magazine portrayed the "Baltic League" as heir to the medieval trading empire, the Hanseatic League. Pehr Gyllenhammer, the visionary chairman of Swedish carmaker Volvo, spoke enthusiastically of Baltic Sea cooperation. "What counts now is regions—not countries," Gyllenhammer told *Newsweek*. "The nation-state has outlived its purpose."[1]

A month later, the French newspaper *Figaro* reported the same phenomenon. Like *Newsweek,* this publication identified the Baltic area and the region joining the Alps and the Adriatic coast as natural superregions. "The bloc between the Alps and the Adriatic," political scientist Francois Fetjo told the French paper, "does not stop at political frontiers. Manifestly, the Venetians feel more affinity with the inhabitants of Vienna than with those of Rome."[2] In the same way, with more negative implications, Jacques Rupnik, an expert on Eastern Europe, identified the Balkans as a superregion.

and Portugal to promote regional cooperation and to counter this danger.

On the other side of the continent, the Danube-Adriatic region, which has never really recovered from the collapse of the Austro-Hungarian empire in 1918, spawned several regional initiatives, many of which overlapped. One of them was a grouping of national governments launched in 1990 by Italian Foreign Minister Gianni De Michelis, himself a native of Venice, on the northern Adriatic coast. It was known at first as the Quadrangular, because four countries belonged (Italy, Austria, Yugoslavia, and Hungary), then the Pentagonal, when Czechoslovakia joined, and the Hexagonal, when Poland joined, and finally the Central European Initiative, when the splitting up of Yugoslavia made it too difficult to keep count.

In March 1992, the ten countries bordering the Baltic Sea formed the Council of Baltic Sea States to work together on a regional basis. The new organization is drawing on the experience and cohesion of the Nordic Council, which links the five Scandinavian nations Sweden, Norway, Denmark, Finland, and Iceland.

The Notion of the Nation-State

To properly identify the superregions requires abandoning the maps we are familiar with. The colored borders outlining countries seem so solid, somehow final and eternal. But the states they portray are relatively new, as is the very notion of a nation-state itself. Historians now tend to date "nation-building," in the modern sense of a mass society pledging loyalty to the concept of its own nationhood, to the French Revolution. The ability to articulate this new concept and to exploit it came really only in the nineteenth century.

Immanuel Wallerstein, a professor at the State University of New York, explains just how new this idea is: "A world consisting of these nation-states came into existence even partially only in the sixteenth century. Such a world was theorized and became a matter of widespread consciousness even later, only in the nineteenth century. It became an inescapably universal phenomenon later still, in fact only after 1945."[5] To back up a bit, historian Eric J. Hobsbawm says World War I was a time "when the map of Europe was, for the first—and as it turned out for the only—time redrawn according to the principle of nationality."[6]

The advocates of nationalism *rewrote* history. Cambridge professor Ernest Gellner writes, "Nations as a natural, God-given way of classifying men, as an inherent though long-delayed political destiny, are a myth. . . ."[7] Nationalism, he contends, either takes preexisting cultures and turns them into nations, or invents them, wiping out the preexisting cultures in the process.

Nationalists, in Europe and elsewhere, created myths to make history look like a long march to the fulfillment of each nation's manifest destiny. The French historian Ernest Renan commented more than a century ago that "getting its history wrong is part of being a nation."[8] France itself is a sterling example. Historian Suzanne Citron shows how French educators, after the reforms of the nineteenth century, indoctrinated generations of schoolchildren with these national myths. Vercingetorix, a Celtic chieftain defending his tribe against the Romans, became a French national hero, along with Charles Martel and Joan of Arc, who were fighting for territorial or dynastic goals.

Citing classic school texts, Citron notes with considerable irony how "our country" has always existed. History starts with it at the beginning of time. "In bygone days, our country was called Gaul, and its inhabitants the Gauls," reads one text. Using terms like "our country" or referring to France as a place before it existed lends history an artificial continuity. "Because they are real right now, these words, projected into the past, bring to life an original, imaginary France. The history of France begins with the myth of France," concludes Citron.[9]

These claims are starting to evaporate in the new Europe, as power seeps away from the nation-states. Or rather, they are being reexamined for clues toward a more fundamental ethnic or cultural identity. Vercingetorix is becoming a symbol not of French nationalism but of Celtic heritage. Europe has always been dynamic, with massive migrations crisscrossing the continent. The rigid boundaries of the nation-state are the exception in European history. Europe is not by nature a "static" place.

Throughout European history, and today more so than ever, people with the most amazing antecedents can be found living in unusual places. In a small town called Annot, for instance, on the road from Nice into the French Alps, is a Hotel Honnoraty. This obviously non-French name is not Irish, as it might seem to be, but Greek. The proprietor claims to be descended from the Greeks who founded Marseilles in 600 B.C., many of whom were driven into the mountains by Caesar's takeover of the Mediterranean port in 49 B.C. In another example, the only noncommunist prime minister of East Germany was Lothar de Maiziere, one of the many descendants of French Huguenot families who came to Berlin when the Edict of Nantes was repealed in 1685. Black Irish, famous for their telltale dark features, are reputedly descended from those survivors of the Spanish Armada washed ashore on the Emerald Isle in 1588.

Migration and intermarriage made Europe a melting pot long before Columbus headed west to India and "discovered" America. French historian Jean-Baptiste Duroselle notes,

> We Europeans of the twentieth century are the product of successive influences—megalithic civilization, Celtic civilization, Latin civilization which admirably spread Greek civilization, Germanic civilization, and, much later, Slavic civilization. All this makes up our very substance, less on the racial level, which is quite secondary, than on the levels of language and civilization. We are almost all members of communities descended from a mixture of at least two or three big groups.[10]

Anyone who has tried to puzzle out the tribal pedigree of a particular region knows what the difficulties are. Throughout much of Europe's early history, mobile bands of warriors, farmers, and their families roamed the continent, including the British Isles, leaving no written records. The historian's main source of information are the trinkets they took with them to their graves. The original Scots, for example, came from Ireland, and Britons lived in Britain before and after the English.

"The ethnic clusters of Europe are whorled and layered, far more complex than any map can display, sometimes almost forgotten," writes Flora Lewis in her book, *Europe*. "They lie below the surface of the nation-states, maintaining ancient links and an almost unconscious pull of kinship which strengthen the roots of the move for European unity. Modern borders haven't really sorted people out in hermetic nationalities; there has long been too much mixing, too much ebb and flow of conquest and settlement for that."[11]

Much of the confusion comes from anachronistic ideas of what makes for a people or a nation. Nineteenth-century notions of nationalism influenced historians and conditioned our own thinking.

In a history of the Franks, the German tribe that gave its name to France, Edward James says that earlier scholars "imagined that a people was a group of men and women with a common language, a common culture and a common racial type, who could be clearly distinguished from their neighbors."[12] Nowadays, historians know that "peoples" are much more fluid than was once thought, moving about and calling themselves whatever seemed most apt at the moment. Inhabitants of a particular region tended prudently to call themselves whatever their ruler called himself. "It identified political allegiance rather than ethnic identity," says James.[13] By the mid-eighth century it seems that most inhabitants of northern Gaul were calling themselves Franks, after their new masters, even though they were actually descended from the mixture of Gauls and Romans who had been living there for centuries.

Another anachronism is confusing historic countries like France or Spain with the nation-states we have today. Prerevolutionary France consisted of a number of vassal regions cobbled together under a greedy dynasty. There were fortified borders, complete with customs controls, between the fiefdoms, and the country bore little resemblance to the centralized, codified state that Napoleon left behind.

These states are not so monolithic as they seem. For instance, Nice, the chief city of the French Riviera, has been a "permanent" part of France for only a century or so, ceded to Paris in 1860 as Italy was being formed. Such annexation is typical of many European territories. Today's nation-states represent the conquest and suppression of one region by another: Castile dominated in Spain, Paris in France, Prussia in Germany, Piedmont in Italy, Muscovy in Russia. In many ways, the current decomposition into historic regions marks a *decolonization*, like that in Asia and Africa following World War II, and generates the same passions.

Europe's Other Frontiers

Many types of frontiers exist in Europe. One obvious divide is a linguistic one, like that between Germanic languages in northern Europe and Latinate languages in the south. This line is drawn fairly clearly through the middle of Europe even though the Roman legions penetrated north of the line into England and the Netherlands, which have Germanic languages, and German tribes pillaged and settled in southern regions.

Another important division is along religious lines. The border between Roman Catholic and Orthodox Christianity in southeastern Europe has been important in history and still inflames passions today. There are also Islamic enclaves in Bosnia and Albania, and Turkey marks the boundary between Islam and predominantly Christian countries. In northern Europe, the border between Protestant and Catholic confessions runs more or less along a line extending the Main River in Germany.

A more modern boundary stems from current economic trends. A group of French geographers, GIP Reclus in Montpellier, identified Europe's industrial core, running from Manchester in western England to Milan in northern Italy, cutting a swath through the Benelux countries (Belgium, Netherlands, Luxembourg) and western Germany and Switzerland. The press promptly dubbed the area the "blue banana" because of its shape and the coloring used by the Reclus mapmakers, and the concept enjoyed a certain notoriety throughout Europe.

One facetious frontier is that between beer and wine, which not coincidentally parallels that between Germanic and Latin languages. Climate seems to be the determining factor—grapes grow in the warmer weather of southern Europe, while barley and hops need the north's lower temperatures. But the frontier follows cultural differences so exactly as to invite speculation about the influence of these beverages. Does beer affect the mind in such a way as to make it easier to speak German, with all its obtuse, ambiguous vocabulary? Does wine lend it itself to clarity and precision in thought like that of Cicero and Descartes? Does beer loosen the tongue and draw people into the pubs that stretch in a band of comfort across Germanic-speaking Europe, while wine, married so well to fine food, gives rise to the refined cuisines of Romance regions? Food for thought.

More seriously, a French expert, Robert Lafont, sees a durable division between northern and southern Europe due largely to physical geography. The north is the region of the plain, washed by successive migrations of Celts, Germans, and Slavs from the steppes of Asia. The south, separated by the Alps and Carpathian mountains, is centered on the Mediterranean basin. Maritime peoples like the Greeks and the Phoenicians expanded westward by sea. "There are two contradictory cultural styles at our origins," comments Lafont: "the culture of the steppe, the horde, the yurt, that of the northern nomad; and the culture of the oar, the sail, the city and the cadaster, that of the Mediterranean."[14]

The borders of the superregions reflect many of these cultural and economic divisions, but paramount is *geography*—the physical intervention of mountains, rivers, and seas. These are the barriers that separated people with different languages, religions, and resources in the first place, or, even more important, the seam that joined them together. Many of the names given to a particular superregion include the geographic phenomenon that does so much to define it.

Seeing historic political patterns in the light of geography is the realm of geopolitics. Friedrich Ratzel, the German scholar whose writings on "political geography" in the nineteenth century laid the foundation for geopolitics, insisted on geography's primacy in the social sciences. Placing geography at the center of all social sciences, in his view, not only freed it from historical domination, but enabled geography to give meaning to historical facts.

Ratzel did not consider geopolitics academic. History illuminated by geography was to teach politicians, generals, and businessmen what decisions to make, he thought. Unfortunately for the world in the twentieth century, Ratzel persuaded German leaders only too well. Both Kaiser Wilhelm and Hitler used these geopolitical arguments to justify German aggression.

Geography does not only affect politics. Immanuel Wallerstein applies the same geographical perspective to culture, dubbing this viewpoint "geoculture." He describes it as "the underside of geopolitics"; the two interact, and both are concerned with boundaries. "Defining a culture is a question of defining boundaries that are essentially political—boundaries of oppression, and of defense against oppression."[15]

The geographical viewpoint can take in a wide spectrum. American writer Robert Kuttner uses the term "geo-economics" to describe how economic strategy now drives international relations more so than military and political strategies. Only by redefining its strategic goals in terms of geo-economics, he argues, can the United States restore its economy to health and contribute to a "plural new economic order."[16] Echoes of this argument could be heard in Bill Clinton's election campaign. This view justifies the new president's creation of a National Economic Council modeled on the National Security Council.

A prime example of geo-economics is the formation of Germany and Italy in the nineteenth century. British historian David Thomson writes that this fundamental redrawing of the European map was certainly due to the ambitions of two states, Prussia and Piedmont, and their exceptional leaders, Bismarck and Cavour. "But the historical significance of these achievements is distorted," he continues, "if they are considered only as political, diplomatic, and military events—the successful results of deliberate man-made policies implemented by two statesmen of undoubted political genius. They were also a consequence of the changing structure of economic and social life in central Europe."[17] Nineteenth-century industrial society required a larger economic unit than the diffuse principalities and provinces in these two territories—it was necessary to unify them to keep pace with economic development.

Nationalism in the nineteenth century aimed precisely to form big nations from such smaller entities, as Hobsbawm argues in his study of modern nationalism, to *build* nations. It was virtually the opposite of nationalist movements in the late twentieth century, seeking to break down existing states into ethnic or religious components. In the earlier view, a nation "had to be of sufficient size to form a viable unit of development," Hobsbawm writes. "If it fell below this threshold, it had no historic justification."[18] And so these nationalists would not consider independence or sovereignty for smaller territories like Sicily, Brittany, Wales—or even Ireland!

Giuseppe Mazzini, one of the leaders of the Risorgimento, the nineteenth-century movement for unification of Italy, thought Europe should consist of just ten countries. One was Italy, of course, "from the tip of Sicily to the Alps" but also including Ticino, the Italian-speaking canton of Switzerland, and Corsica, the island where Napoleon was born. In Mazzini's neat view, each of Europe's peninsulas should make up a single country—the Iberian, by uniting Spain and Portugal, the Scandinavian, by uniting Denmark, Norway, and Sweden. The Balkan peninsula, with Istanbul as main city but under Greek rule, constitutes another country. A "Danubian Confederation" would embrace Austria, Hungary, Romania, and Bohemia (including all of the Czech lands). An "Alpine Confederation" would consist of Switzerland, Savoy (the French Alpine region), and German-speaking Tirol. Germany, in Mazzini's view, should incorporate Holland and Flanders, where Germanic languages are spoken, while France should include the French-speaking parts of Belgium. The British Isles—England, Wales, Scotland, and Ireland—form a single country. Russia and Poland, the Italian statesman conceded, would remain distinct, but should be "associated" in a single entity.[19]

In the late twentieth century, the fact that nations as small as Slovenia, Croatia, and Latvia were seeking and getting international recognition does *not* mean that the threshold for economic viability has been lowered. Rather, the global economy today requires even larger units; that is precisely the motivation for European integration. Mazzini's map, however, anticipated the formation of larger cultural and economic regions within the integrated whole—an early view of superregions.

New nations in eastern Europe are not the only ones to realize that European integration permits greater local autonomy. The same conclusion is behind "independence" movements in western Europe, too. The Scottish Nationalist Party in 1989 adopted the slogan "An Independent Scotland in a United Europe" to signal that European integration finally made it feasible for Scotland to survive economically without being tied politically to England. Likewise, Belgium, cobbled together as a buffer state between France and Germany in the nineteenth century, no longer has the same incentive to maintain its fractious unity and has begun to split into its constituent parts, Flanders and Wallonia.

The nation-state, pundits have begun to say, is becoming too small for many tasks, and too big for others. Europeans do not want bureaucrats in Brussels to decide where schools are to be built or roads improved, but they also see less need for bureaucrats in faraway national capitals to make such decisions. Autonomous regions or small countries seem better qualified to supervise such matters. These regions, in turn, increasingly see the need to cooperate with each other on projects of common interest. These interests do not necessarily follow national borders, but geographic, social, or cultural confines—those of superregions.

Skeptics see all this as so much regional boosterism, or local politicians preening their egos. Even some of those promoting the new autonomy of cities and regions are cautious about the egghead theories sprouting up to explain their actions. Pierre Calfas, director of international relations for the city of Marseilles, makes it clear he wants nothing to do with bananas or crescents, but wants to concentrate on helping the city of Tunis in northern Africa organize its garbage collection. Jean Chemain, executive director of the Chamber of Commerce in Lyons, says succinctly, "The blue banana is an idiocy."

Others see the trend to regionalization as downright dangerous. Ralf Dahrendorf, a German scholar who was longtime director of the London School of Economics, fears the disappearance of the nation-state, which he considers one of the great achievements of civilization. For him, the proponents of a "Europe of Regions" are returning Europe to its "tribal" state. "The tribes and The Great Whole are supposed to replace the heterogenous nation-state," Dahrendorf comments. "That's ill-advised. . . . Tribes do not make Europe; they will wage wars forever."[20]

Dahrendorf, regarding the conflict in former Yugoslavia, sees regionalism as an expression of a narrow and dangerous nationalism. Regional political parties in western Europe, like the Lombard League in Italy, often appear to be right-wing and xenophobic. Nonetheless, although he shares Dahrendorf's horror of "national fundamentalism," Hungarian novelist Gyorgy Konrad sees the dual trend to European integration and local autonomy as a healthy counterweight to centralizing nationalism.

> So that the cult and theater of the nation-state doesn't completely ennervate us, we should take a look at two other trends: at the assimilation of our country in the overall framework [of Europe], and at the emancipation of smaller territories and regions. With regard to the democratization of eastern Europe, the winning of local autonomy from the power centers, from the majority government of the nation-state, cannot be valued highly enough.[21]

Joel Roman, a French political philosopher, suggests viewing the continent as "*post*-national." Europe is not itself to become a nation, but is in the process of inventing a historically new form of political unity, which casts nationhood in a different perspective, relativizing it. "The national identity is not fated to disappear, but without any doubt to become one identity among others."[22] For Roman, learning how to juggle various identities is the challenge facing Europeans.

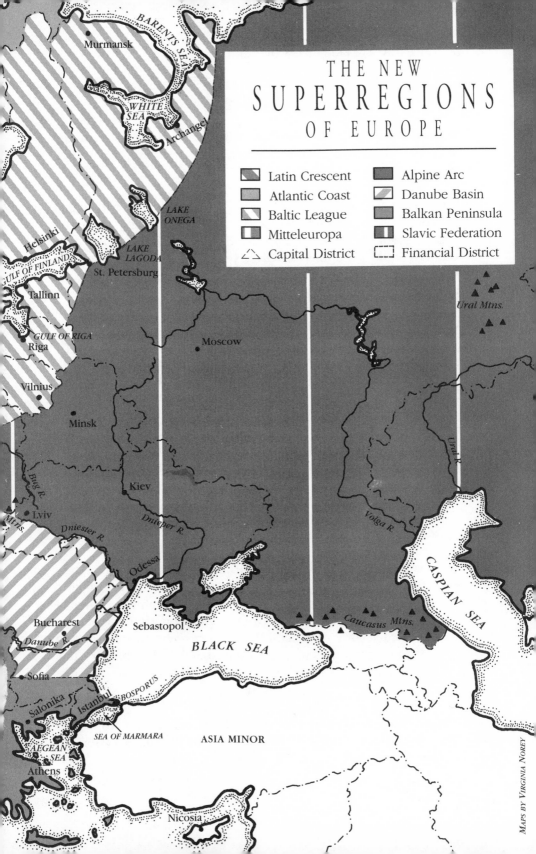

THE NEW
SUPERREGIONS
OF EUROPE

Latin Crescent		Alpine Arc	
Atlantic Coast		Danube Basin	
Baltic League		Balkan Peninsula	
Mitteleuropa		Slavic Federation	
△ Capital District		[ ] Financial District	

Murmansk

BARENTS SEA

WHITE SEA

Archangel

LAKE ONEGA

LAKE LAGODA

Helsinki

GULF OF FINLAND

Tallinn

St. Petersburg

GULF OF RIGA

Riga

Vilnius

Minsk

Moscow

Ural Mtns.

Bug R.

Kiev

Lviv

Mtns.

Dniester R.

Dnieper R.

Ural R.

Volga R.

Odessa

CASPIAN SEA

Bucharest

Danube R.

Sebastopol

Sofia

BLACK SEA

Caucasus Mtns.

Salonika

Istanbul

BOSPORUS

SEA OF MARMARA

ASIA MINOR

AEGEAN SEA

Athens

Nicosia

MAPS BY VIRGINIA NOREY

The Superregions

The superregions discussed in this book follow many of the boundaries already described. On my map, there are eight super-regions and two special districts:

Latin Crescent: The Sunbelt of Europe, this dynamic region stretches in an arc around the Western Mediterranean. It includes most of Spain except for the northwest corner, southern Portugal, southern France, and most of Italy, except for the Alps in the north and the Adriatic region in the northeast. It is the heart of the old Roman Empire and is enjoying a political and economic renaissance. In the long run, however, its future depends on the development of the Mediterranean region as a whole.

Baltic League: This region draws the most immediate benefit from the disappearance of the Iron Curtain, which blocked the traditional commerce around the Baltic Sea. It includes all the areas bordering the Baltic—all of Sweden and Finland, along with the hinterland in Russia down to St. Petersburg, the Baltic republics Estonia, Latvia, and Lithuania, the coastal regions of Poland and Germany up to Hamburg, the eastern half of Denmark, and the corner of Norway east of Oslo. The home of the Vikings and the Hanseatic League, this region has a history of vigorous and prosperous trade.

Atlantic Coast: This region is on the edge of Europe. It includes the islands of Great Britain and Ireland and virtually the entire western coast of the continent, running from northern Portugal, across northwestern Spain, along the western coasts of France, Belgium, the Netherlands, and Germany to Hamburg, through the center of Jutland in Denmark north through Oslo and along the Norwegian-Swedish border. Although much of the coast technically runs along the North Sea, the orientation is to the Atlantic. The ability of this region to act as a bridge between Europe and America and the rest of the world will determine its future.

Mitteleuropa: This is the industrial heartland of Europe, the richest and most powerful of the superregions. The name is German because that people dominates this region. It includes all of Germany between Hamburg in the north and Munich in the south, most of Belgium and the Netherlands, Luxembourg, northern and central France, the northwestern corner of Switzerland, the Czech Republic, and western Poland.

Capital District: This is the triangle formed by Brussels, Paris, and Strasbourg, including Luxembourg City. The main EC institutions are headquartered in Brussels and Luxembourg, while Strasbourg is the home of the European Parliament and the Council of Europe. Paris has provided the main intellectual input for European integration, from the grand concepts to administrative expertise, and remains in many respects the cultural capital of Europe.

Financial District: This is the City of London, the Square Mile, where the concentration of banks, financial markets, insurance, and ancillary services is such that it will remain not only the financial center of Europe, but a major center for global finance.

Alpine Arc: This small region in the Alps mountain range is a microcosm of prosperity and is a bridge between Mitteleuropa and Latin Crescent. Following the arc of the Alps, it includes the Alpine regions of France, most of Switzerland, western Austria, a corner of Italy down to Milan, and a corner of Germany up to Munich.

Danube Basin: This underdeveloped region follows the long path of the Danube River, from the tip of Bavaria east of Munich, through eastern Austria, including Slovakia, all of Hungary and Romania, the former Soviet republic of Moldava, the northern half of Bulgaria, the new republics of Slovenia and Croatia, and the Adriatic coast of northern Italy as far west as Milan. The old Austro-Hungarian empire successfully administered a multicultural state in this area, but at the cost of an economic backwardness which persists to this day.

Balkan Peninsula: This poor, peripheral region is riven with nationalist and religious disputes. It includes Serbia, Bosnia, Montenegro, and Macedonia in the south of the former Yugoslavia, all of Albania and Greece, southern Bulgaria, and the tiny bit of Turkey in Europe. If it can overcome its ethnic problems, it may have long-term chances in cooperation with the Black Sea region and the Near East.

Slavic Federation: This region groups the new nations in the European part of the former Soviet Union—Ukraine, Belarus, and Russia itself west of the Ural mountains, as well as the part of Poland east of Warsaw. Its connection to the massive Asian territory of the Russian Federation and the Central Asian republics of the former Soviet Union make it an important bridge between Europe and Asia.

This map should be seen as a working hypothesis; many people will have ideas about how to improve the names and boundaries of these superregions. For instance, the name Mitteleuropa will surprise those who would take this term, usually translated as Central Europe, to mean rather the area designated as Danube Basin. In fact, however, the translation is not really accurate. The Danube basin is generally called *Ost-Mitteleuropa* in German (East Central Europe).

Other names are conceivable for this central region. Some writers fearful of German reunification speak of it as the Fourth Reich, an unflattering allusion to German aggression during Hitler's Third Reich. Another German term from history, with equally unsavory connotations, is *Grossdeutschland* (Big Germany). I have rejected both as too laden with historical opprobrium that does not really fit today's Germany. Mitteleuropa is itself a threatening term, but that, in the end, goes with the territory. A more neutral name would be one referring to the Rhine, which runs through the region and is central to it. But I like Mitteleuropa because this superregion is literally in the middle of Europe, the heart.

One of the most shocking novelties of the superregions map is certainly the division of France, for most of us the archetype of a centralized nation-state. It would not, however, be such a surprise for French statesmen, who have long known how necessary it was to have a strong capital to keep the country from flying apart through centrifugal force. Flora Lewis recounts that French president Charles de Gaulle "considered their national community dangerously fragile, in constant need of arousal to sustain cohesion."[23] De Gaulle was keen that any European union would be a union of "fatherlands," because "he feared that France would somehow lose itself in the dilution of a larger union."[24] His fears are proving to be well-founded.

In the era of nation-states, it was France's advantage, its glory, to have the country so strongly centralized around Paris. As European integration makes national borders fade, centralization has become a liability. Paris has always been strengthened at the expense of the provinces, which now are relatively weak. This worries Charles Millon, the president of the Rhone-Alpes region, one of the biggest and most dynamic in the country, centered on Lyons. "When there are no more borders, our national territory will be dismembered bit by bit, split up, pulled apart by the strong attraction of big foreign regions which will carve our country up into zones of influence," he warns.[25] It is already happening, as the superregions are formed.

France is but one example of a country experiencing fragmentation. The following chapters will look at each of the superregions in greater detail. First, however, let us examine more closely the two forces underlying the changes in Europe. On the one hand, the integration of the continent continues as a result of new infrastructure and the evolution of European organizations. On the other hand, regionalization is fragmenting the highly centralized nation-state of recent history.

CHAPTER TWO

COMMON EUROPEAN HOUSE

Imagine yourself in a bucolic Burgundy countryside on a quiet, sunny afternoon: the gently undulating landscape, quilted in broad cultivated fields interspersed by clumps of trees and an occasional church spire, traversed by a country lane with a single Citroen *deux chevaux* puttering along. Suddenly, you are aware of a hiss—quiet, insistent, increasing in volume. Then, in the distance, you see a flash of orange just a second long as a sleek train of only half a dozen cars streaks into view. The image disappears behind the next hill, the hiss fades; the chirping birds and chugging Citroen are audible once again, the countryside as lazy as before.

The trim, high-speed trains, known as TGV (*train à grande vitesse*) in French, are imposing in their uncompromising modernity. The long trapezohedral snout of the engine, surmounted by two wide window slits, with air vents slashing the side like a series of gills, together give the machine an appearance of animalistic vitality.

When it first went into service in 1981, the TGV, traveling at 160 miles per hour on specially built tracks, cut the travel time for the 270 miles between Paris and Lyons from four hours to two hours, from city center to center. Counting the time to travel to and from airports, this was quicker than flying, with considerable advantages in cost and convenience as well. The new proximity to Paris, site of so much political and economic power in highly centralized France, invigorated Lyons, giving a needed lift to its regional aspirations. Businessmen, civil servants, artists, and entertainers became more willing to go to Lyons, to visit and even to live, no longer fearing such a trip as an exile, however temporary, from the vitality and opportunities of the capital. The sleepy province became less provincial, more dynamic.

As the line was extended to destinations farther south, cutting travel time to the Mediterranean cities of Marseilles and Montpellier in half, to about five hours, they, too, benefited from the improved access not only to Paris but to Lyons. In 1989, a second line, TGV Atlantique, with even faster trains capable of streaking along at 185 miles an hour, brought similar advantages to Le Mans, Nantes, and Bordeaux along the Atlantic coast in western France. The indefatigable French dispatched their bulldozers to northern France to build the TGV Nord line in time to use the Channel Tunnel in 1994, which would enable train passengers to travel from Paris to London in three hours.

The runaway success of the pioneering French efforts prompted the Community of European Railways in 1990 to draw up a master plan for a network of high-speed train connections throughout western Europe. Their ambitious agenda called for construction by the year 2010 of 5,600 miles of new track—the equivalent of *two* brand-new transcontinental railroads in the United States—supporting speeds of at least 150 miles per hour, and upgrading of an additional 9,400 miles of track for speeds of 125 miles per hour, at an estimated cost of $200 billion at current prices! The new connections would cut travel time from Brussels to Paris, for example, from two hours and twenty-five minutes to an hour and twenty minutes; Brussels to Milan, from ten hours twenty minutes to five hours fifteen minutes; Brussels to Barcelona, from *sixteen* hours thirty-five minutes to *five* hours fifty minutes. Further down the line, so to speak, the fast-train network could be extended to eastern Europe so that some time in the first half of the twenty-first century trains traveling up to two hundred miles an hour could connect Sevilla to St. Petersburg.

The high-speed trains are perhaps the most dramatic example of the revolution in transport infrastructure that is transforming Europe into a single geographical unit. There are other ambitious projects, some already in construction, for express highways, tunnels under water and through mountains, bridges across wide sea channels, canals connecting historic waterways. There are new airports and runways, used by new regional airlines with a new generation of European-built turboprop planes; there are new sea connections via massive "cruise ferries" boasting luxury furnishings and facilities, or catamarans that sluice across straits in half the time of older-generation car ferries.

As travel times decline and transport capacity increases, Europe is growing smaller. Infrastructure, planned on a continental scale and crossing national borders, is making an enormous contribution to European integration. Europe's ability to resolve the inevitable conflicts between big business and environmentalists in building new roads and railways, to mount the finance not only for long-term construction projects but for research and development of new technologies involved, is crucial for the continent's future.

Appreciating this achievement is key to understanding where Europe is going. The building of a Common European House involves not only the deeper political and economic union of the European Community, the extension of this union to northern and eastern Europe, the creation of new structures for security and military cooperation, but also this elimination of geographical barriers to an integrated economy and society. Meetings of traffic analysts and transport planners do not grab headlines in the same way as political summits in splendid castles, but the blueprints for Europe's future are being drawn by engineers as well as by politicians. European integration and the emergence of the superregions is not comprehensible without taking this into account. The fast-train network is a pan-European effort; other infrastructure projects, like the Channel Tunnel, are regional in nature, even though they often have consequences for the entire continent, and will be described in the superregion chapters.

The Geographic Boundaries

Europe's traditional geographic boundaries are the Arctic Ocean in the north; the Ural Mountains and Ural River in the east; the Caspian Sea, Caucasus Mountains, Black Sea, and Mediterranean Sea in the south; and the Atlantic Ocean in the west. French president

Charles de Gaulle often referred to Europe "from the Atlantic to the Urals" to broaden the focus from just western Europe.

These boundaries exclude the Asian regions of Russia and Turkey, as well as the newly independent Central Asian republics and the trans-Caucasian republics of Georgia, Armenia, and Azerbaijan that used to be part of the Soviet Union. The Bosporus and the Dardanelles, the narrow straits separating the Balkan peninsula from Asia Minor, have long been recognized as the division between Europe and Asia. Designating the Urals as the continent's eastern frontier, however, is somewhat arbitrary; in earlier times, this border was drawn farther west, at the Don or Volga rivers in Russia.

The large islands of Britain and Ireland have always been considered part of geographic Europe. Iceland, 570 miles west of Norway between the North Atlantic and Arctic oceans, was settled by Norwegians and long affiliated with Denmark. An independent republic since 1944, it belongs to the Council of Europe, the Nordic Council, and the European Free Trade Association and so usually is included in political Europe. Most of the big Mediterranean islands are affiliated with countries on the continent—Majorca with Spain, Sicily and Sardinia with Italy, Corsica with France, Crete with Greece. The two independent island republics, Malta and Cyprus, belong to the Council of Europe and have applied for membership in the European Community, even though Malta lies south of Tunis in north Africa and Cyprus crouches in the corner of the Mediterranean between Turkey and Syria, five hundred miles east of Athens.

About 690 million people live in the European boundaries described above, approximately half of them in the twelve member countries of the European Community.

In Greek mythology, Europa was the daughter of the king of Phoenicia—a trading empire on the eastern Mediterranean coast in today's Syria, Lebanon, and Israel—who aroused the lust of Zeus, the supreme deity of the Greeks, to the point that he transformed himself into a bull and carried her away on his back to Crete, where they produced three sons together. If the name Europa is derived from Greek, it could mean "large eyes" or "large face"; if it comes from a Semitic language, as some scholars believe, it could simply mean "west," in contrast to Asia, which means "east." Rather than rummaging around too long for hidden meanings in obscure sources, the French historian Jean-Baptiste Duroselle sensibly concludes, "What can be said in the end except that the word 'Europe' derives from a series of historical accidents as haphazard as those by which America was christened after Vespucci," the otherwise unimportant Italian explorer whose first name, Amerigo, was mistakenly used to designate the New World discovered by Columbus.[1]

As terms for an overarching culture or community, the words *Europe* and *Europeans* have had their ups and downs in history. Largely forgotten when the Romans united much of Europe with parts of Asia and Africa in a single empire, they were very much to the fore when Charlemagne sought to create his empire. Most recently, the European Community has tended to appropriate the terms for its exclusive use, so that the twelve west European countries in the EC are called "Europe" and their citizens are "Europeans," leaving out Swedes, Austrians, Hungarians, Poles, and others who share the European heritage.

The rush of applications at the beginning of the 1990s to join the EC, however, seems to suggest that the Community truly has a manifest destiny to embrace the whole continent. The inspired slogan "Europe 1992," launched in 1985 to proclaim the deadline for achieving the Single Market, gave the EC a momentum that drew everyone along with it, especially after the collapse of an alternative in the East Bloc.

With its sights set on economic and political union by the turn of the century, the EC appeared until recently to be on the way to fulfilling a century and a half of dreams of European federalists. Victor Hugo, the French novelist, was one of several prominent Europeans in the mid-nineteenth century taking up the idea of a "United States of Europe." From his first mention of the concept in 1851 in the French Assembly until his death in 1885, Hugo employed all the passion and eloquence at his command to repeatedly describe his vision of a united Europe built on the ideals of the French Republic.[2] British statesman Winston Churchill began urging a United States of Europe in 1930, a proposal he kept bringing up again, culminating in his famous speech in 1946 in Zurich. By pledging Britain's support for such an undertaking, Churchill seemed to imply that the far-flung British empire, with its "special relationship" to the United States of America, would not be included in a united Europe.

French president Charles de Gaulle in the 1960s and British prime minister Margaret Thatcher in the 1980s were among the fervent antifederalist leaders who insisted that the EC remain an organization of sovereign nation-states, rather than a central government of Europe assuming powers in its own right. They stood out as exceptions, though, among European leaders who favored ever-increasing integration. It became less fashionable to speak of a United States of Europe, but federalists nonetheless seemed to have history on their side as the EC juggernaut hurtled along into the 1990s.

Before the bottom fell out from under his feet, Soviet president Mikhail Gorbachev tried to offer an alternative concept to the EC of Brussels with his advocacy of a "Common European House." The U.S. State Department, ever wary of Soviet attempts to coopt Western Europe, bristled at the term. The U.S. point of view was that a Europe contained by its own borders and cut loose from its ties across the Atlantic would inevitably fall under the sway of the hostile colossus to the east.

Ironically, though, the collapse of the Soviet Union cleared the way for western Europe to move into the vacated terrain in eastern Europe with its economic and political systems, and create a Common European House in its own image.

The European Community

Like many other postwar organizations, the European Community had its origins in the desire of a continent ravaged by fascism and war to preserve democracy and maintain peace by pursuing those goals together. The initial organization, the European Coal and Steel Community (ECSC), established by the Treaty of Paris in 1951, was a way of controlling the German steel industry—the "arms of Krupp"—by coordinating production with other European manufacturers.

An organization with much broader goals, the Council of Europe, had been set up in 1949 to foster "common action in economic, social, cultural, scientific, legal and administrative matters." The Coal and Steel Community, though, featured an important innovation, a "High Authority" which could act in its own right independent of the member governments. To Jean Monnet, the Frenchman who designed the ECSC, it was this independent executive, the forerunner of the EC Commission, which made the ECSC "supranational," an entity above the member states, rather than just

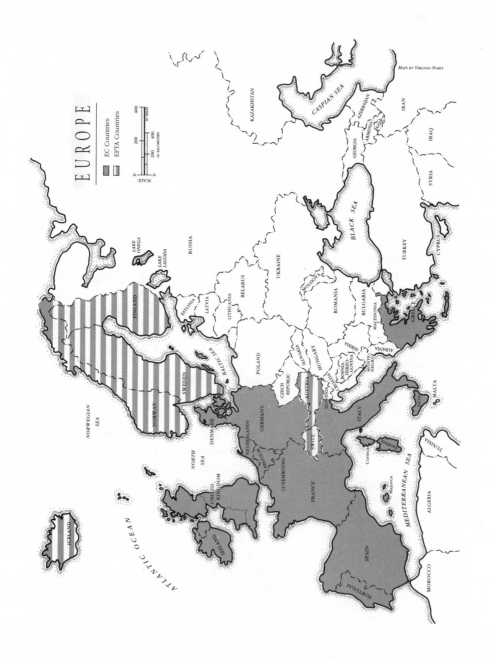

EUROPE

EC Countries
EFTA Countries

SCALE

IN MILES
IN KILOMETERS

ATLANTIC OCEAN

ICELAND

NORWEGIAN SEA

NORTH SEA

IRELAND

UNITED KINGDOM

BELGIUM

NETHERLANDS

LUXEMBOURG

FRANCE

DENMARK

GERMANY

SWITZ.

PORTUGAL

SPAIN

MOROCCO

ALGERIA

TUNISIA

MEDITERRANEAN SEA

Corsica

Sardinia

Majorca

Sicily

ITALY

MALTA

AUSTRIA

CZECH REPUBLIC

SLOVENIA

CROATIA

HUNGARY

SLOVAKIA

POLAND

BALTIC SEA

SWEDEN

NORWAY

FINLAND

LAKE OMEGA

LAKE LADOGA

RUSSIA

ESTONIA

LATVIA

LITHUANIA

BELARUS

UKRAINE

MOLDOVA

ROMANIA

BOSNIA-HERZE-GOVINA

SERBIA

MONTE-NEGRO

MACEDONIA

ALBANIA

BULGARIA

GREECE

BLACK SEA

TURKEY

CYPRUS

KAZAKHSTAN

CASPIAN SEA

GEORGIA

ARMENIA

AZERBAIJAN

IRAN

IRAQ

SYRIA

"international," a cooperation between member states. The conflict between these two notions of what the EC was supposed to be would determine its stop-and-go progress.

In the 1957 Treaties of Rome, which established the European Economic Community (EEC) and the European Atomic Energy Community (Euratom), the initial member states—France, West Germany, Italy, Belgium, Netherlands, and Luxembourg—limited the power of the executive commission so that it did not have the same independence as the ECSC's High Authority. The first president of the new Commission, Walter Hallstein of Germany, set about getting more power for the Commission and for the EC until he ran afoul of De Gaulle, who resisted growing "supranationalism" in the Community. Among other things, France insisted that all major decisions in the EC be unanimous, effectively giving each member state a veto. And so, although the EEC quickly achieved its initial goal of forming a customs union, eliminating tariffs in trade between members, and operating a common regime of tariffs in trade with nonmembers, progress towards the second stage, a Common Market, was slow.

There were watersheds, however. In 1965, the institutions of the three Communities—ECSC, EEC, and Euratom—were merged. In 1973, Britain, Ireland, and Denmark joined the original six members. In 1979, on the initiative of West German chancellor Helmut Schmidt and French president Valery Giscard d'Estaing, two former finance ministers, the European Monetary System (EMS) was formed, linking the exchange rates of European currencies to one another within a narrow band of fluctuation. That year, too, the first direct elections to the European Parliament took place, even though the newly elected deputies still had little real power in the EC's legislative process. Ultimate authority remained with the Council of Ministers, which actually consisted of several functional councils, each one attending to its sector—finance, transport, agriculture—and made up of the respective ministers from the member countries. The EC signed up the southern European countries, Greece in 1981 and Spain and Portugal in 1986, when these countries jettisoned their dictatorships and held democratic elections, even though they were not as economically developed as the other members.

The oil shocks of 1973 and 1979 dampened efforts toward further integration as national governments tried to cope with sharp increases in unemployment and inflation. It was a thankless task that few political leaders survived: In the early 1980s, voters in France exchanged a conservative government for a Socialist one, and those in West Germany and Britain traded leftist governments for rightist.

The EC lost momentum. It had been effectively reduced to administering a program of farm subsidies, if such an active verb can be used for a system that had spun out of control, resulting in massive overproduction that gave us such embarrassing terms as "butter mountain" and "wine lake." In the decade up to 1983, EC farmers, encouraged by the generous subsidies, went from producing 91 percent of cereals consumed in the EC to 116 percent, 96 percent of meat to 101 percent, and 98 percent of butter to 134 percent. The overproduction had to be stored, expensively, or dumped on world markets in a grossly unfair manner. The agriculture ministers who were responsible for the Common Agriculture Program were not responsible for the budget, or for anything, really, except keeping farmer-voters in their respective countries happy. As a result of their shortsighted bounty, the CAP came to account for two-thirds of the EC annual budget. This irritated the British, who felt they did not benefit from the program because of the country's much smaller farming industry and so demanded a budget rebate in compensation. The British budget question—BBQ in Brussels shorthand—distracted the EC from more important matters for a decade, until a compromise was reached in 1985.

It was the arrival in that year of former French finance minister Jacques Delors at the head of the EC Commission that marked a turnaround in EC fortunes. A driven, devoted public servant of the type known fondly in France as a Catholic militant, Delors had the right combination of intelligence, charisma, and persistence to get the EC moving again. A British member of the Commission, Lord Cockfield, drew up a proposal with three hundred specific measures for achieving the original goal of the EC to create a Common Market, with free movement of labor and capital, goods and services. In order to facilitate adoption of the measures, the EC reformed its voting procedures by amending the Treaty of Rome and set a deadline, December 31, 1992, for enacting the directives for a Common Market. The Single European Act, referring to the treaty reforms, and the Single Market, referring to the relaunched notion of the Common Market, became the icons of a fervent new belief in the future of "Europe."

The renewed determination of the EC coincided with an economic resurgence in Europe that made the goal of economic integration seem more attainable. Businessmen started to think more seriously in genuinely European terms. A well-publicized report by Paolo Cecchini of Italy, a former member of the Commission, demonstrated that the Single Market could increase economic growth in the EC by a full 1 percent a year. Nontariff barriers like industrial norms were being removed, paperwork for goods crossing borders was to be eliminated, financial services like banking and insurance could be offered throughout the EC without special licenses in each country. The European Monetary System had fairly well maintained exchange-rate stability in the EC, saving business the losses from currency devaluations or the costs of insuring against that risk. Government and business leaders had a new optimism that trickled down to the man and woman in the street.

After all the false starts, the EC seemed to be finally headed for a genuinely common market. As the EC directives emerged from the Community's legislative machinery, they increased the Commission's power to intervene in the economies of the member states. Economic integration, with a real loss of sovereignty, was an idea whose time finally had come. As Nico Colchester of *The Economist* commented in a July 1992 special report on the EC, "An economic imperative glues today's ambitious European structure together. Much of the authority surrendered by national governments to the EC has gone there not out of idealism, but because that authority no longer works at home. . . . For good or ill, the technology of moving goods, services, people and money around has ousted the European nation as the convenient unit of economic administration."[3] The same functional role that had enabled the nation-state to rise and prosper in the nineteenth century, Colchester concluded, was shaping the EC today.

Small wonder that Delors, latest in a long line of Frenchmen with a federal vision for Europe, was tempted to use the wonderful momentum to steamroller even more ambitious structures for economic and political integration onto the European landscape. He wanted to make another Great Leap Forward right away, using the Single Market as a springboard even before it was in place. Delors and French president Francois Mitterrand feared that any interruption in EC progress toward unity would make a larger, reunified Germany lose interest in the rest of western Europe, and go its own way, with the same fateful consequences as earlier forays of the restless giant. Even chancellor Helmut Kohl agreed it was necessary to "bind" Germany more firmly to the other EC members. Despite the four decades intervening, the Treaty of Maastricht for economic and political union signed in 1992 had much the same mixed motivation of fear and hope as the original Treaty of Paris setting up the first European Community.

European Monetary Union

The word *Erzgebirge*, the name of a modest mountain range separating Germany from the Czech Republic, means "ore mountains" in English. In 1515, a large silver vein was discovered at Sankt Joachimstal, on the Bohemian, or Czech, side of the mountains. Within a few years, the new mine was minting a coin, the "Joachimstaler," which set new standards in fineness and quality. Hundreds of different types of coins, struck by princes and bankers, circulated in Renaissance Europe, and huge exchange fairs were held to clear accounts for merchants who traded in the myriad monies. But the new coin, because of its qualities, gained wider currency than most. The name was shortened to "taler" in everyday parlance, and that word eventually became "dollar" in English.

A few hundred years before the silver discovery in Sankt Joachimstal, Louis IX, the saintly king of medieval France, had minted another silver coin, the "ecu," a French word that also means "shield." The name came to designate various gold and silver coins up through the eighteenth century. In the late twentieth century, thanks to bureaucrats' love for acronyms and a somewhat labored pun, ECU, the European Currency Unit, made the ecu live again. The Treaty on European Union signed in Maastricht in February 1992 proposed to make the ecu the single currency for all of Europe by the year 2000, a counterweight in world trade and finance to the U.S. dollar. Pounds, crowns, marks, and francs were to make way for the ecu.

The Maastricht treaty set out the details of the currency, the European-wide central bank system that would guarantee it, the criteria to be fulfilled by countries eligible to join the European Monetary Union, and the deadlines by which these criteria—limits on inflation, external payments deficits, government spending deficits—must be fulfilled. The European Monetary System set up in 1979 had also called for a European central bank and common currency, but these projects fizzled out in the course of the 1980s because of the wide divergences in member states' finances. The Maastricht treaty tried to rectify that failure by drawing up an "irreversible" timetable. Monetary union would not wait for laggards —the train would leave the station at a set time and those who were not aboard would be left behind.

The supporters of European monetary union claimed that the discipline of a single currency was necessary to bring recalcitrant national governments into line on economic management, and that, in turn, was necessary for the smooth functioning of the Single Market and continued economic prosperity in Europe. Since the Single Market had not yet been established, some argued that monetary union was *not* necessary. The case was made that the EMS, which linked together the national currencies in a flexible band, was sufficient for the purpose.

Critics of monetary union, like Karl Otto Pohl, the longtime president of the German central bank, the Bundesbank, feared that a single currency would deprive weaker economic performers, like the southern European countries, of the mechanism—devaluation of the national currency—they needed to adjust their lagging performance to that of stronger countries. The consequence was glaring in the former East Germany, following its monetary union with West Germany in July 1990: Much of East Germany's industry was rendered uncompetitive overnight and a large portion of the labor force put out of work. Supporters countered that the United States, with its single currency, covers a broad territory with wide divergences in productivity from region to region. Wage and price differentials take account of the divergences.

One of the real driving forces toward monetary union, though, was that the existing EMS lent itself to domination by the strongest currency, which invariably was the German mark. Because the currencies were all tied together, monetary policy in each country had to follow the lead of the dominant member. If Germany raised interest rates, Britain and France had to follow suit or risk coming under pressure to devalue their currencies, which was politically embarrassing. This galled the British and French governments, who were thus blocked from applying monetary stimulus to their national economies even when they deemed it urgently necessary. In the early 1990s, for example, Britain found itself wracked by a prolonged recession but forced to *raise* interest rates, thus exacerbating its problems, in lockstep with the Bundesbank, which was worried about the inflationary effects of reunification in Germany and not about Britain's recession. A European central bank, with representation from each of the member states on a board of governors, seemed to be the best remedy for having the continent's monetary policy dictated by just one member following its own agenda.

Money, of course, is no longer the province of merchants and miners, but exclusively that of princes—namely the nation-states, who have made a national currency with a state-owned central bank one of the great centralizing mechanisms of the modern state. A country's currency has joined the flag and the national anthem as one of the most revered icons of national glory, a symbol in some subtle Freudian sense of the nation's potency. This was especially true for West Germany in the postwar period, with so many of its other national traditions shamed by the war. In a way much less overt than Hitler's rantings and rearmament after World War I, the strength of the deutsche mark served equally well as a vindication of German qualities vis-à-vis the country's erstwhile conquerors.

The European Community's "Democratic Deficit"

The Maastricht treaty also set out certain goals for closer political union in the EC, although in much less detail than the monetary union. The feeling was growing among many European politicians that economic integration must be accompanied by more political integration, that "Europe" as a unit should have the same weight in international politics as it did in the international economy.

These ideas were not new. The French proposed several schemes in the 1950s and 1960s, but these invariably foundered. The European Council (*not* the Council of Europe), the summit of EC heads of state and government that met regularly from 1973 on, became the ultimate forum for political cooperation. In practice, however, the EC leaders rarely found matters of any importance where they could formulate a unified policy.

Building on this experience, the Maastricht treaty made the European Council the centerpiece of the European Union. Cooperation in foreign policy, security, and defense technically would take place outside the EC properly speaking, although the EC institutions—Commission, Parliament, Court of Justice—would be involved in various ways. But the Council, assisted by a secretariat in Brussels, would be the sole legislative and executive body for these "pillars" of the "Union." The idea was to play down control of these sovereign privileges by any supranational institutions and to emphasize the intergovernmental character of political cooperation. The treaty offered few specifics, although it did designate the Western European Union, a moribund organization for military cooperation whose function was usurped by NATO, as the operational arm of a common defense policy.

The treaty had its ambitions, although it was often vague about how to attain them. It tried to replace the original Treaty of Rome with its European Communities, through a European Union, claiming a much wider field of cooperation and integration. It forced the pace of the member states, because its backers were mortally afraid that the EC would slip back into another twenty-year morass of confusion and stagnation if the momentum of the Single Market were not maintained.

In June 1992, a referendum on the treaty in Denmark yielded a small majority against Maastricht. An Irish referendum later in the month overwhelmingly approved the treaty, and a French referendum in September produced a wafer-thin margin in favor of Maastricht. Most countries did not need a referendum to ratify the treaty. Spanish, Greek, and Italian parliaments approved Maastricht, but the British government, faced with growing opposition in its own Conservative Party, was forced to postpone a final vote until 1993. Far from gaining the easy approval expected for it, the Maastricht treaty became increasingly vulnerable to revision or even defeat. The Danish vote alone could have killed the treaty, which depended on unanimous ratification to go into effect. But EC leaders agreed to give Denmark some special exemptions and the Danes approved the treaty in a second referendum in May 1993.

The malaise in the Maastricht debate seemed due in large part to the perceived "democratic deficit" in Community institutions. As the EC bureaucracy in Brussels grew in size and authority, the lack of institutional checks and balances built into most western democracies became more apparent. Civil servants in EC directorates were making decisions involving millions of dollars and thousands of jobs without any parliamentary oversight or control. It was not only that these officials could be susceptible to corruption, but that even the honest and sincere technocrat had too much unchecked power.

The European Parliament had a passive role in the legislative process. At first for the budget, and then in a wider field following the Single European Act, the Parliament could reject or amend legislation from the Council of Ministers, a veto that could be overruled only by a unanimous vote of the Council. To keep them from exercising this sanction, the deputies were consulted more often and saw their influence grow. Parliament also had, theoretically, the right to dismiss the Commission, but the right to appoint a new one remained with the Council of Ministers, as did the initiative for legislation. So the Parliament was not a full partner in the legislative process and did not have the authority or ability to oversee the executive like most national parliaments.

But the democratic deficit that caught up with Maastricht was at the national and regional level. Denmark, perhaps significantly, was the only country where the national parliament routinely reviewed the actions of its ministers in the EC. For the most part, European governments conducted their affairs in Brussels without any debate at home. The sessions of the Council of Ministers took place behind closed doors. In difficult domestic situations, as when Germany wanted to raise its value-added tax, the national sales tax, in 1991, politicians blamed the bogeyman Brussels—in this case, the German finance minister said the EC had mandated a minimum rate and Germany had no choice but to obey. This tactic of using Brussels as a whipping boy sometimes relieved short-term political pressures at home, but in the long run it gave the EC a bad reputation.

It was this lack of democratic accountability, above all, that led to a growing fear of rule by Brussels bureaucrats. It was not the size of the EC bureaucracy—the Commission staff in 1992, including the army of interpreters, was 16,000, one-third the staff employed by the city of Paris, for example—but the lack of control by elected officials that made the Brussels "technocrats" seem prone to willful or arbitrary decisions.

The European Economic Area

Britain instigated talks for a European Free Trade Association (EFTA) in the 1950s as an alternative to the nascent European Economic Community, which was too supranationalist and too interventionist for British taste at the time. London enlisted other West European countries—Austria, Denmark, Norway, Sweden, Switzerland, Portugal—who for various reasons were not interested in joining the EEC, but who liked the idea of a forming a free trade zone with it. Austria, Sweden, and Switzerland, especially, felt that their political neutrality ruled out a close economic alliance with NATO countries, but did not exclude the possibility of a favorable trade regime. And so the Stockholm Convention established EFTA in 1960.

The organization functioned well enough, eliminating most tariffs in industrial trade and regulating exchanges in other sectors. It became willy-nilly a halfway house to the EC. Britain, having at last accepted the changes in economic realities in the postwar world, left in 1972 to join the EC, taking Denmark along. Iceland joined EFTA in 1970, and Finland in 1986, after being linked to it since the beginning through a series of bilateral agreements.

In 1989, EFTA embarked on a negotiating process with the EC to extend the planned Single Market to its members, creating a European Economic Area (EEA). By October 1991, after a marathon session resolving such ticklish issues as how many Spanish trawlers could fish in the Barents Sea off Norway and how many Greek trucks could transit the Brenner Pass in Austria, the parties proclaimed a free trade zone reaching from the Arctic to the Mediterranean, which, with 380 million more or less well-heeled consumers and a gross domestic product of $7 trillion, constituted the biggest economic bloc in the world, bigger even than the proposed North American Free Trade Association linking Canada, Mexico, and the United States. After a last-minute hitch to clarify the jurisdiction of the European Court of Justice, the EC institution that adjudicates any disputes in EC law, the agreement was ready for ratification in the member countries so that it could go into effect with the official opening of the Single Market on January 1, 1993.

But the long negotiations brought home to the EFTA members that if they were willing to get this close to the EC, accepting to a great extent not only its benefits but its constraints, perhaps they would be better off having a voice in shaping its policies as full members. Also, the collapse of communism in eastern Europe in 1989 and in the Soviet Union in 1991 obviated the need for Austria, Sweden, Finland, and Switzerland to worry any longer about neutrality. Austria, in fact, already had applied for EC membership in 1989. In 1992, the other three neutrals all applied to join the EC, hoping to accede at the same time as Austria, in 1995 or 1996.

For all these well-developed, prosperous countries with market economies and democratic institutions, negotiation for entry into the EC is considered a formality. Many of the particular trade issues needing to be resolved when a country joins the EC have already been taken care of in the EEA negotiations, further smoothing the way. In the meantime, because of the EEA agreement, they can enjoy the advantages of the Single Market from the beginning.

Enlarging the European Community

The collapse of communism in eastern Europe in 1989 embarrassed the EC. The Brussels federalists feared that the economic convergence of west European countries they had worked so hard to arrange would be submerged in the poverty and backwardness of the east European countries. So they tried to argue that "Europe," meaning western Europe, must proceed with its plans for greater economic and political union—a single currency, common foreign policy, common security policy—before taking new members on board. In practical terms, it would be much easier to get the twelve west European states to agree on the terms of unity rather than the potential twenty-four members of an expanded Community. Once the institutions were in place, the new members could take it or leave it, but could not negotiate.

There was another consideration. Major enlargement of the Community would entail a thoroughgoing overhaul of its institutions: the number and nominating procedure for Commission members and the extent of its executive powers, the debating and voting methods of the Council of Ministers, the makeup of the European Parliament. An institutional commitment to closer union before this restructuring would ensure that the changes reinforced the supranational character of the EC.

The political and economic situation of the east European countries, however, demanded their inclusion in that market as soon as possible regardless of the pace of economic and political union. It was hardly possible for a European country to countenance life *outside* the Community. The exception that proved the rule was Iceland, which ruled out full EC membership because it did not want to share its two-hundred-mile fishing zone, which generates 70 percent of the country's exports. For most other countries in Europe, though, exclusion from the EC would mean the life of an economic pariah. Having arrogated to itself the title of "Europe," the EC found itself obliged, once the Iron Curtain was removed, to live up to it.

By the end of 1991, the EC negotiated "association" agreements with the three most advanced economies in eastern Europe—Hungary, Poland, and Czechoslovakia. The three countries, who had signed a cooperation pact among themselves earlier in the year, insisted that the EC agreements specify that full membership was their eventual goal, because the precedent for such association agreements, concluded with Turkey in 1963, was used as a tactic for delaying full membership.

The EC argued that the economic gap between these countries and western Europe was too wide to permit full membership in the near future. But one 1991 calculation of per capita income, on the basis of purchasing power parity, put Czechoslovakia's at 66 percent of the EC average, ahead of Ireland with 63 percent or Greece with 58 percent, while Hungary had 53 percent, the same as Portugal. The most populous and poorest of the three east European countries, Poland, had about the same income and population as Spain thirty years previously, and Poland felt EC membership would lead to the same economic boom as it had in Spain.

The association agreements themselves were ungenerous, because they excluded or sharply limited those products—farm goods, textiles, steel—in which the three countries had a competitive advantage. Hungary, for instance, was only allowed to export 5,000 tons of beef to the EC in the first year; in the mid-1970s, when it had a communist government, Hungary exported 100,000 tons of beef to the nine countries of the EC, paying duty on all of it. The spectacle of rich, prosperous western Europe begrudging the desperate east European countries access to its markets drew criticism not only in the countries concerned, but in the EC as well.

As 1992 wore on, the difficulties of ratifying the Maastricht treaty, the strains in the European Monetary System caused by Germany's financing of its reunification, the unsteady course of Russia and other former republics of the Soviet Union, and, not least, the war in the former Yugoslavia were making debates about whether to widen or deepen the EC, to make it supranational or international, seem more and more academic. The EC officially still consisted of twelve member states, but with several others effectively part of the economic sphere, it was actually much bigger. Through various structures and in various degrees, every country in Europe was being integrated into the EC economy. The future seemed to lie in a more flexible structure with varying degrees of participation, depending on need and ability, or, as *The Economist* liked to call it, a "Europe à la carte."[4]

Other European Organizations

International organizations dot the European landscape, testimony to ideas too far ahead of their time or long since out of date. In the surprisingly nimble way otherwise slothful bureaucracies can demonstrate when it comes to self-preservation, they adapt and manage to make themselves useful enough to avoid extinction. They are not driving forces of integration, but they create other networks holding Europe together.

One example is the Western European Union, which had its origins in the Brussels Treaty of 1948, when Britain, France, Belgium, Netherlands, and Luxembourg banded together to formulate a common defense policy in view of the emerging Soviet threat. After a project for a European Defense Community fell through in 1954, the WEU, adding West Germany and Italy, undertook to coordinate West European defense issues, in collaboration with NATO. With NATO doing all the heavy-duty military coordination, WEU subsided into inactivity until French president Mitterrand suggested in 1983 that it become a forum for creating a European "identity" in defense. The notion won enough support to relaunch the WEU. It was an insurance policy of sorts to give Europe a fallback in case the United States decided to pull out of Europe or, as in the case of president Ronald Reagan's Strategic Defense Initiative (Star Wars), if the U.S. went in directions Europe did not want to follow.

When the Maastricht treaty specified that the WEU should be developed as a defense arm for the EC, it was only affirming the role it already had taken on.

A more universal organization is the Council of Europe, established in 1949 to proclaim postwar Europe's commitment to democracy. The number of members increased steadily from the initial ten as applicant countries passed the litmus test of having democratic governments in office. When members like Greece or Turkey experienced military coups, they were suspended until democracy was restored. Thus, at the beginning of the 1990s, when East European countries first elected noncommunist governments, it was the Council of Europe that certified their acceptance into the club of democratic nations by admitting Hungary, Czechoslovakia, Poland, and Bulgaria, bringing membership up to twenty-seven. Once new nations obtained diplomatic recognition, like the Baltic republics, the Council took up contact with them and advised them on setting up democratic institutions, with a view to eventual membership in the organization.

Outfitted from the beginning with a Ministerial Committee and an Assembly of parliamentarians, the Council of Europe had a wide-ranging mandate for cooperation in "economic, social, cultural, scientific, legal and administrative matters." But it lacked the driving force of an independent executive, and was soon overtaken by the EC. Early efforts to merge the two groups met opposition from the neutral countries, who felt they could participate in the Council but not in the EC. The Council continued to be useful, though, particularly in the social, cultural, and legal areas neglected by the EC. One of its first successes was the Convention on Human Rights in 1950, which created the Commission on Human Rights and a Court of Human Rights, where individuals can seek redress for alleged violations of basic rights. The Council has organized more than a hundred treaties and numerous other conventions—like "Legal Status of Children Born out of Wedlock" and "Data Protection Convention"—to harmonize national legislation. It all falls short, though, of the hopes originally put in the institution. As British analyst Clive Archer concluded, "The Council of Europe has not lived up to the expectations of the federalists involved in its creation: it has not provided the legislative, executive and judicial institutions for a federal Western Europe."[5] That became the destiny of the EC.

An energetic Frenchwoman, Catherine Lalumiere, who became secretary general of the Council of Europe in 1989, nonetheless saw much for the Council to do in postcommunist Europe. One new niche, she thought, was to succor would-be EC members, both those already included in the European Economic Area and those outside it. "What is actually coming into being, empirically, is a vast economic space with concentric circles, of which the Community is the center."[6] Those outside the inner circle may have difficulty getting a hearing in Brussels, but they have a voice in Strasbourg, the home of the Council of Europe.

Soon after the fall of the Berlin Wall in November 1989, Mitterrand, alarmed at the prospect of east European countries trying to get into the EC, called for a new "confederation" to bring east and west Europe together, a kind of buffer between the emerging democracies and direct access to the EC. Later, looking more realistically at the obstacles to mounting another new pan-European organization, he conceded that the Council of Europe should rather be strengthened to perform this function, a challenge readily taken up by his compatriot. Lalumiere personally began visiting the independent republics emerging from the breakup of Yugoslavia and the Soviet Union, even venturing to the ex-Soviet Central Asian republics—Kazakhstan, Uzbekistan, Turkmenistan, Tadzhikistan— which few people would consider part of Europe. But their old ties to European Russia and their new ties to Turkey, a Council member since 1949, brought them within the organization's purview.

The Helsinki Process

When Alvar Aalto drew up the plans for Finlandia Hall in the 1960s, he envisioned the concert and conference hall as part of a massive development to create a modern new city center in Helsinki, which would include an opera house, an art museum, a library, and other public buildings. The striking edifice, with its gleaming facade of white Carrara marble, was completed in 1972, in time to host the Conference on Security and Cooperation in Europe (CSCE). But Helsinki failed to follow through on the famous architect's grand plan. So the delegates to the Helsinki conference, like the visitor today, looked out not at the heart of a northern metropolis, but onto a railway freight yard and a sterile parking lot.

Aalto made another miscalculation. He wanted to infuse chilly Finland with some Mediterranean warmth and convinced everyone, apparently without any evidence, that expensive Italian marble could withstand the near-Arctic cold of Helsinki winters better than most other surfaces. This turned out to be wishful thinking, and by the beginning of the 1990s, the huge slabs began to buckle and crack, threatening passers-by with falling chunks of stone. The need to replace the marble posed a problem for the city, because Aalto had designed everything in the hall as a harmonious whole, and any tinkering was bound to diminish the building's aesthetic impact.

In July 1975, long before the facade began to fall apart, the leaders of thirty-five countries met in a solemn summit in Finlandia Hall to sign the Helsinki Final Act. Thirty-three European countries from both sides of the Iron Curtain, together with the United States and Canada, officially ended World War II by recognizing the continent's postwar borders. It was the Final Act's commitment to respect human rights, however, that led to what became known as the "Helsinki process," a series of follow-up meetings to monitor adherence to the treaty's guarantee of basic rights. In the wake of perestroika and then the collapse of communist rule in eastern Europe and the Soviet Union, it would be a mistake to underestimate the role of the Helsinki Act as an internationally recognized moral reference for dissidents throughout the East Bloc.

Western governments, particularly the United States, were skeptical and suspicious when Finnish president Uhro Kekkonen first proposed the Helsinki meeting in the 1960s. Kekkonen had been casting about for a way to divert Soviet pressure on Finland to join the Warsaw Pact. The country was proud of the fact that it had avoided the fate of other Soviet neighbors, forced to accept a communist government and centrally planned economies, even though its foreign policy was severely constrained by the eight-hundred-mile border it shared with the Soviet Union. So Finland, like the East Bloc countries, stoically refused sorely needed Marshall Plan aid after the war and did not join the westward-leaning Council of Europe until 1988.

Some U.S. policymakers saw Kekkonen's conference as a Trojan horse for the Soviet Union to achieve the goal America had worried about for years—the "Finlandization" of Western Europe, or at least of Germany. It was for the same reason that they were cool to Gorbachev's talk of a "Common European House."

By the beginning of 1991, after the reunification of Germany and the collapse of the Soviet Union, this attitude changed. U.S. Secretary of State James Baker joined with German Foreign Minister Hans-Dietrich Genscher, maligned for a long time in Washington as a stalking horse for creeping Finlandization, in assigning an important new role for an institutionalized CSCE. Not content with a modest European house stretching from the Atlantic to the Urals, the two men spoke of a "Euro-Atlantic Community" stretching from Vancouver, on the west coast of Canada at the U.S. border, to Vladivostok, on the eastern coast of Asian Russia. The attractive alliteration seemed to exclude only Japan among the nations of the northern hemisphere, but even that country came to the 1992 Helsinki summit of the CSCE as a "special honorary associate."

At a 1990 summit meeting in Paris, the CSCE reaffirmed its commitment to human rights in a ringing "Charter for a New Europe." It also adopted several practical measures to institutionalize the Helsinki process, establishing a permanent secretariat in Prague, as well as a Conflict Prevention Center in Vienna, and an office in Warsaw to monitor elections throughout Europe. The meeting also provided the framework for NATO and the Warsaw Pact to sign a wide-ranging treaty to reduce conventional armed forces.

By the time of the Helsinki summit in the summer of 1992, the CSCE had outgrown Finlandia Hall. Preparatory work was moved to Marina Congress Center in a new hotel complex at Helsinki's colorful port, and the summit itself was held in the city's commercial exhibition grounds. Following the break-up of Yugoslavia and the Soviet Union, membership had swollen to fifty-two countries. Marina management worried about finding enough flagpoles; newcomer Bosnia-Herzegovina managed to get its flag sewn only in time for the final week of the preparatory conference.

Frustrated by its inability to intervene in the Yugoslavian conflict, the group appointed a high commissioner for national minorities, strengthened its rotating presidency, and registered as a regional organization with the UN so that it could mount military peacekeeping missions. Kekkonen and Soviet leader Leonid Brezhnev, the architects of the original Helsinki conference, were dead and buried, but the CSCE underwent a metamorphosis to try to keep the facade of the Common European House from crumbling away.

After Maastricht

The Maastricht treaty eventually limped its way to ratification, a shadow of itself in letter and spirit. The long debate, close referendum votes, and court challenges weakened the treaty's claim to be a mandate for European unity. Resistance to the treaty served notice to the Commission to trim back its intervention and heralded further difficulties in translating the provisions of the treaty on political union into concrete measures.

In the short term, ratification ensured that the organizational steps toward economic and monetary union—particularly the establishment in 1994 of a European Monetary Institute as forerunner of the European Central Bank—would go ahead. But no one could give reliable odds about how close the national economies would come to the convergence called for in the treaty to achieve monetary union by the end of the decade.

Ratification was important, however, because it allowed the EC, sadder but wiser, to continue its work of integration. The vision of a federal Europe with a strong center that had guided the treaty negotiators had grown dimmer. The treaty had been hammered into a more malleable framework that would permit a more complex, less centralized organization to be built. As such, it fit into the overall pattern of European integration, moving two steps forward and one step back.

Europe needs more flexibility, because the integration already achieved has encouraged greater autonomy and self-determination in the smaller, homogeneous units making up the nation-states that in turn make up the EC and other pan-European organizations. The emergence of these independent-minded regions and their impact on the economic and social structures of Europe are examined in the next chapter.

CHAPTER THREE

CITIES AND THE WEALTH OF REGIONS

When an international traveler arrives at the new terminal in Barcelona's Prat airport, he knows he has reached the Mediterranean. Palm trees three stories high rise gracefully in the spacious hall, while the polished floor gleams in a rosy terra-cotta color. The vast tinted windows on all sides filter through the hazy sunshine, creating a balmy, resort atmosphere.

Barcelona spent $7 billion getting ready for the 1992 Summer Olympics. In addition to expanding the airport, the city acquired two dozen new hotels, 864 acres of new parks, 3 miles of new beaches, 200,000 new trees, a new coastal highway, the Olympic sports complex, a "national" theater for Catalonia, a conference center, and a housing development for 8,000 people, initially for the athletes, which, like New York's Battery Park City or London's Docklands, reclaimed a stretch of derelict shoreline. Barcelona's historic Gothic quarter, its port, the Ramblas shopping street, and the theatrical Gaudi architecture made the city beautiful even before, and the improvements made it stunning.

With more than 3 million people in the metropolitan area, Barcelona is the economic powerhouse of the western Mediterranean. A decade of booming growth prior to the Olympics, which saw real estate triple and quadruple in value, was restoring Barcelona to a preeminence it had not enjoyed since the Middle Ages. At that time, united with its hinterland of Aragon, Barcelona controlled a maritime empire that embraced Sardinia, Sicily, Naples, and half of Greece.

As capital of Catalonia, the region in northeastern Spain that occupies one-fifteenth of the country's surface but generates one-fifth of its income, Barcelona has emerged as one of the champions of regional autonomy in an integrated Europe. Jordi Pujol, president of the Generalitat—the Catalonian governing body that had its origins in Barcelona's prime and may be the oldest representative parliament in Europe—has argued with Madrid and Brussels that his region, which is larger than Belgium and has a language more than a thousand years old spoken by more people than Danish or Finnish, deserves the same type of recognition as these nation-states. The emergence of much smaller countries like Latvia and Slovenia has only strengthened Pujol's case.

Barcelona joins every organization possible that furthers this cause. Catalonia has linked up with three other strong regions that also combine a teeming, prosperous city with a richly developed hinterland—Lombardy with its capital Milan in Italy, Rhone-Alpes with Lyons in France, and Baden-Wurttemberg with Stuttgart in Germany—to form the "Four Motors" of Europe. Barcelona was a charter member of Club Eurometropoles, set up in 1990 to establish political and economic links between eighteen noncapital cities in Europe, as well as Eurocities, a wider grouping to foster cooperation in more mundane sectors of municipal administration. Fortifying its role as an economic pole in the Latin Crescent, Barcelona helped found the "C6" group, becoming the hub of a dual network of six cities, with Majorca, Valencia, and Saragossa on one side, and Toulouse and Montpellier on the other.

Casting about to describe Barcelona, Isabelle Dussutour, executive secretary of Club Eurometropoles in Bordeaux, says, "It's so big, it works with everybody. It's—it's," the young Frenchwoman fumbles, searching for just the right word to convey Barcelona's might and magnificence, "it's *Paris*!" So there.

Catalonia, one of Europe's best-known regions in the wake of the Olympics, is the smallest of the Four Motors, measured by gross domestic product. The largest, Baden-Wurttemberg in southwest Germany, has 9 million people, 50 percent more than Catalonia, but three times the GDP. The Lombardy province in northern Italy is nearly as large as the German region in both population and production, while the Rhone-Alpes region in southeastern France, the smallest in population with just over 5 million people, has a GDP about half that of the two biggest.

With its distinctive language and history, Catalonia is the exception in claiming nationhood for itself. The other regions in the group are political units rather than ethnic. Even Lombardy, the Italian region settled by the German Langobard tribe in late antiquity, makes no ethnic or linguistic claims to autonomy after centuries of intermingling with other Italians. The Lombard League, a local political movement that grew to become the Northern League, has openly called for a separation of industrious northern Italy from the southern half of the peninsula, which it believes to be irremediably suffering from economic stagnation and Mafia corruption; but this is strictly political and common to similar regional movements in northern Italy. Even Catalonia's Pujol has refrained from seeking outright independence from Spain, while pushing hard for more autonomy.

What the four regions do have in common is that they are among the most dynamic cities and regions in Europe, each having enjoyed a resurgence in the 1980s. When they banded together in September 1988 to promote cooperation in business, research, professional formation, student exchange, tourism, culture, environment, and social work, some journalists and businessmen criticized the endeavor as a public relations gimmick to promote provincial politicians. It certainly has worked as a public relations exercise, whatever concrete results might come from the targeted areas of cooperation. The Four Motors have played prominently in national and international media, who, based in the European capitals, normally treated the regional economic centers as marginal (with the exception of Milan, which is Italy's financial and business capital).

The leaders of these four regions have been among the most vocal on the continent calling for a "Europe of the Regions" and a "Europe of the Cities." They want the big cities and regions to constitute a third level of political decision-making in an integrated Europe, on a par with the European and national levels. Networks like the Four Motors, Eurometropoles, and Eurocities have brought mayors and regional leaders together to exchange expertise and to lobby for that voice in decision-making. Well-established regional authorities, like Baden-Wurttemberg and the other provinces (*Länder*) in federal Germany, want to preserve the powers they already have from encroachment by Brussels, while newly enfranchised regions, like Catalonia and Lombardy, want to increase their powers through further devolution in their own countries.

Europe of the Regions

Europe was a continent of cities and regions long before borders of the nation-states were fixed in the nineteenth and twentieth centuries. From the time of the Greek city-state, the *polis,* the liberal tradition of western society was anchored in the notion of a free city, the home of markets, merchants, craftsmen, cathedrals, and universities. Between the eleventh and thirteenth centuries, the time so critical for forming European culture, an urban network grew up across the continent. Krzysztof Pomian, a Polish historian living in Paris, describes this phenomenon:

> During this period, a network of cities emerged on the European map that was to remain unchanged in its main lines until the industrial revolution. From Bruges and Ghent—opposite the English cities, first and foremost London, on the other side of the Channel—the network spanned the Rhineland, southern Germany, Switzerland, the region of the big Italian lakes to Genoa, Florence and Venice. The Rhine cities were the basis for three further branches: One ran to the north to the Hanseatic cities (Hamburg, Bremen, Lubeck, Danzig); one to the south, that ran over Paris, Dijon and the Rhone valley to Marseilles, Barcelona and Valencia; and a third to the east, that crossed Germany and reached as far as Prague and Cracow, Lviv, Vienna and Buda.[1]

This hardy network survived the rise and fall of various kingdoms and empires. The industrial revolution, which fostered the nation-state, also gave rise to new urban conglomerations, while leaving the basic grid of cities remarkably intact. As Bruges's port silted up, first Antwerp and now Rotterdam have taken over as the main western port of northern Europe. Stuttgart, headquarters of Daimler-Benz, Germany's biggest industrial company, has come to overshadow the university town of Tubingen or the cathedral city of Freiburg in southwest Germany. Milan and Turin have replaced Venice and Genoa in importance as industrial manufacturing has become the basis of the modern economy instead of commerce. In many other cases—Hamburg, Prague, Lyons, Barcelona, to name just a few—prosperous medieval cities adapted to industry and became prosperous modern cities.

As economic development continues and the nation-state recedes, the cities are ready to reemerge as major players and to reestablish their own networks. The roll call of cities that initially signed up for Club Eurometropoles—national capitals are excluded from membership—demonstrates a striking historic continuity: Amsterdam, Antwerp, Barcelona, Birmingham, Bordeaux, Frankfurt, Glasgow, Lille, Lyons, Leipzig, Manchester, Marseilles, Milan, Munich, Oporto, Rotterdam, Stuttgart, Turin.

"Europe of the Regions" and "Europe of the Cities" emerged as slogans only late in the 1980s, but the trend has been gathering momentum for some time, largely undetected by a media and public opinion focused on national issues. John Ardagh, a British journalist who has written several books about Europe, saw traces of it early on. In his 1979 book, *A Tale of Five Cities*, he examined five provincial cities in Europe: Stuttgart in southwest Germany, Toulouse in southwest France, Bologna in northern Italy, Newcastle in northern England, and Ljubljana, then in Yugoslavia and now capital of an independent Slovenia. Ardagh writes:

> They are all, in one way or another, involved in the post-war growth of regional feeling. While the nation-states have been groping towards some new unity, there has also been a move in the inverse direction, towards greater regionalism: the two are complementary. This regional trend takes various forms, economic, political, emotional or cultural. In those regions which rightly or wrongly have some sense of their own nationhood— notably Scotland, Brittany, the Basque country—it has even led to separatist campaigns. None of my five towns are in these areas. And yet, in all the five countries featured in this book, and in others too such as Spain, there has been some distinct movement since 1945 towards greater political devolution.[2]

For most of their history, Europeans have identified with their region rather than with a nation. Nationalism generally was not a grassroots movement, but represented the desire of a political elite to create a state. It was the state, then, that instilled a national consciousness in its citizens. British historian Eric J. Hobsbawm recounts the story of the leader of the Italian Risorgimento who told the first parliament of the new state: "We have made Italy, now we have to make Italians."[3] Only 2.5 percent of the Italian population at the time of unification used the language we call Italian for everyday purposes; otherwise they used local dialects. In modern Italian, it is not grammatically acceptable to say, "I am from Italy." The native speaker will call himself "Italian," but go on to say that he comes from Florence, or Tuscany, or Bologna, or Emilio-Romagna, naming his city or region.

Polish novelist Andrzej Szczypiorski tells of an experience he had in the mid-1960s in Germany, evidence of the same strong regional identification in that country. He happened one evening to be drinking wine on a terrace in Baden-Baden, in southwest Germany, with an elderly local gentleman who said that in his opinion the Baden people were not German at all but more like the French—they loved wine, pretty women, and were separated only by the Rhine from *douce France*. Language was their only tie to Germany, he said. By chance, the Polish writer was in Hamburg only two days later and fell into conversation with another gentleman, dressed in a tweed jacket and sailor cap, a pipe clenched between his teeth, who confided that there was no "German" tradition in Hamburg. They were closer to Scandinavia or Great Britain, their customs determined by the sea, with its emphasis on individual liberty, and so on. Szczypiorski was at a loss, hearing two such similar claims one after the other. Confused, he asked his interlocutor where in God's name, then, do "the Germans" live? Without a pause, the Hamburg resident said, "Go to East Germany, that's where the Germans live."[4] Only under a strong, authoritarian state did Germans acknowledge a national identity, Szczypiorski concluded. To reinforce this nationalist feeling, East Germany's administrative districts, like those in postrevolutionary France, deliberately ignored historic regional boundaries. When Germany was reunited in 1990, the old German Democratic Republic was formed into five *Länder* corresponding more closely to historic regions like Saxony and Thuringia.

Bjorn Engholm, a former prime minister of the province of Schleswig-Holstein and a confirmed regionalist, argues that the country's reunification strengthened this sense of regional identity rather than any feeling of German nationalism.

> I don't believe there is a German identity. The German identity would have to embrace the identity of Saxons, the people of Schleswig-Holstein, of Bavaria, of Thuringia, of the Saarland. I don't believe this exists. There is in this Germany grown large so many distinctive features—mental, regional, linguistic, cultural—that are very different. I believe that you can find your identity only in the limited space that you feel you belong to, in a region of Europe.[5]

This sense of regional identity, which never completely disappeared from Europe, has grown stronger in recent years. The very task of building Europe has revivified the regions in both east and west. They see themselves no longer as a brick in the monolithic facade of a nation-state, but as a lustrous tessera in the European mosaic. These regions no longer need to focus exclusively on preserving their dialect and customs, but can contribute to a bigger project—making a modern European society.

The lack of larger ambitions for a long time made these regions petty and provincial in their outlook. The Czech philosopher and dissident Jan Patocka, taking his own homeland as an example, succinctly describes the problem of small regions when blocked from wider horizons.

> It could be said that Czech-speaking Bohemia had a greatness as long as it had the occasion to use its uniqueness for a universal task, such as that of the push toward eastern Europe at the end of the Middle Ages. That is to say, it was great as long as its "Czechness" was not the main subject. The modern Czech nation, which has an explicitly nationalistic agenda, gives way to pettiness.[6]

Bohemia, the principal territory of today's Czech lands, in turn part of Czechoslovakia until that country agreed to split up at the end of 1992, is not an isolated case. Many of the continent's smaller nationalities, particularly in Central Europe, became minorities in a larger state—the Austro-Hungarian or Ottoman or Russian empires —and were reduced to simple self-preservation, which became their sole ambition. Decades of Soviet domination prolonged this single-minded siege mentality. The liberation and integration of Europe creates new possibilities for action. But these peoples are often left blinking in the glare of their new freedom. After years of being dominated by others, they lack a political class to supply leadership. They are the parvenus of the power game. As Patocka points out, regions in the Baltic and the Balkans are facing the same problem, but so are regions in western Europe, like those in Belgium.

In Wallonia and Flanders as in Bohemia, regions must now take the next step, moving beyond petty defensive actions toward building a bigger whole. A Europe without national borders provides a wider field for this constructive activity. The emergence of the superregions is the first sign of how regions are building the new Europe, as they work together across national borders for broader regional interests.

Regional Disparities

Regions come in many shapes and sizes throughout the continent, making definition uncertain and comparison difficult. The bigger countries, naturally, tend to be divided into bigger regions. It can be said with only slight exaggeration that the region of Rhone-Alpes in southeastern France has practically the same gross domestic product as Denmark, Provence more than Greece, and the flat, dull North region of France the same as exciting, bubbling Catalonia. Yet the twenty-two French regions have an inferiority complex vis-à-vis the huge provinces of the former West Germany, which are more or less twice as large. One solution to that problem is the cooperation agreement signed by Brittany and Pays de la Loire in western France, effectively making one big region out of two smaller ones.

That accord has the additional advantage of bringing the city of Nantes, capital of Pays de la Loire, closer to Brittany, where it has historically been the capital. The boundaries of the modern French regions were drawn up in the 1950s to administer funds for economic development without any inkling that they would one day delineate political units, as they did following the devolution of the 1980s. The Paris planners restored the historic names of regions that revolutionary leaders had deliberately suppressed when they carved the country up into counties (*departements*). However, the modern units do not always correspond to the historic regions whose names they bear, or are lumped together with other names to create clumsy hyphenated combinations like Provence-Alpes-Cote d'Azur, called PACA by its friends. Or, as in the case of Rhone-Alpes, the administrative regions join together geographic entities that do not have much to do with each other, like Grenoble, nestling in the French Alps, and Lyons, straddling the Rhone River.

Similar anomalies arise in Spain, where Navarre, the historic capital of the Basque country, was not included in the modern Basque region. Even in Germany, where the provinces trace their ancestry back to historic duchies and principalities, the boundaries are somewhat arbitrary, so that North Rhine-Westphalia sprawls across western Germany with 17 million people while Bremen remains a free city-state with only 660,000.

Eurostat, the Statistical Office of the European Communities, went nuts, literally, trying to iron out the anomalies. It devised a "Nomenclature of Territorial Units for Statistics"[7]—the acronym NUTS, from the French name for the system, quickly found its way into every EC language—which tried to bring some sense into the undertaking by defining three levels of regions. This still posed problems—in the NUTS 1 category alone, population ranged from 253,000 to 17.3 million, and surface area from 200 square kilometers to 215,000. The German provinces, politically the counterpart of French and Italian regions or Spanish "autonomous communities," were put in NUTS 1, while the others were NUTS 2. Nonetheless, the system was a big step forward in getting a comparative picture of regions.

The EC uses these numbers to allocate aid to disadvantaged regions—either those "lagging" behind in economic development or suffering a crippling decline of traditional industries. The effort, which entailed spending of $9.2 billion in 1991 and was scheduled for sizable increases through the decade, is part of the EC's commitment to "cohesion," Brussels jargon for trying to keep regional disparities from growing too wide. Poorer regions, particularly those on the outer edge of the EC, insisted on some compensation for the likelihood that the Single Market would draw business activity to the core regions of the EC, and exacerbate the economic problems in these outer territories.

Just how great a risk they faced was not clear. Researchers at the Center for Urban and Regional Development Studies (CURDS) at the University of Newcastle-upon-Tyne in England studied the impact of consolidation in European industry on regional economies. They were concerned that the effort to build up European "champions" in global industries by merging national units would have a negative impact on regional development. In fact, when the British telecommunications industry began consolidating in the early 1980s, the first jobs to go were indeed those created with government aid in peripheral regions. In a second phase, though, the industry shed capacity in the large big-city operations in London, Liverpool, and the Midlands, in favor of more modern plants in South Wales and Northern Ireland.

The CURDS analysts were rightly skeptical of short-term inducements that failed to keep new investment in the first instance, but the example showed that poor regions could eventually attract industry away from the core areas. They concluded that there were no easy answers. However, the EC policy of nurturing small and medium-sized industries in peripheral regions alone was no guarantee of self-generated growth. "It is now well known that, in areas of such growth, for example, the Third Italy, Baden-Wurttemberg and Silicon Valley, other success factors have been involved. These include the development of a pioneering role in new product or niche markets, a well-developed and integrated institutional support framework for entrepreneurship, and social traditions encouraging the accumulation and exchange of know-how, skills and information," the authors of the study conclude.[8]

The competition for job-creating investment has been one of the main reasons for regions to become more self-conscious and to act independently from national governments. In the past, foreign companies would simply set up a local subsidiary to service a national market. Things have changed in the wake of European economic integration, which is making national markets disappear in favor of a single market across the whole continent. An American or Japanese investor, even a European multinational, now looks at Europe as a whole when it is contemplating a new factory, or sales office, or research center. They scrutinize potential sites for the proper mix of attributes—skilled workers (preferably nonunionized), telecommunications and transportation, quality of life, fiscal and infrastructure incentives—but often are indifferent to which country has the right combination.

In a 1992 study, *Regions of the New Europe,* the consulting group Ernst and Young documented this trend. They found foreign investors measuring one region against another for the right factor mix rather than simply choosing a country by the size of its national market. The study gave examples of typical considerations: the pros and cons of locating a chemical factory in Teesside, in northern England, were compared with those in Milan; the southeastern Dutch province of Limburg as the site of a food-processing plant was weighed against the northern French region of Pas de Calais; labor costs were lower in southern Spain, but so was productivity; on the map, Lombardy looks close to Central European markets but transportation routes are often congested; northern England and eastern Spain are better for manufacturing industry, but for research and development, southeastern England and the southeastern German province of Bavaria were preferable. Companies tended to discard the nation-state as a unit, Ernst and Young found, and to think about markets on a European basis and facilities on a regional basis.[9]

National agencies for regional development, who follow an agenda based on country-wide priorities, were slow to catch on to this change. When Intel Europe wanted to look at a site near Nice for a new factory in the 1980s, French development authorities in Paris discouraged them from doing so, proposing locations in northern France, which they felt needed new jobs more than Nice did. In the end, Intel built its chip plant in Ireland, ignoring Paris's suggestions and frustrating Nice.

By 1992, competition had grown even more fierce. Cities and regions often offered the same resources, although when the proportions varied from one location to another, it was the most nimble and flexible communities that landed new investments. The Colorado firm Storage Technology Corp., for example, wanted to invest $50 million in a European factory to build an online data storage unit, creating 350 jobs. They looked hard at several German sites, including Dresden in the former East Germany, before choosing Toulouse, in southwestern France, instead. The company complained about the high payroll charges in Germany (they are quite high in France, too), but their main objection was the lack of flexibility in Germany in scheduling working hours.

The City as Motor of
Economic Growth

In her seminal 1984 book, *Cities and the Wealth of Nations,*
Jane Jacobs argues that the so-called science of economics has been
barking up the wrong tree since Adam Smith wrote his eighteenth-
century masterpiece, *The Wealth of Nations,* which set the framework for studying political economy in the age of capitalism. Smith,
and generations of economists after him, made a fundamental mistake, Jacobs maintains, in looking at the nation-state as the basic
unit of economic analysis. The assumption was made in the wake
of mercantilist policies designed to enrich one country at the expense of another, which the rising nation-states practiced as a
means of increasing their power. But this nationalist focus was not
necessarily the best way to view capitalist production. According
to Jacobs, "Nations are political and military entities, and so are
blocs of nations. But it doesn't necessarily follow from this that they
are also the basic, salient entities of economic life. . . . Indeed, the
failure of national governments and blocs of nations to force economic life to do their bidding suggests some sort of essential
irrelevance."[10]

The *real* wealth-producing unit in a modern economy is in fact
the city, Jacobs suggests. "Economic life develops by grace of innovating; it expands by grace of import-replacing. These two master
economic processes are closely related, both being functions of city
economies."[11] The city, in Jacobs's view, is a ferment of innovation,
the vibrant site of change and growth. This normally extends to the
city's hinterland as well. For their regions, cities supply markets,
jobs, technology, new activities, and capital.

This view of the city as the main motor of economic growth is
gaining ground in Europe as integration makes national borders fade
away. Robert Koll, an urban economist at the IFO Economic Research Institute in Munich, feels that policymakers in Brussels and
EC member states have underestimated the macroeconomic role of
cities, but are now coming around. "Cities as the spatial conglom-
eration of economic activity gain or lose attractivity for business as
conditions change, but they remain the geographic core."[12]

Changes in the way the world does business are favoring this
trend. The global economy—as Harvard expert and Clinton adviser

Robert B. Reich describes in his groundbreaking 1991 book, *The Work of Nations*[13]—is moving away from the postwar paradigm of high-volume mass production by bureaucratic corporations operating on a national basis with massive fixed investment in plant and machinery. Instead, the modern economy revolves around high-value production, with a higher proportion of "service" input in the form of special engineering or design. The intellectual input in modern production is so high, Reich contends, that old distinctions, like that between "goods" and "services," are no longer useful in analyzing the creation of wealth. The latter-day multinational corporation is a coordinating center for this high-value input, which it shops for around the world, contracting for it in a global web of competing suppliers. It is less and less meaningful, in Reich's analysis, to speak of a corporation as American or Japanese or German—"Japanese" products sold in the U.S. often have a higher level of American input than "American" products.

What a nation, or a region, has to offer in this global economy is not capital—capital knows no borders, savings flow wherever there is a good return—but the skill of its workers and the accumulated expertise in the specialized inputs required in modern production. Jacobs would identify the city as the principal unit of this combination of resources.

The second main factor is the environment a place offers for living and working. "The skills of a nation's work force and the quality of its infrastructure are what makes it unique, and uniquely attractive, in the world economy. Investments in these relatively immobile factors of worldwide production are what chiefly distinguish one nation from another . . . ," Reich writes.[14]

The obvious consequence for government policymakers is to promote education and training on the one hand, and to invest in infrastructure on the other—the two main preoccupations of Europe's public sector on the European, national, and regional levels (and the platform that swept Bill Clinton into office in the United States). The resurgence of Europe's cities both demonstrates the success of their efforts and supports Jacobs's thesis. The EC Commission observed in its report *Europe 2000* that two processes are at work in this resurgence: "On the one hand, there is continued decentralization from the older metropolitan cores in some sectors of lower level economic activity (e.g., routine back-office functions such as typing, coding, accounts processing, etc.). On the other hand, there is a process of reconcentration of higher level economic activities within the older city centers."[15] The report explicitly credits urban revitalization policies in several cases for attracting this high-value work to city centers, and notes that some cities in northern Europe are registering population increases for the first time in two decades.

In his book *Europe of the Regions,* French geographer Jean Labasse looks at the territorial and historical diversity of regions in Europe, and concludes that the city is the unit that in the end determines the shape of a region. "Concerning the geopolitical units in the rank directly subordinated to the national state, it all comes down in principle to identifying the central cities and to determining their respective zones of influence."[16] He cites Catalonia as a prime example of how centuries of interaction and exchange create an organic economic unit between a city and its region. It is precisely this kind of unit that can exert a political authority sufficient to claim the region's "decolonization" in relation to the national capital.[17]

In seeking greater autonomy, European cities and regions are following a tradition dating back to their development in the Middle Ages. Political authority in medieval Europe was split among diverse kings and their barons, among bishops and monasteries whose overlapping claims divided the loyalty of the nascent cities. As a result, cities learned to quietly go their own way, appeasing the wishes of temporal and spiritual sovereigns when necessary, but otherwise concentrating on the business of making life as comfortable as possible. "Western cities," observes the Hungarian historian Jeno Szucs, "could take wing in the spaces left empty by the rivalries of different powers or sovereignties, taking for their own benefit the elements of sovereignty. . . . [T]he cities consequently were able to develop a new form of economy, the autonomous urban economy."[18] This was a specifically western European tradition, Szucs maintains, because in other civilizations, absolute political and religious power usually were concentrated in a single, powerful central authority. It is this tradition of autonomy, eclipsed for the past couple of centuries by the nation-state, that is once again emerging.

Three "Juncture" Cities Prosper

Bracing sea breezes bring the Free and Hanseatic City of Hamburg to life. The pennants flying around the Inner Alster, the river catchment that forms the watery heart of the city, herald its nautical vocation. The sailboats skimming across the Outer Alster, on the other side of the bridge, project the maritime energy of the city, supplying a dynamic counterpoint to the church towers punctuating the low skyline.

Cool, wet, and windy Hamburg does not draw tourists or vacationers, or welcome newcomers. But the city enjoys the highest per capita income of any region in Europe, and, pulled by the new opening to the east, is plunging ahead as one of the fastest-growing cities, too. The main source of that prosperity is the city's large and lively port, situated on the Elbe River estuary seventy miles from where it flows into the North Sea. But Hamburg's wealth derives as well from the low-slung, terraced office buildings along the Outer Alster, housing some of Germany's biggest insurance and media enterprises.

Founded by Charlemagne in the ninth century, a charter member of the Hanseatic League in the thirteenth century, a free city for most of its history except for brief spells under the rules of Napoleon and Hitler, the city-state of Hamburg has come back from the economic setbacks of the 1970s as one of Europe's most successful and aggressive cities. The collapse of the Iron Curtain—the former East German border was little more than thirty miles away—has reopened its historic hinterland, via the Elbe and the canals and rivers feeding into it, to Berlin, Dresden, and Prague and beyond.

Hamburg invested heavily in modernizing its port facilities, restructuring its shipbuilding on a more competitive basis, and creating a suitable environment for new industry. To compensate for the loss of jobs in shipping and shipbuilding, the city aggressively built up its aerospace industry, beating out competitors like Bremen and Munich to land the assembly line for the new Airbus 321, with the first roll-out in 1993, the only assembly of Airbus airliners outside of Toulouse. Hamburg reinforced its aerospace role with the 1992 opening of Lufthansa's $600 million technical center for overhauling wide-bodied jets, the biggest ever investment by the German airline.

Hamburg also fortified its position in tertiary industry. Home of flagship magazines like *Der Spiegel* and *Stern* and headquarters for one of Germany's biggest regional broadcasting networks and the national news program, Hamburg built up its advertising and marketing industries. The city nurtured its insurance and banking activities, expanding in research and engineering. The local economy continued to grow well above the national average in Germany, posting a 4 percent increase in real terms in 1991. Port volume rose 11 percent to 67 million tons in that year, with particularly fast growth in container traffic. Although volume slipped slightly in 1992, the port is expected to handle 88 million tons by 1995, crowding the limits of its capacity, and authorities have begun planning for further expansion.

The city basked in what one official called its "new position in economic geography." Hamburg ran full-page advertisements in international publications, touting the city's location and claiming that "people here have always known how profitable trade without frontiers is."

Hamburg sits at the juncture of three superregions—Atlantic Coast, Baltic League, and Mitteleuropa. Superregion borders, unlike national frontiers, are not dead ends but territories of intensified interchange. Cities located at such junctures are not cut off on one side or another of a line, but radiate in all directions, sending out economic impulses in each of the regions. These border positions seem to offer a potential advantage to cities situated on them. Milan, Munich, Amsterdam, and Lyons are among the border cities that historically have prospered at these regional crossroads.

In the forty-one-year existence of West Germany as a separate state, two cities at its opposite ends vied for economic and cultural preeminence. In the north was Hamburg, reserved and sober; in the south, Munich, boisterous and baroque. Hamburg looked to the sea, Munich to the mountains. Hamburg is a free city, proud of its independence; Munich, the capital city of the Free State of Bavaria, once a kingdom in its own right. Hamburg harbored old wealth, and followed its motto of "more substance than appearance" (*"mehr Sein als Schein"*); postwar Munich became nouveau riche, and flaunted it in rich clothing and other forms of conspicuous consumption. The residents of the two cities detest each other.

Like Hamburg, Munich lies at the juncture of three superregions—Mitteleuropa, Danube Basin, and Alpine Arc. In the same way as its northern competitor, Munich derives enormous benefit from this happy situation.

The city's history is that of the assertive province it is capital of. The Romans conquered Bavaria, at least the part of it south of the

Danube, when Celts were living there. There is no mention of the German tribe that gave the province its current name until the sixth century. Historians have no idea just where the Bavarians came from, or when they settled the territory, but one thing for sure is that they liked it there and tended to stay put. The Bavarians submitted to Charlemagne and became part of the Holy Roman Empire; the territory's East Mark, the buffer between Germans and Slavs, became independent in the twelfth century as Austria. Bavaria became part of the German empire formed by Bismarck in the nineteenth century, although it kept its own king until 1918, when it became a republic like the rest of the German Reich—but separate, always separate.

Munich has had a spotty history in this century, picking up some unsavory connotations. The city was rife with reaction and intrigue in the 1920s, encouraging Hitler to make his first grab for power there in 1923 with the failed Beer Hall Putsch. In 1938, the leaders of Britain and France met in Munich with a now successful Hitler, and agreed to appease him by letting him annex the Sudetenland in western Czechoslovakia. In 1972, during the Summer Olympics in Munich, Arab terrorists took the Israeli athletes hostage; eleven of them were killed after a rescue attempt failed.

But postwar Munich has enjoyed an economic upsurge. Siemens, one of Germany's biggest industrial firms and a world leader in electrical goods, made its new headquarters in Munich after the division of Germany chased them from Berlin. Encouraged by the energetic Franz Josef Strauss, longtime prime minister of Bavaria and one of Germany's leading postwar politicians, other high technology and aerospace firms migrated toward Munich in the 1970s and 1980s.

The majestic onion-domed towers and baroque spires of the city's churches beckoned to a generation of German yuppies who filled the hometown of BMW, frequented the trendy bars in Schwabing, and lived the good life befitting a self-respecting parvenu. Recently, Munich has been suffering from its success. Thousands of BMWs and less exalted makes clog the highways every weekend, blocking the way to the Alps, normally just an hour away to the south. New construction defaces the pristine forests and lakes between the city and the mountains, and housing in the city has become outrageously expensive and virtually unobtainable. As archrival Hamburg overtook the Bavarian capital economically,

Munich officials have had to turn away new investment for lack of suitable terrains to house new industry.

But industries kept coming anyway. When Daimler-Benz acquired the main German aerospace manufacturers in and around Munich and consolidated them into one huge holding company, the Stuttgart carmaker put the unit's headquarters in Munich. In spring 1992, after twenty-four years of debate and delay, Munich finally opened a modern new airport twenty miles from the city center to replace the old one nearer town, which had only a single, short runway. Passenger volume had quadrupled to 11 million in the long period it took to get a new airport built. Already having the second busiest airport in Germany after Frankfurt, Munich hopes with the new facility to build up its position as the second hub for Lufthansa and the main airport for Central Europe.

The severe neoclassical facades in Milan's historic center readily remind a visitor of similar buildings in Munich. With its contained energy, the architecture conveys the power of the Alps separating the two cities. At opposite cusps of the Alpine Arc, Milan and Munich channel much of the activity flowing between northern and southern Europe. Milan, at the juncture of Latin Crescent, Alpine Arc, and Danube Basin, has the same vital drive from its position as Hamburg and Munich. And like them, it is one of the richest and most dynamic cities on the continent.

Milan is the financial and industrial center of Italy, and likes to think of itself as the secret capital of the part of Italy that works. Although a traumatic corruption scandal in 1992 tempered its self-righteousness, Milan has led the movement to somehow separate northern Italy from what it sees as the backward, crime-ridden southern part of the country. Sophisticated, stylish, reeking of money, Milan became the mecca of Italian business and culture in the 1980s. Offered a choice between Milan and Rome, savvy Italian executives invariably chose the former. From the tony ambiance of La Scala, one of the world's leading opera houses, to the understated elegance of Via della Spiga, a pedestrian lane where several of the most evocative names of world fashion maintain their showcase boutiques, Milan offers some of life's finer luxuries to residents and jet-setters from around the globe.

A Celtic city conquered by the Romans in 222 B.C., Milan has a sense of history. It rivaled Rome in size by the time Constantine issued the Edict of Milan in A.D. 313, legalizing Christianity. The fourth-century bishop of Milan, St. Ambrose, mentor to St. Augustine and a churchman of considerable stature himself, made such a profound impact on the city that "ambrosiano" came to be synonymous with "Milanese." Ruled by powerful patrician families during the Middle Ages, the Duchy of Milan in the sixteenth century came under the rule of Spain, and then later of Austria. Napoleon controlled the city briefly, making it the capital of whatever he happened to be calling his domain in Italy from year to year. Milan became part of a unified Italy in the second half of the nineteenth century.

As a financial center, Milan is headquarters for some of Italy's biggest banks and the home of the country's main stock exchange and leading business school. It attracts foreigners, who appreciate the skiing an hour and a half away and the city's other amenities. Businessmen, fashion designers, students will all find their way to the cafés of the glittering Galleria Vittorio Emmanuel, or along the piazza in front of the gleaming white marble of the Gothic cathedral next to it.

These three cities—Hamburg, Munich, Milan—are big, but not metropolises. Each numbers between 1.5 million and 2 million residents. They exemplify Jane Jacobs's view of the city as economic motor; two of them at least, Munich and Milan, also extend their economic pull far into their surrounding regions. With the possible exception of Munich, they are not the first destination for tourists from abroad. Even foreign investors—according to an annual survey by commercial real estate agents Healey and Baker—tended to prefer national capitals like London, Paris, and Brussels or financial centers like Frankfurt, Amsterdam, and Zurich to locate businesses. But these "juncture cities" exemplify the enterprising spirit that makes "Europe of the Cities" and "Europe of the Regions" more than just slogans.

Regional Organizations

In 1985, the Assembly of European Regions (AER) was formed to lobby for regional representation in an integrated Europe. With a secretariat based in Strasbourg, home of the Council of Europe and the European Parliament, the AER had enrolled 179 member regions by 1992, both in and outside the EC. The Assembly became an umbrella organization for existing regional groups. For instance, the Conference of Peripheral Maritime Regions represents coastal regions on the edge of Europe that often get left behind in economic development. The Association of Border Regions tries to rectify the situation of those regions on the edges of their own countries—national railway and highway systems tend to taper out near the frontier, even though the region there might need a liaison to a thriving city or region just across the border. A number of loosely organized groups work to overcome the problems of mountain regions like the Pyrenees or Juras, including, typically, three separate ones for the Alps—western, eastern, and central. The AER established a technical agency, the European Center for Regional Development, to undertake studies and cooperative projects in environment, infrastructure, education, and agriculture. The group has also set up an office in Brussels to lobby the EC Commission.

Border regions were early pioneers of interregional cooperation. One of the oldest, dating back to 1963, is the *Regio basiliensis,* now grouping the canton and city of Basel in northwest Switzerland with neighboring districts in Baden-Wurttemberg in southwest Germany and in the Alsace region in northeast France. In 1978, German and Dutch authorities created a cross-border cooperation around the mouth of the Ems River, on the North Sea coast. In 1986, a pioneering "Euroregion" farther south linked Aachen county in western Germany, the Limburg province in southeast Netherlands, and the Liege region in eastern Belgium. In 1989, the EC drew up several initiatives to help regions cope with the Single Market. One of them was "Interreg," to aid border regions in everything from finding new jobs for customs officials thrown out of work to coordinating joint infrastructure projects.

The creation of the Assembly of European Regions took regional cooperation into a new dimension. The boldest idea, perhaps quixotic, proposed by the regions was to create a second house for the European Parliament, like the Senate in the United States, that would represent the regions in enacting European laws, when and if the European Parliament ever gets real legislative powers. Their model was the upper house of the German federal parliament, the Federal Council (*Bundesrat*), which represents the German provinces and gets to vote on key issues like taxes and treaties. Not surprisingly, the German provinces are among the strongest advocates of greater regional say in the decisions made by the EC.

These German provinces as well as regions in other countries have emphasized the need for "subsidiarity" in European lawmaking. What this jargonistic term, now enshrined in the Maastricht treaty, means is that decisions should be made at the lowest level of government possible, municipal or regional, with higher bodies on a national or European level intervening only when absolutely necessary. The concept, oddly enough, is attributed to Pope Pius XI, who wrote in his 1931 encyclical *Quadragesimo anno:* "Thus it offends the sense of justice to lay claim on what a smaller and subordinate communal entity can bring to a good end for a broader and higher community."

Highly centralized nation-states have rarely practiced subsidiarity in the past, so that mandating the principle in an EC treaty could lead to a huge political step forward for regions, enabling them to claim jurisdiction over a great number of areas currently controlled at a national level. The actual wording of the Maastricht treaty pointedly refers only to two levels of decision-making, European and national. But a principle is a principle, and the newly politicized regions will not be slow in asserting it.

The Politics of Regions

In Western democracies, voters invest their power in politicians, and when voters of a city or region have greater powers, their elected representatives have greater stature, too. Germany provides a case in point: The provinces in the postwar constitution of the Federal Republic of Germany have ultimate authority in key sectors like police, media, education, and culture. They have to negotiate for their share of tax revenues, which are levied by the federal government, but they have a voice in fiscal legislation via the *Bundesrat.* As a result, the prime minister of a German province has an important political base, one that is virtually essential for the party in opposition. Helmut Kohl was prime minister of Rhineland-Palatinate, a smallish province in western Germany, before becoming national chairman of the Christian Democrats and chancellor-candidate. His challengers for the top national government office in Germany included the prime ministers of North Rhine-Westphalia, the most populous province, and Saarland, one of the smallest.

When French regions held their first elections for regional councils in 1988, politicians of the stature of former French president Valery Giscard d'Estaing campaigned for the office of regional president, even though the actual powers of the regions were quite limited. Giscard's political career, in some respects, reflected the trends in Europe. After serving as finance minister and then president of Europe's second-largest nation-state, he became president of the Auvergne region, in central France, and deputy in the European Parliament. France had already created a powerful local political base in the mid-1970s, when it enfranchised Paris residents to elect their own mayor. Prior to that, as for a long time in Washington, D.C., the national government had appointed the top official in the national capital. As popular mayor of Paris, opposition leader Jacques Chirac launched his unsuccessful campaign against French president Francois Mitterrand in 1988.

In Spain, growing regional autonomy attracted politicians of the caliber of Jordi Pujol in Catalonia. In Belgium, which is divided into three autonomous provinces—French-speaking Wallonia, Flemish-speaking Flanders, and Brussels, where both languages are spoken although French predominates—the national chairman of the francophone Socialist Party, Guy Spitaels, created a sensation at the beginning of 1992 when he quit his national post and the chance of leading role in the national coalition government to become executive president of Wallonia. For him, as a Walloon, the region was now the place where things were happening.

The British have bucked the trend toward regionalism. The Conservatives under Margaret Thatcher and John Major have preferred a strong central government, rejecting the extra expense of yet another layer of government. Newly minted regional presidents in other European countries, it is true, did display a marked penchant for spending millions of dollars on handsome new regional government centers. The Treaty of Maastricht itself, the blueprint for the economic and political union of all of Europe, was agreed upon in the spanking new provincial assembly building of the Netherlands' Limburg province, perched prettily on an old fortress island in the Meuse River, built at a cost of $90 million. Whatever the cost, commented *The Economist* regarding British objections to regional government, "other Europeans seem to think a bit of extravagance is a price worth paying for local democracy."[19]

The EC Commission quietly encouraged regional aspirations. While the Commission itself continued to increase its own powers, ultimate authority in the EC rested in the Council of Ministers, consisting of the national officials of the member states. A common desire to make inroads in national government authority prompted the Commission and the regions to join forces. As Giles Merritt, a longtime observer of EC politics, comments of regional leaders: "They quickly identified the EC Commission as a natural ally, because Brussels' best chance of weakening the powers of the member states' central governments lies in increasing those of local governments."[20]

Obviously, if the principle of "subsidiarity" ever does take root in European politics, Brussels will find itself tussling with regional officials, too. But in the time-honored tradition of divide and conquer, the Commission continued to support regional autonomy, if ever so discreetly, so as not to annoy the national governments too much.

Autonomy and Integration

Capping more than two decades of devolution of power, the Belgian parliament early in 1993 approved a constitutional amendment formally declaring Belgium a federal state made of three autonomous regions—Flanders, Wallonia, and Brussels. The country is a prime example of how European integration encourages increased regional autonomy. Created in 1830 as a unitary kingdom, Belgium entered into a currency union with Luxembourg in 1921 and an economic union with the Netherlands and Luxembourg in 1944. After the war, it was a founding member of the European communities and has been a fervent supporter of political and economic integration.

At the same time, since the 1970s, the national government has steadily devolved power to the constituent regions, so that it now retains direct control only over defense and foreign policy, internal security, the budget, and social security. Even sensitive sectors like agriculture and foreign trade have been put under regional authority. Belgium is a showcase example for the impact of the dual trend in Europe toward integration and decentralization.

This two-track development has prepared the way for superregions to emerge, as increasingly autonomous regions form bigger groups within an integrated Europe. In Belgium's case, the rise of Mitteleuropa as a superregion, which takes in all of the country except for a narrow strip on the coast, reinforces its overall integration. In many larger countries, however, regions gravitate toward different groupings—France and Germany each have territories in four different superregions. The following chapters examine each of the eight superregions and the two special districts in turn, describing their boundaries and the sources of their internal coherence.

CHAPTER FOUR

LATIN CRESCENT: EUROPE'S SUNBELT

The A8 express highway along the French Riviera between Marseilles and Nice stays just far enough away from the coast that drivers are not distracted by views of the Mediterranean. Taking the Valbonne exit just after Cannes, however, turning away from Antibes up into the hills, a motorist quickly reaches some of the most glorious scenery on earth.

The French Riviera, Cote d'Azur as the French call it, is not just a beach. It is an enchanted landscape, a sliver of land between mountains and sea, white rock scantily clad in green shrub, shaded by Mediterranean pines and plane trees. Even during the French school vacation in July and August, when it becomes deplorably congested, the Riviera can seduce the most skeptical visitor.

The sea sparkles in a deep sky blue, veritably azure, which the gleaming white buildings of Antibes and Juan-les-Pins throw into breathtaking relief. The Provencal light that has enthralled painters like Van Gogh and Picasso reflects gaily off the green of the pine and oak and the patches of reddish soil showing through the scrubby growth of grass and herbs.

Ahead, on the horizon, silver-topped mountains shimmer in a blue haze, beckoning the tourist farther into the Alps. The mingled fragrances of wild thyme and rosemary and pine needles waft through the sun-baked hills. The magic juncture of mountains and sea prompted the ancient Romans to call this province the Maritime Alps, which is still the name of the county in modern France.

Following the direction signs amid the sensual splendor of the countryside, skirting the bulldozers and graders widening the two-lane feeder road, the driver arrives quickly at the administrative headquarters of Sophia Antipolis, one of the oldest and largest industrial research parks in Europe.

Promotion officials at Sophia Antipolis claim that productivity of high-technology researchers rises 20 percent when they relocate to this paradisiacal environment, once the preserve of jet-setters and vacationers. The denizens of this science park sport the healthy, bronzed look that sun and sea air invariably produce. Sophia Antipolis is a tranquil place. At least two-thirds of the land within the park's boundaries must be left virgin. After a couple of initial structures turned out to be eyesores, buildings had to conform to strict specifications in height and follow as much as possible the contours of the land.

Antipolis is the ancient name for Antibes. The Greek can mean "the city opposite" or "the anti-city." Sophia is the Greek word for wisdom. It is also, by a curious chance, in its French version of Sophie, the name of the wife of Pierre Lafitte, who founded Sophia Antipolis in 1972. Lafitte's goal was to create a city, or anti-city, of wisdom, that would rival research parks in other countries and spur economic development in the region, too dependent on tourism, which was defacing the environment, and agriculture, which had long since reached its limits.

By 1992, 850 companies had come to Sophia Antipolis, employing nearly 15,000 people. The park is ready to double its original 6,000 acres by 1995 and to open two satellites to the east and the west later in the decade. Located in a triangle formed by Cannes, Nice, and Grasse—glamorous names evoking a milieu of movie stars, millionaires, beaches, and yachts—Sophia Antipolis slowly is changing the image of the Riviera.

Oh so slowly. Jacqueline Mirtelli, director of promotion and marketing for the park, says it is hard to surmount rampant prejudice about the region's playboy atmosphere to lure multinational companies to Sophia Antipolis. Many northern Europeans refuse to take the Riviera seriously as a place to work. American companies, familiar with the virtues of Sunbelt living, have been easier to convince. Digital Equipment, the computer firm, arrived in Sophia Antipolis in 1979, becoming one of the biggest operations in the park by the 1990s, after it moved its world headquarters for telecommunications research to the Mediterranean site and lifted employment to more than eight hundred persons. Rockwell International, Dow Chemical, Dow Corning, and Wellcome are among other multinationals with research operations in the park.

Sophia Antipolis is positioning itself as the hub for a "High Technology Highway," a network of research parks comprising similar "technopoles" in Montpellier, Toulouse, Barcelona, and Valencia to the west, and Turin, Milan, and Genoa to the east. The group, set up in 1990, aims to promote joint research projects and foster cross-fertilization of new companies. Its goal is to create Europe's version of the Silicon Valley, where education, research, and industrial centers interact to produce innovations in technology and to commercialize them successfully.

The leap into high tech along the Mediterranean coastline is a major factor in the resurgence of the region, one of the most historic in Europe. The crescent formed by the Italian and Iberian peninsulas, capped by the stretch of France linking the two, has been conquered, settled, and cultivated by successive waves of Greeks, Romans, Goths, Franks, Arabs, Bourbons, and Bonapartes. The heart of the Roman Empire, the region has preserved the essence of Latin culture, enriching it over the centuries with the evolution of the Romance languages and their societies.

Lacking coal and iron and the Protestant work ethic, the Latin Crescent missed the industrial revolution in the nineteenth century and has the reputation now of being economically backward, hindered by archaic institutions and customs from keeping up with the rest of Europe and the industrial world. A world, as the cliché would have it, rooted in the simple pleasures of family, good food, fine wine—a peasant society with a veneer of modern civilization.

But this stereotyped view of southern Europe no longer corresponds to reality. The Latin Crescent superregion is one of the most economically dynamic in the world. "Countries that are more dynamic are rare: only Japan and some newly industrialized countries (Brazil, South Korea) just barely surpass the Mediterranean states," a group of French economists comments in a study of EC member countries bordering the Mediterranean.[1] The phenomenon is not particularly new, but awareness of it has taken a long time to pierce through the prejudices.

Italy, for instance, doubled its gross national product in the 1950s, registering average growth of 5.3 percent, a pace it kept up until the oil shock in the mid-1970s. Post-recession growth has been slower, but above the EC average. By the 1990s, Italy fulfilled its longtime slogan *"il sorpasso"* in surpassing Britain as the fifth biggest market economy in the world.

In Spain, once Franco gave free reign to government technocrats to liberalize the economy, the country bounded forward to catch up with Europe. In the period between 1961 and 1973, gross domestic product grew at an average annual rate of nearly 7 percent in real terms, lifting Spain into tenth place in global economic ranking. Following the oil shocks and accession to the EC, Spain paced Europe with annual growth approaching 5 percent. The development in Portugal was largely parallel.

Southern France, meanwhile, experienced its own revival. Languedoc-Roussillon, the region extending to the southwest from the Riviera along the Mediterranean coast, registered a sizzling 9.1 percent annual growth in per capita income in the 1980s, well ahead of the Paris or Lyons regions. By 1990, the four major regions of southern France, out of twenty-two in the country, accounted for 25 percent of new jobs being created nationwide. "This percentage," according to an analysis entitled *The Revenge of the South*, "virtually unknown, confirms the reality of the reversal of the movement that used to operate between the north and south of the country."[2]

The industrial revolution of the nineteenth and early twentieth centuries was marked by massive immigration from the rural south of France to the industrialized north. Now that trend has reversed, and it is the south that has experienced a net immigration of more than a million persons between 1975 and 1990. Nor are these for the most part retirees seeking a warmer climate, but young people, often college graduates looking for their first jobs, or those in mid-career who want a different lifestyle.

The Revenge of the South, written by a group of sociologists, explains that such "immigrants" from northern France are often seeking freedom for individual expression, and are not motivated exclusively by economic considerations. For instance, there is the Paris subway worker enamored of lavander who goes south and becomes a producer of honey and perfume; a university instructor fond of turquoise who relocates to make jewelry; a photo engraver adept at masonry who goes into the building trade.

The migrants, these sociologists found, are usually young, with young families. They are seeking independence—from self-employment to their own house and garden—and are willing to take a cut in pay. Wages are generally lower in the south, and family income is reduced further because the spouse usually does not find work right away. Often the migrants must create their own employment, as the above examples show. Sometimes they find local residents unreceptive, but establish a social network with fellow immigrants.

The EC study *Europe 2000* listed other reasons for migration from northern Europe's industrial heartland to southern Europe. Congestion in northern industrial centers has driven up real estate prices and lowered quality of life. At the same time, the growth of "knowledge-intensive" industries means that many jobs are no longer linked to a specific area where natural resources happen to be located or where sheer economies of scale demand a large concentration of employment. The EC study calculated that only 50 percent of employment at the beginning of the 1990s was tied to a specific place, compared to 70 percent thirty years ago.[3] It is precisely the college-educated knowledge-industry worker who puts a higher priority on quality of life and happily relocates to the heady atmosphere of the Mediterranean.

There is another worldwide trend that contributes to this movement. Big multinational companies have realized that bureaucratic organization often stifles innovation. They have sought to decentralize as much as possible, and particularly to provide an entrepreneurial environment for research and development activities. At the same time, these huge, rich companies are trying to channel part of their massive cash flow into promising new enterprises founded by outsiders, creating "nurseries" for innovation. Both activities find their fruition in the research parks that are flourishing throughout the industrialized countries, particularly in congenial climates like those in California or the Mediterranean.

If the trend in southern Europe escaped notice for a long time, it has now forced itself into the public's awareness. A French journalist in 1989 signaled the arrival of a new competitor for Europe's industrial north in the following terms: "It is the red arc of the high tech civilization which, from Valencia to Tuscany via Barcelona,

Madrid, Montpellier, Nice, Milan, Turin—with a pointer to Toulouse, another pointer toward Lyons—stretches across the Mediterranean."[4]

The EC Commission wrote in its 1991 study: "Economic growth and prosperity is spreading outwards from its traditional heartland in northern Europe. A new arc of development is being created running from northern and central Italy through southern France to northern and eastern Spain. . . . The core of economic activity in Europe is likely to be split between these two areas over the next decade."[5]

From *Condottieri* to the "Third Italy"

It is not always easy for the Latin economy to move into modern times, as the meteoric career of Carlo de Benedetti demonstrates. De Benedetti was a dynamic entrepreneur in his early forties in 1978 when he bought into Olivetti, a tired typewriter manufacturer headquartered in Ivrea, a city in the Alpine foothills near Turin. De Benedetti brought capital from a family firm and management expertise from the Fiat auto group, where he was briefly chief executive before falling out with the Agnelli family that owns Fiat. His rigorous cost-cutting and decisive move into computers quickly turned the company around.

De Benedetti seemed to represent a new generation of professional managers in Italy, a departure from the tradition of family-owned and managed companies that dominate the economy. A trim, dashing figure with a brilliant smile, De Benedetti became an articulate champion for capitalism in an Italy ridden with communism and terrorism. His energy and charisma not only captivated Italian investors and the press, but also gave a new image of Olivetti, and of Italy as a whole, to foreign businessmen.

De Benedetti was a maverick, excluded from the small Establishment of families like the Agnellis and the Pirellis that effectively controlled Italian industry and finance. As time went on, though, it became clearer that De Benedetti was perhaps not so different, that his main motivation in all his entrepreneurial activity was to storm that exclusive group and force entry into it.

In his hurry, he began to make mistakes. He plunged into an

investment in the ill-fated Banco Ambrosiano, run by the shadowy Roberto Calvi. Put off by Calvi's secretiveness, De Benedetti sold back his shares only weeks after joining the bank. Less than a year later, Calvi's corpse was found hanging under Blackfriars bridge in London, and Ambrosiano was exposed as an imbroglio of fraud and embezzlement that implicated everyone from the Vatican to the conspiratorial P-2 Masonic lodge and the Mafia—all that gives Italy a bad name as a morass of crime and corruption, and not at all in keeping with De Benedetti's Mr. Clean image. But his quick exit seemed to spare him any consequences from the bank's collapse.

Worse was to come, though. When De Benedetti launched a bid for Societe Generale de Belgique, a sprawling holding company that controls a good portion of Belgian industry, a combination of Belgian networking and French capital handed him his most disastrous defeat. The press, which had lionized De Benedetti for so long, scented blood and began hounding him. In 1992, as the global market for computers crashed, De Benedetti was forced to take over active management of Olivetti again to stop its slide into the red.

At this critical juncture, De Benedetti was convicted of fraud for his role in Ambrosiano and sentenced to six and a half years in prison. An Italian court decided that he had used his knowledge of wrongdoing at Ambrosiano to exact a high price for his shares, thus perhaps hastening its downfall, rather than reporting what he knew to the authorities. The verdict was appealed and De Benedetti will stay out of prison in the *years* it takes to decide the appeal. Whatever the outcome of the court process, though, the verdict finished off the myth of De Benedetti as the forerunner of a new type of businessman in Italy.

All along, though, there were those who saw the true economic renaissance in Italy elsewhere. The parvenus celebrated in the press were too much in the traditional dynastic mold to promise any lasting change. Besides De Benedetti, there was Raul Gardini, who built up the Ferruzzi sugar trading group of his in-laws before overtaking himself and handing it back to the family, and Silvio Berlusconi, who made a fortune with raunchy television programming as broadcasting in the Latin countries was opened up to private interests. These ruthless tycoons with their huge egos were like the *condottieri,* mercenary army captains who sold themselves and their troops to the highest bidder during the long period of warring among Italian city-states.

While these colorful personalities captured the headlines, whole new manufacturing centers mushroomed throughout central Italy and along the Adriatic coast in the form of small entrepreneurial companies making high-quality products that found markets throughout the world. It became known as the NEC model (Northeast-Center), and gave birth to a "Third Italy" between the industrialized north and the underdeveloped south. In this new industrial region, small companies, in traditional sectors like clothes and shoes as well as in machine tools, motors, electronic music instruments, and many other readily exportable manufactures, were linked by family ties to suppliers, making for a supple production chain that could react quickly to new demands in the market. Seasonal workers, moonlighters, often working at home and kept off the books, enabled this industry to adjust capacity rapidly. Benetton, the retail clothing chain which purchased its brightly colored knitwear from a network of such small firms, is a famous example of this phenomenon.

"As spectacular as it was, the individual success of *condottieri* like Agnelli, De Benedetti, Berlusconi, or Gardini has in fact less significance than this semi-artisanal pullulation," a French study of the Mediterranean economy asserts.[6] The same is largely true throughout the Latin Crescent, where the explosive growth of small and medium-sized industry has driven the surge in the economy. Moonlighting is so prevalent throughout the region that economists now feel that unemployment figures do not accurately reflect the real state of affairs in these countries—a sizable number of able-bodied workers are happy to collect an unemployment check while actually working full-time on an "informal" basis. Unemployment in Spain is estimated to be closer to 10 percent in real terms, rather than the persistently high 15 percent of official statistics.

The Latin Ascendancy

As in the other superregions, history can provide important clues to understanding the essence of the Latin Crescent. The Roman Empire looms through the centuries as the dominant influence, and it is worthwhile to review that heritage before looking at other current trends that define the region.

There was no evident reason why Rome, a village in Latium con-

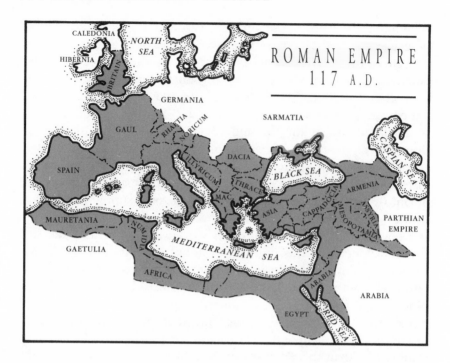

trolled by the Etruscans, should have come to dominate the ancient world. Historians have explained it with Rome's military discipline, its political institutions, its simple alphabet, its engineering skills. Like the Japanese today, the Romans rose to their hegemony through sheer genius in a land lacking most natural resources.

By the end of the Third Punic War in 146 B.C., when victorious Roman legions razed Carthage, the city in modern Tunisia that controlled the western Mediterranean, Rome ruled all of Italy and the northern rim of the Mediterranean, including Greece and the western tip of Asia Minor in the east, and most of Spain and Portugal and southern France in the west. This western region, including Italy, forms today's Latin Crescent. It was the zenith of the Roman Republic, which successfully blended monarchy, aristocracy, and democracy in its government of Senate, consuls, and tribunes elected by the citizens. Later conquests, notably by Julius Caesar, extended what became the Roman Empire clear around the Mediterranean rim and northward in Europe to the Danube, the Rhine, and Scotland.

With its rule, Rome brought its language and laws and assimilated its subjects into a cohesive, prosperous political unit. So durable were the Roman institutions, and the culture it adapted from Greece, that even the so-called barbarian invasions in the fifth century, Belgian scholar Henri Pirenne argues, did not really disrupt the political or social continuity of the empire.[7] Most historians consider A.D. 476, when the German chieftain Odoacer deposed the last emperor of the Western Empire, as the date marking the end of that half of the empire. But in Pirenne's view, the Western Empire, even without an emperor, survived more or less intact until it was divided up in the eighth and ninth centuries by the Franks and the Moslems.

During this long interval, *Romania,* the civilization established by the Romans, persisted and even prospered throughout the former empire. It was during this time that Latin, taken over by the invading Germans, became vulgarized and started to develop into the Romance languages. The division of the Western and Eastern empires has left its traces till now in language, alphabet, and religion. The Western Empire, the basis for the Latin Crescent superregion, remained Latin despite the imposition of German rule.

The Franks eventually conquered much of the territory and Charlemagne briefly united Christian Europe. Although the successor kingdoms provided a semblance of political unity for centuries, southern Europe continued to go its own way, preserving its Latin traditions.

Southern Italy, as so often in its history, was separated from central and northern Italy under Byzantine and later Norman rule. Central Italy came under the sway of the pope, where it would stay until the nineteenth century, while northern Italy developed into a region of warring city-states.

In Provence and Languedoc, the two Mediterranean regions of southern France, a civilization grew that flowered in troubadors and chivalry, and was united eventually under the counts of Toulouse. In the eleventh century, Count Raymond de St. Gilles of Toulouse was one of the leaders of the First Crusade. In the thirteenth century, however, Toulouse found itself on the receiving end of a "crusade." The spread of the Albigensian heresy in Languedoc was seized upon by the king of France as a pretext to brutally subjugate the southern realm and eliminate it as a separate culture and language.

The "*langue d'Oc*," a dialect that used *oc* for yes instead of *oïl* like the northern *langue d'Oïl,* which became French, survives today in modified form as Occitan, although it is not widely used. But southern France resisted annexation by the north as long as it could, with disconcerting obstinacy. "Even in the twelfth or thirteenth century an inhabitant of southern Gaul or 'France' might have resented being called 'French,' " writes British historian Edward James. "The south had been conquered three times by the northerners, in the sixth, the eighth and the thirteenth centuries, but still they preferred to keep their own identity."[8] That tenacious cultural border runs from Bordeaux across the Massif Central south of Vichy to Briancon, just southeast of Grenoble on the Italian border—the northern border of the Latin Crescent.

Meanwhile, in Spain, Christian rulers gradually reconquered the Iberian peninsula from the Islamic invaders, taking Cordoba in 1236, the longtime seat of the Moslem caliphate, and reducing the Moslem presence to a tiny kingdom of Granada, which was vanquished in 1492. It was under the victorious Ferdinand and Isabella, who sponsored Columbus's voyage, that Torquemada took over the Spanish Inquisition and turned it into a lasting symbol for the Church's iron grip on the country.

Roman Teaching and Latin Enterprise

Since the reputed arrival of St. Peter in Rome, the Roman Catholic Church has strongly influenced the entire region, as it did all of Europe and later much of the rest of the world. But it is in Italy, France, Spain, and Portugal that the Church has always been strongest, resisting heresy and imposing its belief and practices on the people.

There is a school of thought that the Catholic religion was mainly responsible for the economic backwardness of the Latin countries in modern times. Given the wealth and prosperity of Italy, Spain, France, and Portugal in previous centuries, this thesis applies mostly to the industrial age. Reduced to its essentials, this theory holds that the Catholic Church, promising rewards in heaven and preaching acceptance of poverty, robs the faithful of any incentive to make a fortune. Most Protestant persuasions, on the other hand, put their faith in predestination, and consider material prosperity a sign of God's favor for those chosen to enter heaven.

A professor at Rome's La Sapienza university, Mario Rivosecchi, contends that Catholic countries have inherited the Roman tradition of *res publica,* putting the highest priority on the public good.[9] Like the Romans, Catholics emphasize laws and political institutions as a framework for an economy to function well and take care of everyone. Protestant countries prefer a laissez-faire liberalism that permits individuals to accumulate wealth, but does not always protect the poor, who presumably are slated for eternal damnation anyway.

It is a diverting theory, but too neat to fit the sloppy facts of real life. In Franco's government of technocrats, it was members of Opus Dei, a secretive, reactionary order of laymen in the Catholic Church, who pragmatically liberalized the Spanish economy so that it could compete in world trade. Belgium, nearly 100 percent Catholic but chockablock with smokestack industry, puts the lie to Protestant supremacy in leading the industrial revolution; it is full of people happy to accumulate a fortune. Likewise, the social security network created in Germany by Bismarck, a reactionary Protestant, served as a model for modern nations to safeguard a minimum welfare for their citizens.

Looking at economic structures themselves, it is tempting to characterize southern Europeans as patriarchal, dominated by family-owned enterprises. Labeling Italian magnates like Agnelli and Pirelli patricians or even *condottieri* identifies them with a specifically Latin past, harkening back to the Medicis. But the Protestant Wallenberg family in Social Democratic Sweden had an economic dynasty to match any Agnelli or Medici. In Germany, medium-sized family-owned companies are the backbone of the economy.

Southern Europe is widely seen to be backward in finance, even though northern Italy is the historic cradle of modern banking. In a schematic view, you could say the stock market is the main financing vehicle in the Atlantic Coast (notably in Britain and Netherlands), the banks are paramount in Mitteleuropa, and the state in Latin Crescent. But of course all three sources are significant throughout Europe. As De Benedetti amply demonstrated, finance need not be a hindrance to economic success in southern Europe.

Many of the economic structures considered to be archaic and endemic to southern European culture seem rather to be stages of economic development that are left behind as the region catches up with the rest of the continent. A whole new generation of Span-

ish and Italian yuppies are pursuing wealth as avidly as their counterparts in other industrialized countries. Into the 1980s, the civil
service continued to hold such an exalted position in France that
it attracted the cream of the country's high achievers; by now,
bright French graduates are likelier to pursue a career in the private
sector, bypassing the legendary Ecole Nationale d'Administration in
favor of a business school.

Economic development is changing social behavior even more
profoundly. The cliché has it that southern Europe, because of the
Catholic Church's opposition to birth control but also because of a
putative Latin attachment to large families, produces swarms of
lovely *bambini* who are the darlings of their big-hearted mothers.
After decades of rapid economic growth, however, birth rates
throughout southern Europe have plunged. Keeping in mind that a
fertility rate of 2.1 children per family is the standard to keep a
population unchanged, the demographic revolution in the Latin
Crescent can be documented by noting that the fertility rate in 1990
in France was 1.8, in Spain, 1.6, and in Italy, 1.3. Even projecting
a slight increase in these rates, the population of Italy by the year
2030 could be just 70 percent of its 1985 population of 57 million![10]
Italian women today are doubtless still big-hearted, but more likely
to be found, smartly dressed in a designer suit, working in a big-
city office than staying at home with the children.

As in France earlier and perhaps Spain afterward, Italian fashion
and design have given the country a chic image. Style is what genuinely distinguishes the Latin region most. Milan and Paris vie with
each other for the title of world fashion capital, with Milan given a
slight edge in recent years. Germans may engineer the best cars in
the world, but Italians generally design them. Olivetti won prizes
for its design of typewriters, then computers. It is the same imaginative flair that makes the French leaders in computer software;
Europe's biggest firm for specially tailored software packages, Cap
Gemini Sogeti, was born in Grenoble. Catalan architects like Ri-
cardo Bofill achieve global recognition. Centuries of prosperity and
culture, magnificent achievements in art, literature, and urban architecture while the rest of Europe lived in huts, have given the
Latins a clear edge in artistic creativity.

It seems a natural outgrowth of the passion and animation we
associate with the voluble Mediterranean people. To walk down
Madrid's Paseo del Prado at midnight on a summer evening, with

fountains gaily lit and throngs of pedestrians and cars creating a friendly din, is a contrast to venturing out at the same time in London, Berlin, or Chicago. In Naples, a coffee break with colleagues, particularly in nice weather, takes much longer than the half minute necessary to down the sip of rich brown elixir, because it is a time of welcome leisure and human warmth, less efficient in an economic sense than the mechanical quarter of an hour to fetch a plastic cup of watery vending-machine coffee in the north, but so much more pleasant—and perhaps better for productivity in the long run.

And there is the climate. The Latin Crescent lifestyle depends in large part on the agreeable weather in the Mediterranean region. Is it really a surprise that when economic conditions permit, so many people voluntarily relocate to where it is warm and the sun shines?

The Terrain of the Latin Crescent

The tunnel of Fourviere is a terror for European truckers and motorists. Until completion of the bypass in 1993, the narrow tunnel in the heart of Lyons was the main road link between Spain, Portugal, southern France, and the north of Europe. About a mile long, the tunnel burrows under a hill crowned millennia ago by the Roman forum of ancient Lugdunum, as Lyons was called in Latin. On any given workday, 100,000 vehicles, 15 percent of them trucks ranging up to the massive forty-ton piggy-back trailers, trundled into the tight space, often backing up traffic for miles in both directions on the A6/7, the *"Autoroute du Soleil"* or "Highway of the Sun" that runs through the Rhone valley.

The Rhone River, which flows out of the Alps through Lake Geneva to empty into the Mediterranean near Marseilles, is not the longest river in Europe, but the valley it forges between the Alps to the east and the Massif Central, the wide plateau to the west, have made it a main thoroughfare between northern and southern Europe since Caesar's legions marched to conquer all Gaul.

Even today, a road map of France shows a fairly empty spot around the Massif Central. The highest point is only 6,000 feet, and most of it is much lower, but the range covers 33,000 square miles—an area bigger than South Carolina or Scotland, even though the formation is virtually unknown outside France. As a businessman in Lyons remarked, "It's not very high, but it's hard to get through." An express highway to span the plateau region, linking Bordeaux to Geneva, has remained largely at the blueprint stage for decades and is more than half a century from completion at the present rate of construction.

For the foreseeable future, then, the main channel for land transport to and from the Iberian peninsula will continue to be through Barcelona, skirting the Pyrenees to the west, via Perpignan, Montpellier, Nimes, Valence, and Lyons. Traffic from Marseilles and Nice also passes through the Rhone Valley. Once the highway linking Turin and Valence via Grenoble is finished, further traffic will be funneled through Lyons. And so that city, which has enjoyed a boom period since the Iberian traffic started to flow, is likely to continue its rapid growth.

In many respects, the Massif Central is as "natural" a frontier as the Pyrenees. It divides the plain of northern Europe from the Mediterranean coast, marking the boundary of the Latin Crescent. Here is the way British writer John Ardagh describes it:

Many times I have made the 400-mile car journey south from Paris to Toulouse and it is always exciting, on the final lap, to cross that mysterious cultural frontier that separates Europe's north from its south. After winding over the lovely western foothills of the Massif Central, the *route nationale* descends at last into the broad valley of the Garonne where suddenly the sun beats stronger, the air is drier, and the ancient villages with their red-tiled roofs have the unmistakable flavor of the Midi.[11]

Such geographical barriers — the Alps are the best example — are useful as frontiers when needed, but they can be surmounted when the will to do so is strong enough. The Pyrenees themselves, a genuine mountain range with its highest point over 11,000 feet, have long been claimed as a "natural" border between Spain and France. But the Pyrenees did not block unified administration of territory on both sides under the Romans, Visigoths, or Franks. For centuries, the Kingdom of Navarre united the Basque provinces on both sides of the western Pyrenees. Roussillon, a region on the northern side of the eastern Pyrenees, was finally ceded to France only in the seventeenth century after five centuries joined to Spain.

Today, major highways pass on either side of the Pyrenees along the coasts, connecting Perpignan to Barcelona in the east and Biarritz to Bilbao in the west. Two major road and tunnel projects are planned to breach the mountain obstacle. One through the Puymorens pass in the east would provide a direct link between Toulouse and Barcelona; the other, at Somport in the west, would open a route from Bordeaux to Saragossa and the whole of central and eastern Spain. Dynamic growth in the triangle formed in northeastern Spain by Saragossa, Valladolid, and Burgos—driven by massive European investment after Spain's 1986 accession to the EC—is even beginning to counterbalance Barcelona's weight in the region. Roger Brunet, an economic geographer based in Montpellier, sees Saragossa as a key pole in the new economic axes being formed in the Latin Crescent. A new freeway connecting Saragossa to Madrid has reduced driving time from four and a half hours to two and a half hours.

Farther to the south, on the eastern coast, Valencia, where Ford Motor was an early and big investor, is surging, while even farther south, in the Almeria region of Andalucia, an agricultural renaissance is taking place. Almeria, one of the chief port cities for the Romans in ancient times, is Spain's biggest agricultural success story since the war, due to hothouse growing under plastic on the coastal strip south of the city. The manager of a local cooperative explains their goal, "Our job is to produce what Europe produces at a time when Europe cannot climatically do so."[12] The climate—3,000 hours of sunshine annually and an average temperature of 65 degrees Fahrenheit—helps the Mediterranean region rival colder Holland, which has a head start in hothouse technology.

The project in southern Spain has been so successful that it is attracting imitators. Almeria must continue to develop its technology to keep ahead of potential new competitors in northern Africa. And so southern Spain is trying to create an extension of the High Technology Highway that runs through the core of the Latin Crescent farther north. A 415-acre research park has sprung up in Malaga in the hopes that the resort area's sunshine and 20-odd golf courses will entice high-tech investment. The government also plans to transform the site of the 1992 Expo in Sevilla, in western Andalucia, into a research park.

In general, such is the vitality of the economy in the Latin Crescent that it seems to be overflowing into the moribund and underdeveloped extremities of the superregion, in southern Italy and southern Spain. One enterprising building contractor in Bari, a port town in southeastern Italy, has carved out a profitable niche for himself: He constructs new facilities tailored to meet the exacting specifications of high-technology research. Even southern Portugal, boosted by EC subsidies, is making progress. Setubal, just south of Lisbon, was mired in misery and on the verge of famine in 1980. A decade later, Volkswagen and Ford were producing passenger vans there.

Toulouse: *La Vie en Rose*

Toulouse, with its high-performance industrial enterprises in high technology, exemplifies the dynamism of the Latin Crescent. The city, located in southwest France midway on the isthmus between the Mediterranean Sea and the Atlantic Ocean in the foothills of the Pyrenees, counts 2,300 high-tech companies in its environs, many of them in the aerospace industry.

Toulouse is evocative of New Orleans, or rather the inverse, since the French city was founded in the fourth century B.C., two millennia before New Orleans. Toulouse's three-story red brick structures, with their sober, elegant facades and wrought iron railings, resemble those in the French Quarter. The vivacious night life also recalls New Orleans. The pink shimmer of the city's red bricks in the sunset has prompted the French to call it *"la ville rose,"* the Rose City, a pun on *la vie en rose.*

The capital of the refined Languedoc civilization in the Middle Ages, Toulouse's history in modern times has been closely linked to aviation. After the success of fighter pilots in the First World War, France worked hard to build up its airplane industry, prudently concentrating it far away from the German border, in the opposite corner of the country—in Toulouse. The pioneer French aviator Pierre Latecoere inaugurated airmail when his airline linked Toulouse to Buenos Aires in 1928.

It was a French-German joint venture in aviation formed in 1970, however, that set the stage for the city's recent prosperity. Airbus Industrie, which later took in British and Spanish partners, was launched to produce commercial airliners that could take on the dominant U.S. manufacturers in world markets. Most people in the industry, including some among the original partners, did not give the fragile trans-European venture much hope for success.

Assembly of the new jetliners was set for the Toulouse facilities of Aerospatiale, the state-owned French manufacturer, then known as SNIAS, which had built the Caravelle and Concorde aircraft. Airbus's top executives spent so much of their time in the venture's infancy showing skeptical customers just how solid the aircraft was that headquarters also was quickly moved to Toulouse from Paris.

Two decades later, Airbus had delivered more than eight hundred aircraft and had firm orders for nearly a thousand more in six basic models covering all major flight ranges and seating capacities. Although U.S. manufacturers complained constantly that Airbus benefited from government subsidies that gave it an unfair competitive advantage, it was primarily the quality of the product that enabled the European venture to sell its aircraft to one hundred-some customers and capture nearly two-fifths of the global market for aircraft seating more than a hundred passengers. The success of Airbus forced many, inside Europe as well as out, to change their ideas about the continent and what it was capable of. Americans have had trouble accepting that Europeans could make inroads in one of their traditional fortes, contends Jean Pierson, the French chief executive of Airbus. "They are still asking why the Europeans are building aircraft when they can sell perfumes and wine."[13]

In the new assembly hangar for the long-range 330/340 model, which cost $200 million and with 70,000 square meters floor space claims to be the largest building in Europe in surface area, robots rivet the wings and fuselage sections together, an innovation in aviation construction. While the aircraft parts arrive in super-guppies — large transport planes specially designed to shuttle components between the venture's various manufacturing sites — from all over Europe, the robots were developed in Toulouse by a special research team of Aerospatiale in collaboration with local manufacturers in Toulouse and Bordeaux.

More than anything else, Airbus's glamorous success has made Toulouse a magnet for high-tech industry and the lifestyle accompanying it. The city claims to be the second biggest space industry center in the world after Los Angeles, with one-third of Europe's employees in the sector — the Ariane rocket and Hermes manned space shuttle programs are headquartered in Toulouse. The French government's huge space research agency, employing 2,000 people, has generated a host of commercial spinoffs, like Spot Image, which markets satellite photos, creating thousands more jobs in the sector.

Nor is it just high-tech industry that benefits from the pull of Airbus. With the medium-haul A321, Airbus will assemble a plane outside Toulouse for the first time, in Hamburg. As a compensation, though, the Rose City will be allowed by the consortium to handle interior finishing for the widebody long-haul A330s and 340s, opening up a lucrative new business for local producers. City fathers hope that the specialized materials needed to furnish the aircraft will enable Toulouse to revive its textile industry, once a mainstay for the local economy.

The rapid expansion of the aerospace industry in Toulouse has generated spectacular growth in another important sphere—education. Although the city's university dates back to the fifteenth century, there were only 1,200 students in 1960. By 1987, Toulouse was host to *fifty times* that number of college students—with 64,000 young men and women enrolled in three universities, four schools of engineering, three aviation schools, a military school, a business school, and other specialized institutes. Toulouse has become France's biggest center of higher learning after Paris. The concentration of educational and research facilities in the city, which has a population of only 600,000 in the metropolitan area, has moved Sorbonne geographer Georges Benko to note, "The university and industrial landscape in the southeast of Toulouse has no equivalent"—a startling concession from a Parisian.[14]

From Lisbon to Venice

The borders of the superregions follow the historical and geographical features of the territory. The foregoing discussion gives us a start in tracing the boundaries of the Latin Crescent, which we can now examine in greater detail. As with the other superregions, these borders have been established after careful consideration of many factors. Keep in mind, though, that superregion borders are broad, permeable demarcations and not hermetic frontiers. And they are anything but immutable.

The borders of the Latin Crescent to the east, south, and west seem at first glance easy enough to define because these are bodies of water at the extremities of Europe. The Adriatic Sea, that long arm of the Mediterranean that separates the Italian and the Balkan peninsulas, marks the eastern boundary, while the Western Mediterranean, separating Europe from Africa, is the southern border.

As soon as we designate the Atlantic Ocean in southern Portugal as the western boundary, however, the problems begin. There is, of course, a reasonable argument for including all of Portugal in the Atlantic Coast region. Even Sevilla, for that matter, faces to the Atlantic via the Gualquivir River. Columbus sailed from there to find America and it was the port of entry for all the riches flowing to Spain from the New World. The Atlantic Arc association of coastal regions does include all of Portugal and western Spain. But the new infrastructure, investment, and trade flows that have followed Spain and Portugal's entry into the EC tie twentieth-century Lisbon and Sevilla to Europe via the Latin Crescent and justify their inclusion in this superregion. In a more notable example, the new high-speed train from Sevilla to Madrid cost a stunning $4 billion, but cut travel time from six hours to less than three.

People still speak Portuguese north of Lisbon, of course, a language derived from Latin, as is the Galician language spoken in the northwestern corner of Spain (in fact, Portuguese actually evolved from Galician). But Oporto, the main city in northern Portugal, has clearly cast its lot with the Atlantic regions, taking a leadership role in the Atlantic Arc. As for Galicia, it is, in the words of British writer John Hooper, "as wet and lush and mournfully beautiful as the west of Ireland,"[15] — authentic Atlantic Coast territory. It has a visible Celtic heritage, complete with bagpipes. So the northern boundary of the Latin Crescent follows a line from Lisbon to Bilbao, hugging the coast around the Bay of Biscay to pass south of Bordeaux in an arc across the Massif Central south of Grenoble, through Milan to reach the Adriatic at Venice.

This northern border should be visualized as a particularly wide band, especially where it passes through France. Although Bordeaux is an Atlantic Coast city, it experiences the tug of a true border town toward the Latin Crescent. Lyons, in the words of a city father, "is the most southern of northern cities," a city of Mitteleuropa, but important for the Latin Crescent, too.

The region includes some of the lower Alpine ranges, like the Maritime Alps on the French-Italian border, which beckon so alluringly toward Sophia Antipolis, and the Ligurian Alps along the Italian stretch of the Riviera. Most precisely, this northern border should pass just to the south of Grenoble. Claude Maudelonde, director of a mini-research park called Micropolis, in a small city fifty miles south of Grenoble with the unlikely name of Gap, points out that the weather changes dramatically across the Bayard pass just north of Gap on the road to Grenoble. On the southern side, in Gap, the sun shines most of the time; in Grenoble, there is less sun, more rain. Local pilots refer to the *trou* of Gap (the gap over Gap, so to speak), where the clouds open up and the sun shines. Grenoble belongs wholly to the Alpine Arc, whereas Gap is still in the Provence-Alpes-Cote d'Azur region of France stretching down to the Mediterranean; so it seems best to draw the Latin Crescent border between the two cities.

Milan, as we have seen, lies at the juncture of Latin Crescent, Alpine Arc, and Danube Basin. The mountain region north of Milan, including South Tirol, belongs to the Alpine superregion, while the crook of Adriatic coast in the northeast corner of Italy belongs to the Danube Basin region by virtue of history as much as geography.

On the map, this superregion looks like a crescent moon. It has a population of about 90 million, making it one of the bigger superregions.

Mare Nostrum: The Mediterranean Rim

The Latin Crescent forms the main part of Europe's southern border. The region's future, and to a certain extent Europe's, depends on its interaction with its neighbors along that border, across the Mediterranean in northern Africa. As the superregion grows closer together, this fundamental reality is becoming more evident.

The Imperial Palace of Pharo crowns the point guarding the entrance into Marseilles' old port, which is now used exclusively for pleasure craft and small fishing vessels. The palace, built in the nineteenth century for the Spanish-born wife of Napoleon III, Empress Eugenie, commands a dramatic view of the Gulf of Lions to the east and a panorama of Marseilles' pastel hills to the west. It sits grandly in the center of twenty-four-acre park which also contains the city's university, a school of journalism, and an institute of tropical medicine.

The Pharo palace, long underused to house the city's technical services, occupies one of the most splendid sites along the entire Mediterranean coast. Since 1993 a completely refurbished palace, containing conference rooms and reception halls, office and research space, dining rooms, auditorium, and underground parking, serves as a center for "Euro-Mediterranean" encounters, a meeting place for countries, regions, cities, associations, and other institutions from around the Mediterranean rim. The main purpose of the new center is to promote dialogue between southern Europe and its neighbors bordering the great "sea between lands." As Marseilles' mayor Robert P. Vigoroux declared when he announced creation of the facility: "Europe in its entirety will take up its legitimate ambitions only by rigorously ordering its relations with its southern flank."

The need to come to terms with Europe's Mediterranean neighbors preoccupies many policymakers in France and elsewhere in the Latin Crescent. Demography alone raises the issue—the population in southern Europe will remain stable or even decline in the coming decades, while that of the other Mediterranean nations, for the most part developing countries with a much lower standard of living, will see their populations double or triple. In 1990, there were 163 million people living in EC countries along the Mediterranean and 223 million in the others; by 2010, it is estimated there will be 167 million citizens in the EC Mediterranean countries and 324 million in the others.

This is not so worrying in itself, especially since birthrates in some of the non-European countries are also showing a tendency to fall. The danger lies rather in the poverty of these countries— per capita income in 1989 was $640 a year in Egypt, compared with $17,820 in France—and the resurgence of Islamic fundamentalism in these largely Arab nations. In short, Europeans in their heart of hearts are afraid that millions of hungry, fanatic Moslems, lured by the riches of the prosperous countries on the Mediterranean's northern shores, will invade their cities, diminish their wealth, and disrupt their societies.

Marseilles is a case in point—Moslem immigrants, for the most part from the Maghreb countries across the Mediterranean, account for one-eighth of the city's population of 800,000. The National Front of Jean-Marie Le Pen, a rightist, xenophobic political party, has gained a significant following in France by playing on fears of a Moslem invasion.

Spain has experienced an increase in illegal immigrants from Morocco. Unscrupulous fishing-boat operators have been ferrying refugees across the treacherous Strait of Gibraltar; many of them perish in the crossing, their corpses washing ashore in Spain, like those of the Haitian refugees trying in vain to reach Florida. The influx of foreigners has provoked new right-wing extremism in Spain, where paramilitary groups attack and murder clandestine immigrants.

Animosity between Moslems and Christians is as old as Islam, beginning with the seventh- and eighth-century jihad that swept across North Africa and into the Iberian peninsula. That conquest transformed the Mediterranean, which had been an economic unit since its settlement in ancient times and a political unit through the long centuries of the Roman Empire, dividing it for the first time into two opposing camps. "Islam destroyed the Mediterranean unity that the Germanic invasions had let survive," writes Belgian historian Henri Pirenne. "What had been a great channel of communication is today an unbreachable barrier."[16]

Islam and Christian Europe seemed irreconcilable in history. French historian Fernand Braudel regrets that when the Spanish drove the last Moslems out of Granada, they did not continue their reconquest of Moslem territory across the Strait of Gibraltar, to restore the unity of the Mediterranean under European rule. "It was a tragedy for Spanish history that . . . this new war of Granada was not pursued with more determination," says Braudel. Spain's "failure to pursue the war on the other side of the Mediterranean is one of the great missed opportunities of history. . . . Spain, half-European, half-African, failed to carry out her geographical mission and for the first time in history, the Strait of Gibraltar 'became a political frontier.' "[17]

Europe launched its ultimately unsuccessful Crusades against the "infidel" over a period of two centuries, and resisted the Moslem tide mounting the Danube basin as the Ottoman Turks extended their empire to the very gates of Vienna. This age-old enmity makes the ideological hostility between Soviet communism and Western capitalism that has terrorized our century seem like an interlude.

It is unlikely that the new Euro-Mediterranean center at Pharo palace can bridge such an historic chasm, no matter how many conferences it holds. Andalucia in southern Spain, one of the European regions the longest under Moslem rule, also wants to promote dialogue between Europe and Islam. Oil sheikhs, no doubt comforted by the presence of the magnificent Alhambra in Granada and the Moorish cast of architecture in southern Spain, have settled in a villa colony around Marbella. Madrid turned out to be an inspired choice to inaugurate the Mideast Peace Conference in 1991.

But the first bridges are likely to be those built on more pragmatic grounds. The Medcities Network established in 1990 in Barcelona could show more immediate success with its nonpolitical objectives of cleaning up the environment and promoting commerce and tourism. Under the auspices of the Mediterranean Environmental Technical Assistance Program, itself sponsored by international heavyweights like the World Bank and the European Investment Bank, the network linking one large port city from each of the eighteen Mediterranean nations established a permanent secretariat (in Marseilles), a steering committee, and a no-nonsense agenda on managing water resources, taking care of solid and toxic wastes, preventing marine pollution, and improving coastal lands. The tasks are enormous: proper sewage facilities alone—as untreated wastes flow into the sea not only from the developing countries on the southern rim, but from civilized Athens, too—could cost anywhere from $25 billion to $100 billion. The Mediterranean basin, incredibly, accounts for fully one-third of the global tourism market, so the participants have a profound economic interest in maintaining their environment for that reason alone.

The Latin Crescent is beginning to look at the positive side of the situation. The Maghreb, which has enjoyed long periods of prosperity in history, has a rich potential for economic growth and development. The latest in a series of attempts to organize cooperation in this North African superregion was the formation in 1989 of the Union of the Arab Maghreb by Algeria, Libya, Morocco, Mauritania, and Tunisia. Along with numerous projects in the economic and cultural spheres, the association has embarked on a regular 5+5 dialogue with European countries in the western Mediterranean— Spain, France, Italy, Portugal, and Malta. However, political crises like the UN sanctions imposed on Libya in 1992 to force extradition of suspected terrorists, or electoral triumph that same year of Islamic fundamentalists in Algeria and the subsequent coup d'etat by the army, demonstrate just how problematic such attempts at dialogue will continue to be.

The idea is taking hold nonetheless that cooperation between southern Europe and other Mediterranean countries might create an economic zone that could begin to vie with northern Europe. Gilles Martinet, a French diplomat, urges as part of the overall political and economic realignment in Europe "the creation of a true Mediterranean pole in the Community."[18] He points out that in the mid-1980s French foreign minister Claude Cheysson was the first to call for a "Mediterranean pact" between the southern European and the Maghreb countries. Economist Henri Regnault sees the growth of the Latin Crescent as a way to "anchor" Europe in the south. "The emergence of a Latin bloc, if it is confirmed, would constitute a major event inside the European Community and in the northwest Mediterranean," says this expert. "The emerging Latin Europe should combine Latinity and 'Mediterranean-ness' and provide a Mediterranean anchorage to the whole of Europe, putting an end to a purely economic view of continents, which cannot alter geographic proximities and the security requirements that go with it."[19] Alain Minc, the French writer and polemicist who first alerted his compatriots to the new emergence of Mitteleuropa, suggests that rather than try to combat the Germans on their own territory in northern Europe, "The French would do better to get interested in the south, which has extraordinary potential."[20]

Some northern firms have already learned how to take advantage of the Mediterranean connection. The Swedish firm Ericsson set up a subsidiary in Spain to supply that country's telephone monopoly, Telefonica. Before long, however, the Spanish unit was developing its own products tailored to the needs of the nearby export markets along the southern rim of the Mediterranean (as well as to Latin America). Likewise, when the German chemicals giant Hoechst put a unit in Portugal to profit from lower production costs, the subsidiary soon found itself innovating new products for the Maghreb market, particularly Morocco.

But the progress will be short-lived if trade remains a one-way street. In their own interest, the European countries will have to open their markets to imports from these developing countries, beyond the oil and gas supplies flowing from Algeria and Libya. "The search for complementarities should operate in both directions," says a joint European-Arab study of the region's economy.[21] Economies of scale in the north as well as in the south can assure the future equilibrium and success of the Mediterranean economy, the study concludes.

In 1991, Arab countries on the southern rim of the Mediterranean bought 37 percent of their imports from EC Mediterranean countries, while those EC countries realized 3.2 percent of their imports from the Arab countries. In absolute amounts, the Arab countries actually had a trade surplus with their EC neighbors because of the much greater volume of trade in the EC countries.

The Latin Crescent is clearly well positioned to profit from the fast-growing North African market. If it helps this region to develop, it will create vast new economic opportunities, and will be the middleman between a wealthy northern Europe and a dynamic threshold economy, with all the obvious benefits. It is probably the key to maintaining its own high growth rates and catching up with Mitteleuropa in relative and absolute terms. And it is certainly keeping in the Latin tradition established by Rome of making the *mare nostrum*—"our sea," as the ancient Romans referred to the Mediterranean—a prosperous economic unity.

Latin Renaissance

In 1993, an investigation that started with local corruption in Milan took on increasingly national implications in Italy as several prominent politicians, such as former prime minister Bettino Craxi, were implicated in the scandal. Related probes reached even higher, touching Giulio Andreotti, many times a prime minister and for years the single most powerful politician in Italy. The scandals pitched the nation into a wrenchingly painful adjustment of its entire political system.

The phenomenon seemed to have several causes. For one thing, criminal infiltration of public life and corruption, nurtured over decades, reached proportions that were simply unsustainable in any reasonably democratic society. For another, the collapse of communism in eastern Europe robbed the Christian Democratic party and its allies of their historic justification for monopolizing political power in Italy. The right could no longer claim to be a bulwark against an antidemocratic communist regime. The Italian public no longer felt obliged to put up with the inefficiency, corruption, and crime that accompanied decades of Christian Democratic rule. The brutal assassination in 1992 of two anti-Mafia prosecutors was not a sign of Mafia strength, Alexander Stille argued in *The New*

Yorker[22], but an act of desperation borne of fear that politicians were no longer able to guarantee the protection they had provided for so long.

There can be little doubt, though, that the dynamic forces generated by economic growth in the Latin Crescent region also contributed to the political crisis and catharsis in Italy. It is no coincidence that regional parties like the Northern League became agents of political change in the country, driving a wedge into the monolithic power structure. These parties represented the trend prevalent throughout Europe: the desire for local populations to take responsibility for their own welfare and to benefit from the opportunities afforded by an integrated Europe. When Italian carabinieri finally tracked down and arrested top Mafia boss Salvatore Riina in January 1993, a commentator in the Turin daily *La Stampa* wrote, "With the arrest of Riina, Italy enters Europe."[23]

This cleansing influence led to almost comical consequences elsewhere in the superregion. Already in 1990, Jacques Medecin, the longtime mayor of Nice and notorious ally of organized crime in the city, fled ignobly to South America to avoid criminal charges, heralding the end perhaps of the systematic corruption that has blocked development on much of the Cote d'Azur. In Spain, the scandals surrounding the Socialist Party began to multiply after its long years of uninterrupted power. Regional parties gained in strength, and they held the balance of power after the Socialists lost their absolute majority in June 1993 national elections.

The recessionary trends of 1992–93 slowed down growth in the Latin Crescent, as elsewhere in Europe. But the pause encouraged a consolidation and refurbishment of political and economic structures in the region that would foster further growth once the business cycle swung around. The superregion dynamic continued to force the pace of modernization as southern Europe strove to catch up with the north. The slowdown also confronted the Latin Crescent with the challenge posed by the opening up of eastern Europe, and the shift in the continent's center of gravity in that direction. Like the Atlantic Coast, the Latin Crescent risked increasing marginalization. The superregion that profited the most from integration in western Europe had the most to lose as that integration was extended eastward. Or so it seemed.

But the profound reach of the Italian probes, which surprised everyone in and outside the country, provided new evidence of

Latin Crescent vitality. Even while top executives of state-owned companies were being led off to jail, the government pushed through legislation to privatize much of public-sector industry, a favored terrain of political patronage and corruption. The sell-off promised to open up whole new sectors of business to the entrepreneurial drive that made the Third Italy such a success. If carried to its conclusion, the clean-up of local government in southern Italy and Sicily would mean that the European aid flowing to these underdeveloped regions, due to be increased in the wake of the Single Market and the European Economic Area, could finally find its way into productive investment rather than lining Mafia pockets.

The restructuring of Italy represents one of the clearest examples of how the dual trends of integration and regionalization are transforming Europe. It is not by chance that Latin Crescent, one of the first superregions to emerge in Europe, became the first to evidence the capacity for self-renewal contained in the dynamic of superregions.

CHAPTER FIVE

BALTIC LEAGUE: TRADING PLACES

For three sunny days in June 1992, Tallinn, capital of the newly independent Baltic republic Estonia, gladly welcomed an influx of hundreds of west Europeans who helped relieve, however briefly, the country's dire need for foreign exchange by spending their deutsche marks, Finnish marks, Swedish kroner, Dutch guilders, Swiss francs, and other hard currencies. The visitors belonged to official delegations sent by sixty-eight cities in northern Europe to the twelfth Hanseatic Diet of modern times.

The diet in question, of course, referred to a formal governing assembly, like a parliament, and not to a low-calorie eating program. The primary order of business was to drink beer at the score of special stands set up for that purpose, dance to the folk and rock music that filled the cobbled lanes and central square of the historic town, and shop for bargains in the city's refurbished stores.

The delegates from Germany, Poland, Netherlands, Finland, Sweden, Norway, Latvia, and Lithuania met in working sessions to discuss projects for economic cooperation and tourism. But the meeting, like the others that had preceded it in eleven previous years in other cities, mostly was a summer holiday festival harkening back nostalgically to a time in the Middle Ages when the Baltic Sea and the cities around it constituted a prosperous trading empire, the Hanseatic League. The loose confederation of cities, with the German port city of Lubeck as its capital, controlled commerce in the Baltic absolutely during its heyday from the fourteenth to the sixteenth centuries, and exercised a virtual monopoly on trade in the region extending from Novgorod in northern Russia to London.

Tallinn, known in history by its German name Reval, was the first city in eastern Europe to host the modern Hanseatic Diet. Its well-preserved historic center, with fifteenth-century guild houses and aristocratic mansions, was a fitting venue for the event, so mindful of the past. The gentle Estonians, who then and now have little in common with the thrusting German merchants of the Hansa, were happy to have the hard currency, even if somewhat bewildered by the happening.

Sitting in one of the makeshift sidewalk cafés in front of City Hall, Estonia's foreign minister, Jaan Manitski, in a German television interview, appealed to foreign businessmen for sympathy with his country's desire to lessen its dependence on Russia, which had accounted for 90 percent of Estonia's national income when the smallest of the three Baltic republics was part of the Soviet Union. Manitski, an Estonian émigré who grew up in Sweden and served for a time as financial manager for the popular music group Abba, defended Estonia's introduction of its own currency (called, ironically in view of the minister's previous job, the "kroon") as a step toward economic sovereignty.

Estonia, like Latvia and Lithuania, has had trouble persuading foreign investors to put money into the Baltic republics. Not even nearby Finland has been much help. Several times a day, hydrofoils skip quickly across the fifty miles of water separating Helsinki, the capital of Finland, from Tallinn. The Estonian language is related to Finnish—both belong to the select group of Finno-Ugrian tongues that differ radically from other European languages. As a result, the two countries share many cultural traditions.

In the year following Estonia's independence, Finns mounted nearly half of the 250 joint ventures in Estonia, but few of them were able to conduct any business right away. Estonia Engineering, majority owned by a Finnish machinery group, spent most of its initial months handling barter and countertrade deals. Estonians exchanged fish, hides, powdered milk, cheese, and butter for necessary imports. Foreign investors worried about the effects of breaking away from Russia on the local economy, and hesitated to make commitments. They also worried about the thousands of Red Army officers and soldiers who seemed reluctant to leave the territories they had guarded for fifty years.

Scandinavian farmers and fishermen shared their expertise with their Baltic counterparts, students traded places, but there was little concrete investment in Estonia or its neighbors. Even three Estonian factories making prefabricated homes failed to attract any foreign investors, although the prefabs would have found a ready market in Russia to house the further thousands of soldiers who were actually leaving eastern Europe.

Such experiences have dampened Estonian expectations, but the ghost of the Hansa still haunts the Baltic. The advent of communism in Russia early in this century had ended the sea's long history as a highway for commerce. "Instead of a sea joining shores," comments Olof Ruin, a political scientist in Stockholm, "the Baltic was transformed into a moat that separated and divided."[1] Now that communism is gone, many hope the Baltic can reclaim this role, "as in the time of the Hanseatic League, when merchant ships went freely from port to port, along the shores of the Baltic, and there weren't any nation-states yet."[2]

The Hansa (the word originally referred to any cooperative organization) joined a string of German towns along the Baltic coast —Lubeck, Hamburg, Wismar, Rostock, Stralsund, Danzig (Gdansk), Riga, Reval (Tallinn)—that eventually extended westward along the North Sea coast to Bremen and Frisian towns in what is now the Netherlands, and southward, to towns in the Baltic hinterland. The League set up trading posts, or counting houses, in foreign countries, to store goods and keep careful control of transactions. The main counting houses were in Novgorod, about three hundred miles northwest of Moscow, the preeminent Russian city in that period; Bergen, in Norway, where the "German bridge" of rebuilt merchant houses today makes the city's port so colorful and picturesque; Bruges, the elegant trading center for Flanders; and London, already then a leading commercial center. The Hanseatic League's network of cities maintained a monopoly on trade between northern and southern Europe, exchanging furs, timber, metal, wax, amber, dried fish, and hemp from the north for wine, textiles, salt, spices, and other luxuries from the south.

The Hansa's German merchants pursued Baltic trade in the wake of the Teutonic Knights, a military religious order that turned its crusading zeal to Christianizing the pagan Baltic territories after the Europeans were chased out of the Holy Land in the thirteenth century. The Knights established a domain along the eastern shores of the Baltic that endured until the sixteenth century, when they converted to Protestantism and secularized their state. They ruthlessly suppressed the local Baltic tribes, including one called the "Pruzzi," who left their name behind in what came to be known as Prussia.

The Hanseatic merchants took over the trade originally conducted by the Vikings, who in previous centuries crossed the Baltic from Sweden and eastern Denmark and traversed Russia via the Dnieper and Volga rivers, to trade or pillage as far as Byzantium and Persia. The Hanseatic League marked the zenith of peaceful commerce in the Baltic. As nation-states came of age in the seventeenth century, Sweden became master of the sea, extending its dominion along the western and northern shores and seizing much of the German territory on the southern and eastern coasts. In the eighteenth century, Peter the Great's fascination with the sea led to the foundation of a new Russian capital, St. Petersburg, directly on the Baltic, and to the retreat of the Swedes. In subsequent decades, a vastly expanded kingdom of Prussia vied with Russia to control the sea. The defeat of Germany in World War I and the victory of the Bolsheviks in Russia began the division of the Baltic that was completed at the end of World War II, when the Iron Curtain was drawn across it.

Baltic Networks

More than in any other superregion, the removal of the Iron Curtain from across the Baltic seemed to unleash decades of pent-up longing for contact. A plethora of new organizations established overlapping networks across the sea, at various levels. In June 1991, the Union of the Baltic Cities came into being at a conference of thirty-some municipal authorities in Gdansk, Poland, the home of the Solidarity trade union and under its German name, Danzig, a key member of the Hanseatic League. In March 1992, the Council of Baltic Sea States brought together the ten countries bordering the sea at a national government level. Meanwhile, businessmen and local politicians in the western Baltic formed a North European Club to lobby for improved infrastructure in the region. A Baltic Chamber of Commerce was set up in Kiel.

Whereas the revived Hanseatic Diet had a more festive character, and other calls for restoration of a Hanseatic League seemed tinged with nostalgia, the new organizations had practical, down-to-earth goals. The first president of the Baltic Cities union was Anders Engstrom, an energetic deputy mayor of Kalmar, on the east coast of Sweden two hundred miles south of Stockholm. The new group's secretariat was housed initially in Gdansk, and the first working committees were set up to study cooperation in telecommunications, environmental protection, transport, and maritime industry.

The North European Club was even more general in its geographical reference. Cofounded by the chairman of Volvo, Pehr Gyllenhammer, and the prime minister of Schleswig-Holstein, Germany's northernmost state, Bjorn Engholm, the club was a western initiative, but came in response to the growing integration of Europe and the opening to the east. The group pledged support for "Ars Baltica," a cultural exchange program in the region, and talked about other joint regional projects like a "Baltic Academy of Sciences" and a "Northern European Business School." But the main emphasis of the business-backed group was to promote transport infrastructure in the Baltic—a bridge to link Denmark with Sweden, a tunnel joining Denmark to Germany, improved road and rail links between Malmo in southwest Sweden and Stockholm on the east coast, and Turku in southwest Finland and Helsinki in southeast Finland—specifically to prepare the ground for high-speed train connections.

Many of these groups played on their geographic bond in the Baltic Sea rather than on the historic connection of the Hanseatic League. This betrayed a certain resistance along the northern rim of the Baltic to the term Hansa, which carries overtones of German dominance. More to the point, many of the most important Baltic cities—St. Petersburg, Helsinki, Stockholm—did not exist at the time of the Hanseatic League, or were not so prominent as they are now.

This did not stop a heated competition in marketing the region's history. When SAS, the joint Scandinavian airline, started calling Copenhagen its "Hansa Hub" and its flights to Russia and the Baltic republics "the Hansa Hopper," Luft*hansa,* the German airline, threatened court action to curtail such indiscriminate use of what it considered a trademark. SAS responded succinctly, "The history of the Baltic Sea region is not the property of Lufthansa."[3]

In Estonia, the nationalist historian Tunne Kelams called for the Baltic republics and Kaliningrad, the Russian exclave squeezed between Lithuania and Poland on the Baltic coast, to form a free trade zone affiliated to the EC and called "Hanseatic Region Baltikum." This appeal to a superregional history is the only way, he feels, that the republics can wrest true sovereignty away from Russia. To promote this, Kelams suggested a "Hanseatic Highway" from Hamburg to St. Petersburg.[4]

Booming Hamburg embarked on an ambitious office complex amid the historic red-brick warehouses of its harbor area, called the Hanseatic Trade Center. The management promised to set aside 10 percent of the office space to rent to East European companies at half price.

In much of the region, though, uneasiness about German domination tempers enthusiasm for labeling everything Hanseatic. A Swedish professor, Kristian Gerner, puts it this way: "A slightly somber perspective is that the Baltic states and Poland above all will become a kind of hinterland for the expansive German economy. . . . A modern Hanseatic League, dominated by the Germans and with its center in Schleswig-Holstein and Hamburg, will then shape the future."[5] As in the original Hanseatic League, Germans will control the region's economy while the local population will supply the proletariat, Gerner fears.

Those who share his fears prefer to concentrate on the geographic unity based on the Baltic itself. An early target of regional cooperation was the badly polluted environment. The Baltic Sea's narrow link to the ocean means that the water is exchanged on average only every forty years or so. The numerous rivers flowing into the Baltic bring fresh water, too, but also industrial waste, agricultural fertilizers, and sewage. In addition, air pollution from factory emissions in Poland and the Soviet Union for years contributed to the problem. The Baltic became too acidic and had too little oxygen, harming plants and fish and making many beaches unusable.

Already in 1974, the countries bordering the Baltic signed the Helsinki Convention to reduce risk of pollution from oil and other hazardous substances. The Helsinki Commission was set up in 1980 to monitor adherence, but progress under the communist regimes in the East Bloc was slow. Several specific protocols, for instance against sulphur dioxide emissions, were agreed to subsequently. A summit meeting in 1990 in Ronneby, on Sweden's southern coast, reaffirmed the goals of the Helsinki Convention and set a deadline of 1993 for coming up with a detailed plan to cut down pollution.

The change in regimes in the East has meant more open discussion of the problems, but concrete results are still slow in coming. The parlous economic state of Russia, the Baltic republics, and Poland makes it difficult for them to stop emissions from low-quality fuels or inefficient factories. Nor do they have the funds needed to invest in antipollution processes, sewage treatment, or extra safeguards like double-hulled oil tankers. The Nordic countries themselves, however, have been leaders in cleaning up the environment and developing antipollution technology. It is one type of aid they should be able to provide their neighbors across the Baltic relatively quickly, especially since it is in their own interest to do so.

Bjorn Engholm, prime minister of Schleswig-Holstein from 1988 to 1993 and for a time national chairman of the Social Democratic Party, was a strong proponent of regional cooperation in northern Europe. "The Europe of the future will no longer be determined by nations, but by large cooperating regions," he said in cosponsoring the North European Club with Volvo chairman Pehr Gyllenhammer.[6] In his first speech to the state parliament as prime minister, he described northern Europe as one of the continent's "regions of the future," and "the '*Mare Balticum*' as a region of thriving economic and cultural contact."[7]

In a 1990 seminar on "The New Hansa" in the Finnish island port of Kotka, on the border of the Soviet Union, Engholm was even more explicit. "We Europeans do not just focus on the nation-states, as we did at the turn of the century, or on ideological blocs that existed over the last forty years, but rather to a growing extent on the political, economic and cultural situations in our neighboring countries." He continues, "The new European supraregions [sic] will not be defined by national boundaries alone—and I might add, they shouldn't be."[8]

Politicians all over Europe were echoing these themes, but northern Europeans seemed particularly susceptible to the idea. One of the more successful organizations for regional cooperation during the Cold War was the Nordic Council, which linked Finland, Sweden, Norway, Denmark, and Iceland. The group realized many helpful projects—notably a passport union—in the narrow field left it by superpower politics. The Nordic Council feels that it can be a model as regional cooperation comes into its own. Anker Jorgensen, a former prime minister of Denmark, spoke as president of the Nordic Council to the Gdansk conference of the Baltic Cities union, telling them, "The future united Europe will consist of the regions of Europe. I believe that the regional aspects of the new European architecture will become increasingly politically important."[9]

Engholm himself sees many of the qualities normally considered to be Scandinavian as prevalent throughout northern Europe, and important for integrating the region. These include "a certain circumspection, a seeking after consensus, a less theoretical and rather pragmatic attitude towards life, a definite interest in equality and justice," he told one interviewer.[10] They are qualities the Germans like to attribute to "the cool North," and in the eyes of many southern Europeans contribute to making the northerners simply very dull. But they are useful for making international cooperation work.

Europe's Other Mediterranean

The Baltic Sea has been called Europe's second Mediterranean —*not* because of its climate, which is the antithesis of the dry, sunny weather in the south—but because it, too, lies "between the lands." Completely surrounded by Europe, the Baltic is the continent's one truly inland sea. In German and Swedish, it is called the "East Sea."

With a surface of about 160,000 square miles, the Baltic is one-sixth the size of the Mediterranean. It is a relatively shallow sea, opening to the North Sea and the Atlantic Ocean beyond through three narrow straits threading their ways through the islands between the Jutland peninsula and Sweden—the Great Belt, the Little Belt, and the Oresund. Because of this narrow connection to the ocean, the Baltic, like the Mediterranean, is hardly affected by tides.

The Baltic runs from the southwest to the northeast, splitting into three main branches in the north—the long Gulf of Bothnia, which separates the Scandinavian peninsula from Finland; the Gulf of Finland, separating Finland from Estonia and poking into Russia at St. Petersburg; and the much smaller Gulf of Riga, creating a sheltered harbor for the Latvian capital. Much of this northeastern area freezes over during the winter, closing ports on average anywhere from one month in Riga to five and a half months in Karlsborg, at the northern tip of the Gulf of Bothnia in Sweden.

The Baltic League superregion includes all the territory bordering on the sea. It begins at Oslo, where the Skagerrak and Kattegat waterways funnel traffic from the North Sea through the straits into the Baltic. It includes the southeastern corner of Norway, all of Sweden, and the Danish and German territory east of a line running through the center of Jutland to Hamburg. As with the Atlantic Coast border going west from Hamburg, the Baltic League border going east follows the coastline. The Baltic League, like the other coastal region, lies very much in the economic tidal pull of Mitteleuropa.

The border runs east through Germany, not too far from the coast, along what one authority has dubbed the Baltic Arc. Raoul Blanchard, a French geographer who taught at Harvard, describes it this way:

On the hills around the Baltic, where the end of the glaciers was stationary for a long time, a topography consisting of hills and depressions in great disorder was developed: we shall call this the Baltic Arc. . . . From Jutland to Lithuania, for a distance of 750 miles, a belt of hills which are connected to each other, and which parallel the coast line which they have determined, form a kind of arc made up of hills, sometimes of very low elevation, other times, especially in the east, a thousand or more feet high. The general form is that of crescents which parallel the coast. . . .[11]

The border of the Baltic League follows this arc, to the south of Hanseatic coastal cities like Lubeck, Wismar, Rostock, Stralsund, Szcecin, and Gdansk. The superregion border, now running along next to the Slavic Federation, turns north, following the eastern borders of the Baltic Republics—Lithuania, Latvia, and Estonia. These territories, though small in relation to the Soviet Union that ruled them for half a century, are every bit as big as many West European countries, although much more thinly populated. Lithuania, the biggest, is twice the size of Belgium, with two-fifths the population, about 3.7 million people. Estonia, the smallest, is significantly bigger than the Netherlands, but with 1.6 million people has only one-ninth the population.

The Baltic League also includes the unfortunate Russian exclave of Kaliningrad, now sandwiched between two independent countries, Poland and Lithuania. One of the glories of Prussia as Konigsberg, the city was the home in the eighteenth century of Immanuel Kant, a key figure in the history of philosophy—very much the home, for Kant, who lived to be eighty, never once traveled any distance from his beloved Konigsberg. But Kant's city was leveled in World War II and became part of the Soviet Union afterward. The Russians sealed it off for military use—its port usually does not freeze over—and only started rebuilding it in the 1960s, with the result that it is, as a *Financial Times* reporter notes, "arguably the ugliest city in the Baltic."[12]

The superregion border continues northeastward, paralleling the coast, through St. Petersburg, which straddles the border between Baltic League and Slavic Federation. The border continues northeast, taking in the important lakes Ladoga and Onega, up to the White Sea port of Archangel, and perhaps a bit beyond to the Kanin Peninsula, which juts out into the Barents Sea. Thus, the Baltic League includes all of Finland and Russia's Kola Peninsula, with its strategic port of Murmansk and extensive raw material resources. It was Russian czar Peter the Great's dissatisfaction with the limited sea access afforded by Archangel that prompted him to seize a stretch of Baltic coast from Sweden and build St. Petersburg there. This northern extremity of Europe will be directly affected by the developments in the Baltic Sea region.

Although Baltic League covers a large region, most of it is thinly settled. The territory's population is about 43 million, making it one of the smaller superregions.

The Western Baltic: The Oresund Region

The Nordic countries (including Iceland) conduct about one-fifth of their foreign trade with one another, another fifth with Germany, and a further two-fifths with the rest of Europe. Denmark and Sweden are particularly close trading partners—bilateral exchange accounts for 12 percent of Denmark's trade and 8 percent of Sweden's.

The locus of economic cooperation between the two countries is the Oresund region. The Oresund, sometimes called simply the Sound in English, is a narrow strait of water connecting the North Sea to the Baltic, separating Denmark from Sweden. Only three and a half miles wide at its narrowest point, at Helsingor, the putative site of Hamlet's castle, the Oresund measures about eleven miles between Copenhagen and Malmo, the Swedish city facing Denmark across the Sound. One of the three channels leading out of the Baltic, the Oresund, along with the Great Belt, is most used by shipping.

The Oresund region is one of the two cross-border territories targeted for special support by the Nordic Council (the other is the Nordkalott area where Norway, Sweden, and Finland are joined at the northern tip of the Scandinavian peninsula). The rich and populous Oresund region, embracing the provinces of Sjaelland in Denmark and Scania in Sweden, represents 4 percent of the surface of the two countries but nearly 25 percent of the combined population.

For several years, Denmark and Sweden have been lurching unsteadily toward approval of a multibillion-dollar project to connect Copenhagen to Malmo with a bridge and tunnel across the Oresund. Aside from the cost, in the neighborhood of $3 billion, potential environmental dangers have slowed down agreement. Opponents of the bridge fear that the structure, and the construction itself, would hamper the already feeble exchange of water between the Baltic and the North Sea, which makes the ecology of the Baltic very fragile. Also, another ambitious link, an eleven-mile bridge and tunnel across the Great Belt, has suffered numerous problems and delays. Originally targeted for completion in 1993, the Great Belt connection is not expected to be finished before 1997 because of these difficulties, which included faulty boring machines, near-disastrous flooding, and escalating costs. The Oresund project probably could not be finished before the turn of the century.

Not to be discouraged, business leaders on both sides of the Oresund promoted visions of a thriving North European commercial metropolis created by the new link. The bridge would cut the travel time between Copenhagen and Malmo, at least half an hour by hovercraft, to just minutes, while greatly expanding capacity. Copenhagen, with 1.7 million people, is already the biggest city in northwestern Europe; joining Malmo and its hinterland to the Danish capital via the new bridge would create a metropolitan area of 2.3 million people. It would also supply the missing link for a fixed connection between the Scandinavian peninsula and the European mainland, thanks to the Great Belt project to the west and the existing connection across the Little Belt. A third major project envisions a bridge or tunnel crossing the Fehmarn Belt, a strait to the south of Copenhagen separating Denmark from Germany. Now the main ferry route for highway and train traffic between the two countries, the Fehmarn Belt, about as wide as the Oresund between Copenhagen and Malmo, would be an even more direct route between Scandinavia and the continent.

Copenhagen lies on the eastern edge of Sjaelland, the largest of the Danish islands in the passage between the Baltic and the North Sea, spilling over onto Amager, a much smaller island separated from Sjaelland by the port. For six hundred years, up to the seventeenth century, the kingdom of Denmark included the fertile territory of southern Sweden across the Oresund. The Oresund bridge, according to its backers, will restore Copenhagen to the center of this economic unit. A paid advertising supplement in the *International Herald Tribune,* sponsored by local businesses and development agencies, explicitly sounds the superregion theme: "A new economic map of Europe is being drawn—not following national boundaries, but according to areas and peoples bound together by shared trading ties and common local interests. Oresund is a dynamic new center of growth in the Europe-of-regions that is taking shape."[13]

Besides the two industrial and commercial centers, Copenhagen and Malmo, the metropolitan area embraces the educational and research center of Lund, twelve miles northeast of Malmo along the express highway. A 1977 educational reform in Sweden, consolidating many independent schools with the University of Lund, transformed the seventeenth-century university into the biggest institution of higher learning in Scandinavia. In addition, the Ideon research park, founded in 1983, has become the biggest industrial research center in Scandinavia, with two campuses in Lund and a new facility in Malmo.

The third largest city in Sweden, Malmo has been pushing hard for the Oresund bridge, and has drawn up plans for a new city subway to use the bridge and transport passengers between the two city centers in half an hour. The city renovated its stock exchange building, poised picturesquely in the harbor area across the street from the central train station, into a stylish office and conference center. Southern Sweden, with its well-established research facilities and high quality of life, wants to attract high-technology industry and research from abroad, becoming a northern version of the French Riviera's Sophia Antipolis.

Support for the bridge also comes from as far away as Goteborg, Sweden's second largest city and home of Volvo, 150 miles north on the western coast. The ubiquitous Pehr Gyllenhammer, chairman of Volvo, has been dreaming of millions of car owners driving all the way to, or from, the continent. Oslo, another 150 miles distant along the coast, would also benefit from the improved accessibility.

Denmark, which staged a model economic turnaround in the decade to 1992, wants to extend its successful strategy throughout the region. Caught before in a downward spiral of weak currency, payments deficits, and mushrooming foreign debt, the country implemented strict controls on public spending, trimmed production costs to foster exports, and, by all accounts, simply became more aggressive in business. The result: Export sales boomed, yielding a string of payments surpluses that enabled the country to start paying off its foreign debt. A prominent success, for example, is Lego, whose plastic building bricks have captured toy markets throughout the world in an industry recently dominated by low-wage Asian producers.

In the 1990s, new export opportunities in the eastern Baltic— in Poland, the Baltic republics, and Russia—beckoned to Danish industry, appealing to management and labor alike. "Europe is moving in a northeasterly direction, and this will benefit Denmark," says Jorgen Eckeroth, an economist at the Danish trade union confederation, LO.[14] The Oresund bridge, the moves by Sweden and Finland to join the EC, the growing network of Baltic cooperation, all reinforced this trend.

The Eastern Baltic: St. Petersburg

The Oresund metropolitan region in the western Baltic, with its ties to Lubeck and Hamburg in the south, and Stockholm and Oslo in the north, promises to become a major pole of economic growth.

At the opposite end of the Baltic sea, St. Petersburg offers the potential to create a counterweight.

It was no accident that Peter the Great had to start from scratch when he wanted to build a new Russian capital at the eastern tip of the Gulf of Finland. The marshy land at the mouth of the Neva River hardly lent itself to habitation; the building of St. Petersburg cost many lives as well as an enormous amount of money. As the Russian poet Yevgeny Yevtushenko wrote in an essay about the city, "St. Petersburg is a marsh paved with human bones."[15] The completed city sprawls over forty-two islands, with more than a hundred bridges stitching it together.

Peter the Great's capital grew into a city of such grandeur and harmony, however, that it ranks today, even after seven decades of communism have left it shabby and dilapidated, as one of the truly beautiful cities of Europe. The glorious baroque and neoclassical facades of the Neva embankment, where the Winter Palace houses the fabulous Hermitage Museum, can still overwhelm even the most jaded tourist. The elegant canals and streets intersecting the Nevsky Prospect drew literary giants like Pushkin, Gogol, and Dostoyevsky, who, along with the thriving ballet, music, and drama of the capital made St. Petersburg one of Europe's cultural meccas in the nineteenth century.

The new capital took on the mantle of Novgorod, one of the most powerful cities in Russian history, now receded into obscurity in the shadow of St. Petersburg. In the thirteenth century, under its most famous prince, Alexander Nevsky, Novgorod became the preeminent Russian power. About a hundred miles south and east of the site of St. Petersburg, Novgorod was already important in the ninth century as a trading post for the Vikings. These hardy Norsemen sailed the short length of the Neva to Lake Ladoga, then south along the Volkhov River to Novgorod, just north of Lake Ilmen, across the lake and farther south up the Lovat River to the Valday Hills, where they carried their boats over to the headwaters of the Dnieper, which carried them south past Kiev to the Black Sea and Constantinople. Novgorod later became the easternmost trading post of the Hanseatic League and the main outlet for Russia's foreign trade.

Peter the Great wanted a new capital on the Baltic because he liked the sea, but also because he feared the intrigues of the claustrophobic Kremlin. It was in St. Petersburg, though, that revolution finally toppled the czars in 1917, enabling the Bolsheviks to seize power. The Soviets moved the capital back to Moscow, but honored Peter's city with the name of the man who brought communism to Russia. As Leningrad, the city earned a lasting place in history for its truly heroic resistance to the German army in a siege lasting nine hundred days during World War II. An estimated 1 million of the city's residents perished in the siege!

Leningrad, always an industrial center, became an important site for heavy industry, particularly military. As a result, the implosion of the Russian economy that followed the collapse of communism hit the city hard. However, given its industrial and cultural resources, as well as its geographic position, St. Petersburg, as it now calls itself again, is widely expected to be in the vanguard of economic recovery in Russia. By virtue of its very size, it seems destined to dominate the eastern Baltic, while remaining important for development in the rest of Russia as well. With 7 million people in the metropolitan region, St. Petersburg poses a challenge for Finland, with a total population of 5 million. But there are rewards as well; as one Helsinki wag notes, "The Finns no longer need to go to London for the opera. You can see *Boris Godunov* in St. Petersburg, too."

The Baltic Triangle

Toward the middle of the nineteenth century, the Finnish poet Elias Lonnrot tramped through the wooded hills between the lakes Saimaa and Ladoga, north of the Baltic Sea, recording the folk tales and legends of the local population, handed down through generations in an oral tradition. He fashioned these tales from the Karelian isthmus into a long poem, the *Kalevala*, that became the Finnish national epic. In the nationalist resurgence of the nineteenth century, many peoples who had lived without a state of their own through the centuries relied on such heroic epics to reform their language and make up for their lack of history.

Finland, which became an independent state only in 1917 in the wake of the Russian Revolution, was a prime example. Descended from Finno-Ugrian tribes, a different language family than most Europeans, the Finns lived for centuries under Swedish rule, and then from 1809 to 1917 under Russian domination. Even as an independent country, Finland was widely perceived as not enjoying full sovereignty in the shadow of the Soviet Union. During the Cold War, Finland's policy of accommodation toward its superpower neighbor resulted in the unsavory notion of "Finlandization." Following World War II, Stalin annexed a good portion of the beloved Karelia province, prompting more than 400,000 Finns—11 percent of country's total population—to uproot their homes and move westward to stay within the new Finnish borders.

Finlandization had its rewards. Through barter-like agreements with the Soviet Union, Finland obtained many raw materials, notably oil, in exchange for manufactured goods like clothes, shoes, furniture, and ships, particularly icebreakers. Finland found markets for up to one-fourth of its exports in this manner, and mounted large construction projects—hotels, hospitals, harbors, whole new subdivisions—in the Leningrad metropolitan area, in Estonia, and, yes, in Karelia.

The collapse of communism in the Soviet Union opened up new perspectives for Finland in the triangle at the eastern end of the Gulf of Finland, formed with the populous St. Petersburg and the culturally related Estonia. While there was some talk of trying to get the rest of Karelia back—there are 500 associations of Karelian refugees with 73,000 members who now openly lobby for the return of their homeland—the prospect of more open borders to the east was sufficient for most Finnish firms. Ironically, the economic collapse in the former Soviet republics at first threw the Finnish economy, too, into a tailspin.

Helsinki, which styles itself "Daughter of the Baltic," was a small fishing village until czar Alexander I designated it as capital of the autonomous Grand Duchy of Finland in 1812, three years after Russia won the territory from Sweden. The historic capital of Finland was Turku, called Abo by the Swedes, which was situated in the southwest corner of the country, facing Stockholm across the Gulf of Bothnia. The czar wanted a capital nearer to his own court, and Helsinki lies a hundred miles closer to St. Petersburg. Today Helsinki is poised to supply goods and services to the sprawling Russian metropolis, which presumably will be one of the first regions in Russia to regain economic equilibrium.

The Finnish feeling for Karelia is more than nostalgia. The Saimaa canal, first opened in 1856 and widened and refurbished in the 1960s, connects an important system of lakes in eastern Finland to the Gulf at the port of Vyborg, or Viipuri in Finnish, the capital of Karelia that is now in Russian territory. Vyborg, like many other eastern Baltic ports, has suffered the ravages of war and Sovietization, but Finnish writer Johannes Salminen recalls its history as the "Alexandria of the Baltic," a cosmopolitan city like the legendary Mediterranean port that was a crossroads of many cultures. In its heyday in the nineteenth century, Vyborg was a Babel of Finnish, Russian, Swedish, and German; residents who mastered all these tongues called it "learning to walk on all fours."[16] The Finns now look for vastly increased trade through the canal and a renewed Finnish presence in Vyborg.

Vyborg is one of several Baltic ports in the former East Bloc with ambitions to establish a "free trade zone" to promote economic development. Although the term changes from case to case, it generally includes the possibility of moving goods in and out of the zones without paying tariffs or other taxes. Thus encouraged, domestic and foreign firms provide jobs for the local population—who do pay taxes—and other economic benefits.

St. Petersburg itself bruited about the notion soon after it recovered its name that it would become a free trade zone, but did not specify what that meant. Kronstadt, a strategic naval base on a small island fifteen miles west of St. Petersburg in the Gulf of Finland, declared its goal of becoming a "Baltic Hong Kong," a free enterprise zone for foreign businesses. The town's mayor, Viktor Surikov, a naval retiree like one-fourth of Kronstadt's residents, says it was British prime minister Margaret Thatcher who first gave him the idea of a new role for the island. Kronstadt, which was closed to foreigners for two hundred years, quickly became a popular destination for Finnish tourists. Initial plans to turn nineteen old fortresses into hotels, yacht clubs, nightclubs, and casinos promised to make Kronstadt more like Macao, a smaller enclave in China devoted to leisure and entertainment, than industrious Hong Kong.

Kaliningrad authorities also expressed the wish to turn their region into a kind of Hong Kong. Despite the city's deplorable appearance, it does have an ice-free port, vestigial road and rail connections to Berlin, and military plants that could be converted to civilian industry if German or other foreign investors could be persuaded to provide the capital. Likewise, Szczecin, farther west along the coast at the mouth of the Oder River, the postwar border between Poland and Germany, would like to exploit its connections to Berlin with a free trade zone. Their model is the *maquiladora* type of zone on the U.S.-Mexican border, where U.S. investment has created half a million jobs for Mexican workers. The port, known as Stettin in German, is the heart of the old German region of Pomerania, which straddles the border. In November 1992, local authorities announced the creation of a Euroregion Pomerania in the border territory.

Just how many free trade zones would actually function or prosper was difficult to judge in the immediate aftermath of the collapse of the centrally planned economies in the east. The idea had obvious appeal because the zones by definition are carefully circumscribed and benefit from a clear set of rules supplied by a central authority—better than the messy birth of a market regime in the economy as a whole.

In March 1992, the Baltic republics—Lithuania, Latvia, and Estonia—signed several documents with a view to creating a customs union and "free trade zone" among the three countries. A top priority is to improve transportation and communications between the countries along a north-south axis paralleling the Baltic coast. The Soviets favored the east-west axis linking the republics individually to Moscow.

Now, the "Via Baltica" has been conceived, running from Tallinn four hundred miles south to the Polish-Lithuanian border, and eventually on to Warsaw to intersect with the planned Trans-European Highway connecting Gdansk to Istanbul. In the concept of its promoters, the Via Baltica would extend to Helsinki via ferry.

The project modestly envisions the use of existing roads, which in the first stage, through 1995, would be repaired and upgraded, and fitted out with a minimum of services for international use. A second stage, through 2000, would bring new intersections and bypasses and more services, and finally, in the third stage, through 2010, the route would be built up into a dual-lane express highway on the model of western Europe's network. The concept appealed immediately to many Finnish firms involved in road construction, from asphalters to manufacturers of sophisticated electronic equipment that monitors ice formation on highways. Finland's big oil refiner, Neste, has begun building shiny new service stations along the route.

Separate plans to construct highways linking Helsinki to St. Petersburg and St. Petersburg to Tallinn would create a land connection around the triangle. Farther west, the German federal government is drawing up plans for its own Baltic Highway to run between Lubeck and Szczecin along the former East German section of the Baltic coast. Like many highway projects in crowded and ecologically minded western Europe, however, this proposal faces considerable opposition. Nonetheless, there was consensus among western and eastern residents of the region that improved infrastructure was a precondition for economic growth. A background paper on transport for a parliamentary conference on Baltic Sea cooperation in April 1992 in Oslo noted, "The development in the field of transport and communication is a fundamental necessity for increased trade and cooperation."[17]

A "Baltic Boom"

Although it covers a vast terrain, the Baltic League is one of the most compact of the superregions because of its sharp geographical focus on the Baltic Sea. Partly for that reason, it already has one of the strongest identities. Its diffuse structure of overlapping networks makes it one of the most advanced superregions. Above all, there is a widespread awareness of the regional dimension, and an understanding of the role and functioning of a superregion.

Two political analysts articulate this consciousness well in another background paper prepared for the 1992 parliamentary conference on Baltic cooperation:

The region is the networks. The region is emerging as more and more groups in society make links and connections across borders and across the sea. The Baltic Sea region essentially consists of these networks and it has its power and potential in the strength of the networks. . . . A Baltic Sea region will be neither an alternative to, nor a local branch of the EC. Instead we will see an increasing—not yet settled—division of labor between the EC-level, state [national] level and the level of trans-regions (like the Baltic Sea). . . . Baltic Sea region institutions will not become an apparatus for big decisions. They first of all have the role of creating the conditions for the networks to unfold. Although complex and perplexing, the many different activities by business groups, environmental activists, town, harbor authorities, universities, and cultural institutions *are* what makes the Baltic Sea region dynamic and valuable in the positioning of Northern Europe on the new European map—not least the map of the new *economic* geography.[18]

In their quiet, unobtrusive way, the residents of this superregion are laying the groundwork for a "Baltic boom"[19] once the effects of the west European slowdown and the east European economic implosion have worn off. With their capacity for modest, pragmatic cooperation, the northern Europeans could lead the way in making this "neo-medieval"[20] structure of overlapping authorities work, just as it did in the time of the Hanseatic League.

CHAPTER SIX

ATLANTIC COAST: EUROPE'S EDGE

On December 1, 1990, Philippe Cozette, a Frenchman, and Graham Fagg, an Englishman, both dressed in hardhats and overalls, chipped through the thin layer of rock that separated them and shook hands. That hole marked the completion of the first of three tunnels under the English Channel, exactly three years after work had begun. In 1991, laser-guided tunnel-boring machines with monstrous disks twenty-eight feet wide finished the other two. Sometime in 1994, Eurotunnel plans to phase in transport of passengers and vehicles in specially built trains, traveling through the thirty-mile-long tunnel in half an hour. Interspersed among the shuttle trains carrying cars, trucks, buses, and their occupants, high-speed passenger trains are supposed to cover the distance between London and Paris in just three hours. In its first full year of operation, Eurotunnel hopes to carry nearly half of the 60 million people expected to cross the Channel each year.

The press hailed the tunnel breakthrough as an end to Britain's "isolation" as an island. Two earlier attempts to build a tunnel—in the 1880s and the 1970s—had failed; the completed tunnels mark the first fixed link between the continental mainland and Britain in

6,000 years, from the time seawater flooded into the channel scooped out by retreating glaciers.

Such acclaim reflects the view of Britain as an island fortress serenely indifferent to a "Europe" separated by twenty miles of water and radically different mentalities, of a "Britannia" ruling the waves, an imperial seapower with a global history far above the niggling territorial strifes of the continent. But this view hardly corresponds to the full reality of an island that was settled or conquered by continental peoples at least five times in its history—by the Celts, the Romans, the Anglo-Saxons, the Vikings, the Normans—and whose current monarch is descended from a German prince who preferred to rule England from his home in Hanover, Germany. If Britain was finally strong enough by the sixteenth century to repel the Spanish Armada, and discourage later invaders like Napoleon and Hitler, its participation in the battle of Waterloo and the landings in Normandy hardly qualify it as "isolated."

The Eurotunnel is simply the modern version of the galleys, ships, and ferries that have linked the British Isles to the rest of Europe since before recorded history. In an age when hovercraft and catamarans carry cars and passengers across the Channel in thirty-five minutes, and jet airliners cover the distance between London and Paris in forty minutes, the Eurotunnel offers a significant increase in capacity, but no real qualitative difference in the relationship of Britain to its neighbors. The fact that the project could be completed now, as a private commercial venture, points to an imperative need arising from the intensity of existing relations. Along with other major infrastructure projects, like the proposed Gotthard railway tunnel through the Alps or the bridge across the Oresund linking Copenhagen to Sweden, it is the physical expression of the political and economic integration of Europe.

The drama of a project on this scale does jolt our historic consciousness, however, and makes us more aware of how much Britain, and Ireland, are part of Europe. Like the rest of those regions on the western edge of the continent, the British Isles face the challenge of turning their position on the geographical margin into an asset. Throughout history, the Atlantic coast regions from Norway to Portugal have found wealth and power by sailing along that coast or venturing west, across the sea, to other continents. In the wake of fundamental changes in the world economy, the Atlantic

Coast superregion is slowly groping its way to redefine that role as a bridge between Europe and the rest of the world.

The Coastal Frontier

Columbus, so the story goes, found irrefutable evidence of an Atlantic route to the Indies when he visited western Ireland and saw a mummified corpse, perhaps that of an Eskimo, washed ashore there. No one knows for sure just when or where Columbus made his discovery, but in the port of Galway, a smallish city midway along the coast, a discreet stone and plaque recall its significance. Where mummies could go, reasoned the Genoese seafarer, so could well-equipped sailing ships.

Ireland's Atlantic coast does not offer too many harbors for oceangoing ships, and Columbus found the sponsors for his project on another Atlantic coast. He sailed under the Spanish flag across the Atlantic, so that Spain eventually colonized half of the New World he found. Other European powers facing the Atlantic—Portugal, England, and France—claimed their shares, too, of the largely unsettled territory. For all of them, the opening to the west brought increased prosperity and power, in varying rhythms, for centuries.

The peoples on Europe's western coast have throughout history found their fortunes and built their empires by sailing west across the oceans facing them. The Vikings from Norway and Denmark colonized Iceland, conquered Ireland, and occupied much of Britain and coastal France by traversing the North Sea in their longboats. Spain, Portugal, France, and England crossed the Atlantic to settle vast colonies in North and South America. Holland and England became commercial superpowers through their sea trade around the globe.

The Atlantic coast was the bridge between a European civilization at its peak and a world of primitive tribes or earlier civilizations in decline. The Europeanization of the world that marks our modern era was launched in the continent's Atlantic ports. In return, the wealth of the world—gold, cotton, tobacco, tea—poured into Europe through these ports, creating one golden age after another on this western edge of Europe.

Along the Seaboard

The Atlantic Coast superregion runs the length of the continent's western seaboard, and includes the islands in the Atlantic, notably Britain and Ireland. The coast faces variously the Atlantic Ocean, the North Sea, and the Norwegian Sea.

From the north, the border of the Atlantic Coast region follows the Norwegian-Swedish border through the mountain ranges that form the backbone of the Scandinavian peninsula, diverging from that border directly north of Oslo down to the Oslo fjord, so that the city lies on the frontier between Atlantic Coast and Baltic League. The fjord leads into the Skagerrak, an arm of the North Sea that turns south to divide the Scandinavian peninsula from Jutland as the Kattegat, the gateway into the Baltic Sea.

The superregion border runs south through the center of Jutland, the peninsula forming the bulk of Denmark, down to Hamburg, in Germany. This dynamic and prosperous port city, as we have seen, occupies a privileged position at the juncture of Atlantic Coast, Baltic League, and Mitteleuropa. The border follows the coastline west of Hamburg, past the cities Bremen, Groningen, Amsterdam, Rotterdam, Antwerp, and Calais to Le Havre, at the mouth of the Seine. Along here, the border is at its blurriest. The ports and the coast belong to the Atlantic Coast region, but how far inland the border should run is hard to say. Not very far, though, because Dutch cities like Nijmegen and Eindhoven, even Utrecht, are Mitteleuropa cities. Obviously, this border region, like the Atlantic Coast as a whole, is very much in the pull of powerful Mitteleuropa.

At Le Havre, the Atlantic Coast border turns due south, running through Tours, with Poitiers to the west and Limoges to the east, to a point south of Bordeaux, at about Agen on the Garonne River north of Toulouse, where it runs into the Latin Crescent border running east and west across its path. The Atlantic Coast follows this border west, along the curve of the Bay of Biscay, skirting the Pyrenees to the east and crossing southwest through Spain to Lisbon, which is on the border between Atlantic Coast and Latin Crescent.

The superregion thus includes all the western French territories united with England under the Plantaganets—Normandy, Brittany, Anjou, Poitou, and Aquitaine—as well as northwestern Spain and the northern half of Portugal. And, of course, the British Isles— Britain, with England, Scotland and Wales, and Ireland. The super- region embraces a population of approximately 110 million.

It is a long and diverse territory, which seems to have at least as many differences as things in common. But the commonalities are not negligible: from Norway to Portugal via England, France, and Spain, these great maritime powers all enjoyed a golden age of trade and adventure with overseas empires. Trade and an opening to the west are the key to the region's future, too. Other similarities, in mentalities and customs, conditioned by the shared experience of the sea, are more subtle.

Claude Lacour, an economist at the University of Bordeaux, de- scribes the Atlantic Coast region as a chain of interlinking common interests. While northern Norway and central Portugal may seem poles apart, there is a chain of interests—Norway and Scotland, Scotland and England, England and Normandy, Normandy and Brit- tany, Brittany and Poitou, Poitou and Aquitaine, Aquitaine and Basque Country, Basque Country and northern Spain, northern Spain and northern Portugal, northern Portugal and central Portugal. Such a view allows for subregions to emerge; Lacour himself is a proponent of more intense cooperation on a subregional level and actively supports a South European Atlantic Arc.[1]

Twentieth-century politics and economics reinforce the geo- graphical unity of the Atlantic Coast. What pulls the region together most is the common threat of being pushed to the periphery of Europe. Many of these places—Scotland, Ireland, Wales, Brittany, northwestern Spain, Portugal—are already among the poorest and most economically depressed in Europe, and risk falling further be- hind in an integrated Europe centered on Mitteleuropa.

The popular "Blue Banana" image of Europe's economy shows London and southeast and central England as part of the European Community's industrial powerhouse, which continues in a swath through the continent down to Milan. For that reason, the Atlantic Arc Commission, a regional grouping in the EC, bypasses southeast England, although it finds it necessary to include the area in some of its statistical presentations to avoid distorting the picture. I think that history and future potential both argue for putting the super- region border across the Channel to the east—that the fortunes of coastal Holland, southeastern England, and western France have been linked in the past to those of the rest of the Atlantic Coast, and will be in the future.

The one exception is the role of London as financial capital for Europe. This function, discussed in detail in Chapter Eight, "The Special Districts," extends beyond the narrow limits of the City of London itself, the Square Mile, because it embraces the entire culture of financial services nurtured by London's preeminence in finance, from banking to accounting to insurance. It is artificial, on the face of it, to try to separate out the economic strands of financial services from the rest of the British economy, in southeast England or throughout the country. And yet, in a very practical way, the global money markets have done just that—London's premiere role in foreign exchange and Euromarkets have no connection to the standing of the British stock or bond markets, or with the strength of the pound sterling as a currency.

Some partisans refer to the Atlantic Coast region as a Celtic Axis, evoking the region's long domination by Celts, or a Celtic Fringe, specifying those areas—in northern and western Scotland, central and northern Wales, western Ireland, Cornwall, Brittany—where a version of Gaelic, a Celtic language, is still spoken and Celtic names and traditions still survive. These pockets of Celtic heritage on the edge of Europe are the last outposts of a people who spread out from their home in central Europe across the continent, from the Balkans to the British Isles, pillaged Rome in the fourth century B.C., and dominated Europe for a millennium until the Romans and then the Germanic tribes drove them west, virtually into the sea.

Precisely because of this broad European history of the Celts, it would be misleading to designate the Atlantic Coast region as Celtic. Nor would it do justice to the subsequent settlers of the coastal region. Rather, the European west should be seen as similar to the rest of the continent—the result of many cultures overlaying one another in successive waves of migration.

However useful history may be in finding patterns and relationships, and however colorful the folk heritage, there has to be a limit to how meaningful historical claims are. Otherwise you have a case like Ian Adamson, the Ulster nationalist who argues that Northern Ireland should belong neither to the United Kingdom, as it does now, nor to the Republic of Ireland, which has claimed the six northern counties since it won independence in 1920, but should be a sovereign nation in its own right, because there is a historical justification for a British-dominated state in the region. According to Adamson, the original inhabitants of Northern Ireland were the "Cruthin," who were driven across the Irish Sea to Scotland by the

Celtic Gaels who took over the whole island. The Protestant settlement of the Ulster Plantation mandated by London in the seventeenth century enabled the descendants of the Cruthin to return, after thousands of years of absence, to their original territory, restoring their rightful heritage to them, which they should now be allowed to sovereignly govern, his argument goes. Colorful as it is, the claim, based on thin historical evidence, is hardly compelling as a solution to the vexed political situation in Northern Ireland today.

The North Sea Link

Through much of its history, Norway was politically united with Denmark, until in the nineteenth century it was affiliated with Sweden, for ninety years up to 1905, when Norway went its own way. In the twentieth century, Norway has usually been seen as a Siamese twin of the more populous and prosperous Sweden, but the mountains running the length of the Scandinavian peninsula historically have kept the two countries apart, with Norway seeking its fortunes far to the west across the North Sea and the Atlantic, and Sweden pursuing power in the Baltic. While Sweden remained neutral in World War II, Norway was occupied by the Germans, a status it fought and resisted throughout the war. Because of this, Norway has been a steadfast member of the North Atlantic Treaty Organization since the war.

The country has historic links to its neighbors across the North Sea. The most famous "link," of course, took the form of Viking raids that began with the descent of the Norsemen in 793 on the undefended monastery of Lindisfarne, at the northern tip of Northumbria near the Scottish border. Norwegian Vikings occupied the Shetland and Orkney islands—which they kept until the fifteenth century!—and used northern Scotland as a staging post for their settlement of Ireland.

While the Norwegian Vikings were busy with the northern and western regions of the British Isles, their comrades from Denmark drove deep into England, and established the "Danelaw" throughout northern and central England, levying a heavy tax—the "Danegeld"—on the Anglo-Saxon inhabitants. The Anglo-Saxons themselves were distant cousins of the Danish Vikings, since they

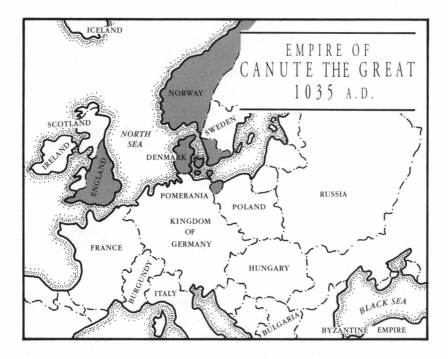

EMPIRE OF
CANUTE THE GREAT
1035 A.D.

had followed much the same route across the North Sea in the fifth century, when Angles, Saxons, and Jutes left territory in present-day Denmark, Germany, and Netherlands to settle in the land the Angles gave their name to. At one point in the eleventh century, King Canute the Great of Denmark briefly united southern Sweden, Denmark, Norway, and England in a single empire.

Later that century, the histories were to grow more intertwined when the Normans, themselves descended from Danish Vikings who had settled in northern France, crossed the narrow straits of Dover to defeat the Anglo-Saxons at the battle of Hastings. The event changed history. "On the eve of the Norman Conquest of 1066 the future of the British Isles seemed to be largely linked to Scandinavia," muses U.S. historian Hugh Kearney. "Had the battle of Hastings turned out differently the future of the British Isles for many centuries might have lain with Scandinavia, an alternative course of events which the historian cannot dismiss as an impossibility."[2]

The stretch of the North Sea between Scotland and Norway continues to link the two territories together. When *The New Yorker* writer A. Alvarez went from Aberdeen on the Scottish east coast to spend some time on an offshore oil platform in the North Sea, he noted with surprise that the nearest railhead was in Bergen, Norway.[3] Since the oil and gas fields were discovered in the 1960s, Britain, Norway, and the Netherlands have carefully circumscribed their respective fields and cooperated in exploiting the energy resource.

Aberdeen, on the east coast of Scotland, has become the center for the North Sea oil industry. It numbers a thousand companies in the oil and gas business, many of them foreign, so that you can hear, as a Scottish Development Agency publication put it, "the accents of Norway, the Netherlands and the USA mingling with the local dialect."[4]

The North Sea continues today to be more of a bond than a barrier. Passenger ferries ply between Bergen and Newcastle-upon-Tyne—Norwegians will come to Newcastle for a weekend of shopping and a night on the town. Harwich, on the east coast of England, has regular ferry service to Hamburg and to Holland. When they want to visit companies or customers on the continent, investment managers in Edinburgh find it more convenient to fly to Schiphol airport in Amsterdam than to London for connections. Port authorities in Rotterdam and Humberside, in northeastern England, pooled their marketing resources in early 1993 to promote the Humber-Rotterdam connection as the preferable alternative to the Channel Tunnel for freight traffic between the continent and northern England, the Midlands, Scotland, and Ireland.

The politics of our generation shape our perceptions of geographical space, making us "forget" other relationships that have been important in the past. This is particularly true of the Atlantic Coast region. Gordon Donaldson, a former history professor who is now Her Majesty's Historiographer in Scotland, points out that Scotland's nearest continental neighbor is Norway, three hundred miles away, a good hundred miles closer than the Netherlands, the next closest point. "These simple geographical facts, which did much to shape events for centuries, are often ignored, for no better reason than that Scotland is part of an island which extends southwards until it is separated from the European continent by only twenty miles of sea at the Straits of Dover."[5]

Perhaps nothing illustrates the ambivalence of the coastal location better than the divergent fates of the territories surrounding the North Sea. North Sea oil and gas have buoyed the standard of living in Norway, but employment in traditional activities like smelting and whaling has declined. Norway's insistence on resuming whaling activities in defiance of international agreements is a sign of its desperation on this score.

At the same time, two of the wealthiest and most populous conurbations in Europe face each other across the North Sea—Greater London, with 12 million people, and the Randstad, Holland's metropolitan sprawl along the coast from Amsterdam to Rotterdam, with 5 million. Two of the biggest European multinationals, Shell and Unilever, straddle the North Sea as Anglo-Dutch joint ventures. Shareholders, management, and headquarters for both firms are divided between the two countries. Rotterdam, adjacent to the busiest waterway in the world, the English Channel, is the preeminent port in the world. Its astonishing growth in the postwar period, fueled largely by Europe's rapidly increasing need for imported oil, affirms once again the importance of the Atlantic Coast region as the gateway between Europe and the rest of the world.

Manchester: An Enterprising City

One of the historic gateways lies in the west of England. When Manchester built its Ship Canal a century ago so that oceangoing vessels could bypass the Liverpool port thirty-five miles away and dock in Manchester itself, the city was fighting for its economic life. Unless it could cut the cost of transferring goods to Liverpool and loading them there, many of its industries faced bankruptcy. Against bitter opposition from the Liverpudlians, the canal was completed in 1894 and Manchester quickly became the third largest port in England.

In the late twentieth century, Manchester once again is fighting back from traumatic decline after its thriving textile, coal, and steel industries died out. The Ship Canal, largely derelict and infested with rats in recent decades, is being redeveloped as an office and residential complex, complete with a World Trade Center and an opera house designed by Britain's renowned architect, the late Sir James Stirling. A century after it built the canal to attract ocean traffic, Manchester is investing heavily in more modern means of transportation. It has expanded its airport in the past decade to enable passenger traffic to triple, from 4 million to 12 million, mak-

ing the facility, according to the city's promoters, the fastest growing airport in Europe. A massive new international terminal, costing
a cool half billion dollars, went into service in 1993. Together with
another terminal and a new runway slated for later in the decade,
the investment will permit traffic to double again, to 24 million
passengers a year.

The enterprise that built the original Ship Canal—which Michael
Middleton, former director of Britain's Civic Trust, called "the last
epic achievement of Victorian engineering"[6]—and made Manchester one of England's most prosperous cities, is enjoying a renaissance. The redevelopment of central Manchester shows an
undeniable flair: converting the Victorian railroad station into a
sports and exhibition center, turning harbor warehouses into hotels, and creating the world's first "Urban Heritage Park" on the
site of the ancient Roman fort, where a sprawling Museum of Science and Industry and Granada TV's studio tour round out the Roman ruins to attract tourists.

In one of his historical thrillers set in 1939, Ken Follett refers to
Manchester as a "grimy industrial city"—certainly the picture any
of us might have had, if we had a picture at all of Manchester. But
Follett would probably be kinder in describing the city today, or
the one that should be there in the year 2000, if the visionary plans
of the city council and three development corporations take form.
Many of the grand Victorian buildings have been sandblasted clean,
recovering much of their original splendor. A sleek new tram glides
quietly through the center of the city. The Metrolink, which began
service in 1992, is the first new tramline in Britain since the old
generation died out in 1962, and shows again Manchester's knack
of keeping a step ahead of other British cities. The "supertram,"
which runs on suburban railroad tracks as well as the new track
laid for it in the city's streets, will eventually link the center to the
redeveloped dock area and the suburbs. Greater Manchester has a
population of 2.5 million; the North West region of England is the
country's most densely populated, so that 6 million people live
within a thirty-mile radius of the city center, and 11 million within
a fifty-mile radius.

In the early 1990s, many parts of Manchester were still run
down, others were building sites, but enough of the new construction was up to make the ambitious projects credible. At the docks,
in Salford, the gleaming office towers of Exchange Quay look sus-

piciously like London's ill-fated Docklands on a smaller scale (the developer in fact built the Harbour Exchange in Canary Wharf). Like Canary Wharf, Exchange Quay has had trouble lining up tenants as a result of Britain's sluggish economy—only 15 percent of the space was rented by the end of 1992 and managers expect it to take four or five years to achieve full occupancy. In neighboring Trafford, next to the oldest and biggest industrial park in Europe, bulldozers had cleared the way for more offices and apartments and a large new freight terminal for shipments via the Channel Tunnel.

Manchester is positioning itself to benefit from the same decentralizing trends seen elsewhere in Europe. Just as many French firms and families are leaving Paris for southern France, so British companies are fleeing the congestion and pollution and expense of London. ICI, one of the country's biggest companies, located the new headquarters for its specialty chemicals division in Manchester; the BBC transferred its Youth Programmes Unit from London; the British Council, the government-sponsored organization that promotes British culture throughout the world, moved its head offices there.

The focus of Manchester's hopes during this period was its bid for the summer Olympic Games in the year 2000. The city had already made a run for the 1996 games, losing out to Atlanta. But the well-oiled bid team mounted a new effort for the millennium games. Feeling that Margaret Thatcher's laissez-faire philosophy—no public money for Olympic structures—had hurt their earlier effort, Manchester officials enlisted the support of her successor as prime minister, John Major, who had a more flexible policy on public spending and, besides, was a big sports fan. Clever as they are, the Mancunians (the designation for residents of Manchester comes from the medieval Latin name for Manchester, *Mancumium*) cadged a $100 million pledge from the central government, most of it to be spent *before* the International Olympic Committee handed down its decision in September 1993. So even if they lost out, Manchester would still get a new velodrome, a sports arena, and a cleared site in the eastern part of the city suitable for an Olympic stadium.

The Olympic bid itself was another manifestation of the city's ambition to be, as its promotional literature puts it, "a European Supercity of the 21st century." With the Olympics, they wanted to put Manchester on the new map of Europe, the way the games did for Barcelona in 1992. As Bob Scott, head of the Manchester campaign, told the press during the Barcelona Olympics, "The biggest thing I see is that having the games in Barcelona has shifted the geographic and economic axis of this country. Madrid isn't the beginning and end of every story—and never will be again."[7] Substitute Manchester for Barcelona and London for Madrid, and you have Manchester's dream scenario for 2000.

The Atlantic Connection

Even though it failed to land the Games, Manchester has made its point. Like Barcelona, the city stands to benefit from shifting perceptions of economic strength. The property crisis in London and the severe effects of the recession in the South East disillusioned many who believed that the corner of England nearest the continent would prosper first and foremost from European integration. The cosmopolitan capital, London, for a long time attracted investment from the rest of the United Kingdom and from abroad. In the 1970s, American and then Japanese high-technology firms began planting subsidiaries along the M4 express highway running from London to Bristol on the west coast. What counted for them was the proximity to London and to Heathrow airport. The "M4 Corridor" came to have a glamorous reputation around the globe. "Thus," comments French geographer Georges Benko, "this region has become a gateway for economic exchange between the EEC and other continents."[8]

In the meantime, though, the gateway has widened. American high-tech firms have invested in Silicon Glen in Scotland, the valley between Edinburgh and Glasgow, and Japanese investors have flocked to Newcastle-upon-Tyne in the northeast of England, and to southern Wales, while western Ireland has made terrific tax concessions to successfully attract foreign investment. The congestion and high costs driving British firms out of the South East are prompting foreign companies to seek alternatives, too—but still in the superregion of the Atlantic Coast.

Why this preference for the British Isles? Many reasons are advanced: skilled industrial work force (and docile after Thatcher tamed the trade unions), relatively low wage costs, English language and Anglo-Saxon legal system (comfortable for Americans and more familiar to the Japanese than others). Added to that are the incentives from active and well-funded development agencies in Scotland, Wales, and Ireland, and urban development corporations in England. But the most obvious reason should not be overlooked: The Atlantic Coast superregion is *closer*. Landing at Shannon or Heathrow, or Manchester or Glasgow, may save only a couple of hours over a continental destination, but jet travel is a matter of hours. In its presentations to American manufacturers, Liverpool argues that unloading goods in western England will get them to central Europe more quickly—once the Channel Tunnel is fully operational—than docking at Rotterdam or Hamburg.

Whatever the reasons, Britain has continued to attract new investment. The *Financial Times* reported that in the twelve months to March 1992, overseas companies approved 332 projects in the United Kingdom, providing 50,000 jobs. These included a $300 million investment in Wales by the Japanese electronics firm Sony and a $200 million installation in Humberside, in northeast England, by the American consumer products company Kimberly Clark. Nearly two-fifths of all U.S. and Japanese investment was targeted on Britain, the newspaper said.[9]

Success does not come automatically in a case like Manchester's. The Ship Canal redevelopment resulted from the collaboration of an imaginative city councilor in Salford, the city authority on the west side of the canal, an architect from London, and a Manchester entrepreneur who mortgaged his own house to get the project started. Liverpool, a half-hour drive away, provides the contrast. The city of the Beatles managed to transform the derelict central dock area, built a century and half ago, into a congenial ensemble of shopping center, business park, luxury apartments, and a Maritime Museum that draws 3.5 million visitors a year. But the Albert Dock, the success story of the Merseyside Development Corporation, is set in a depressing industrial city in visible decline. A city council deeply divided by ideology blocked development in the 1980s, so that Liverpool badly trails more progressive authorities like Manchester and Birmingham.

A shopping center alone cannot spur an economic renewal, even though a number of regional development officials seem to think so. The shopping malls of the late twentieth century—with their dreary round of franchised clothing chain stores, soap and candle shops, fancy stationery and imported wicker furniture stores—stand as monuments of futility if no industrial investment accompanies them to strengthen the basis of the local economy.

In Newcastle-upon-Tyne, in the northeast of England, new shopping centers draw crowds, while downtown merchants have kept a robust share of the retail business. The region struggled hard to recover from the decline of its heavy industry. "Like bringing coal to Newcastle"—coal mining was a byword for the city after generations of shipping coal down the coast to stoke the furnaces in London. By the 1990s, all of Newcastle's traditional industries— coal, steel, and shipbuilding—have virtually disappeared, employment in these sectors dropping from 30 percent of the local work force during the postwar period to 3 percent now.

Energetic efforts to attract new investment, particularly from abroad, have brought 360 foreign companies to the region in the past few years. The Japanese have led the push, with Nissan employing 5,000 at Washington (the supposed home of George Washington's ancestors), and Fujitsu operating a semiconductor plant at nearby Durham. The region has moved aggressively to take part of the North Sea oil and gas bonanza from Aberdeen, north along the coast in Scotland, so that two hundred local firms, employing 20,000 people, profit from the offshore energy industry.

One seasoned analyst of the North East worries that the job-creating investment in the region is foreign rather than native. He misses the driving energy of local entrepreneurs with a personal stake in the region. It is a concern shared in other areas where jobs depend on decisions made far away in foreign countries. Investment is a two-way street, as Unisys, an American computer company, reminded everyone when it shut down its plant outside Edinburgh in 1991, with a loss of 700 jobs.

A little reflection can temper this worry. The underlying fear is that in a crunch, foreign investors with different priorities will favor operations closer to home, and will close down their factories abroad first. In its more irrational form, this fear becomes a nightmare of domination, with arbitrary layoffs and closings visited upon this far colony simply to cause suffering for its inhabitants.

But markets rather than arbitrary decisions are what open and close factories. A location that is close to consumers or a transportation network, a work force that is skilled, productive, and competitively priced, an environment that is attractive—these are the fundamental criteria that lure and keep investment, from whatever source. More ephemeral incentives—tax breaks, infrastructure investments—may tip the balance in the initial choice of location, but will not determine the long-term future. When General Motors experienced a severe crisis in 1992, it did not close down its plants in faraway Europe—its main source of profit!—but made deep cuts in Detroit and other U.S. facilities.

Big changes in the structure of an economy can lower the value of this factor mix, resulting in factory closings. But that is true whether the owner is a local entrepreneur or a foreign multinational. Local ownership did not save the shipbuilding industry in Newcastle or Glasgow—global trends in demand and production costs condemned these operations. A local subsidiary is vulnerable to bad decision-making in a foreign headquarters, but if the market fundamentals remain constant, the operation will have little trouble finding a smarter owner.

Similar fears rose in another Atlantic Coast territory, when Japanese investors began buying into prestigious Bordeaux vineyards in the 1980s. There were of course many Frenchmen who protested the "loss" of a national heritage into foreign hands. But, as one editorialist noted trenchantly, the vineyards were not going anywhere—they would always remain where they were, in France. It is relatively unimportant for the local job situation who collects the profit on the production and marketing of the wine. It is more important of course, and the legitimate worry of the Newcastle analyst, that these profits do not accumulate locally, a source of further investment in the region. Even so, if genuine investment opportunities are there, capital from somewhere should find them.

Decentralization in England

England abounds with other examples of economic vigor. East Anglia, the bulge of the island northeast of London, registered an 8.7 percent increase in population in the decade to 1991. Cambridge, the famous university town in the west of this region, has built up one of Europe's most prestigious science parks, with more than 500 high-tech firms, while the "Peterborough Effect," referring to the city thirty miles northwest of Cambridge, has become a byword for investment synergy.

The swath of territory through Birmingham, sandwiched between Manchester and the M4 Corridor, has earned the sobriquet "Northern Playground" for its ability to attract industry fleeing the crowded South East. The Bournemouth-Southampton area on the southern coast and the South West have seen stirrings of investment interest, making real estate in historic Winchester, conveniently halfway between London and the South West along the M3 express highway, some of the most expensive property in the country.

Beneath the gloom of recession that gripped Britain in the early 1990s, there were undeniable signs of vitality. Because the South East, and London in particular, was the hardest hit by the long slump, the gloom bulked disproportionately large in the national media, all headquartered in the capital. Britain's traditional political centralization, ruthlessly fortified in the Thatcher years, masked the country's economic regionalization.

As in so many other cases, Thatcher's Britain bucked the prevailing European trend toward devolution. While France and Spain were creating directly elected regional governments and giving them new responsibilities, Britain in 1986 abolished the one regional authority it had, the Metropolitan County Council. These councils were too messily democratic for Thatcher's taste, controlled by Labour leftwingers or Tory "wets," both advocates of the government intervention that was anathema to the longtime prime minister.

The lack of regional authorities makes the economic development in Britain so haphazard and sporadic. The splintering of political authority hampers effective cooperation even in those areas that successfully restructure. The city information office in Manchester, for instance, refuses to tell a visitor anything about the Salford Quay development two miles away across a narrow strip of water, because *that* is the responsibility of Salford city authorities. Elsewhere in Europe, cities are flexing a new-found autonomy and surmounting historic rivalries to cooperate in regional development, while English cities succumb to a political diviseness fostered by a central government bent on preserving and expanding its power.

Yet, as John Osmond argues persuasively in his book *The Divided Kingdom*, the United Kingdom is experiencing the same centrifugal pressures for decentralization as other European nation-states. More critical than the perennial debate on devolution for Scotland and Wales, with their vestigial claims to nationhood, are the divisions within England itself. It is the English, who for so long have subsumed their identities in the Greater England of the U.K., who are most in need of new solutions. "There has been no English Parliament since 1536 and today there is no English Office or Secretary of State for English Affairs,'' Osmond notes, whereas the Welsh Office and Scottish Office are supervised by Cabinet ministers.[10]

As a result, English identity by default has focused on the institutions of state—parliament and monarchy—housed in the capital, and nourished in the "Home Counties" surrounding London, the prosperous South East, which has perpetuated its domination of the U.K. for centuries. Michael Steed, a political scientist, identifies the core of English identity as the territory within a 120-mile radius of London, south of the line Liverpool-Hull, and east of the Welsh border. Nor is it a coincidence, Steed and Osmond contend, that this is the area directly colonized by the Romans for four centuries. Outside this core region, the Romans extended a military rule over the Celtic tribes, but did not settle or assimilate the local population in the same manner. It was precisely this core area, four centuries after the Romans left, that was able to resist the incursions of the Danish Vikings, keeping the Kingdom of Wessex independent.[11]

What it means in latter-day Britain, these analysts conclude, is that the areas outside this core—the South West, the North West, the North East—need to free themselves from the domination of the South East and follow their own paths to prosperity. Consciously or not, this is what these regions are in the process of doing. Nor can it be long before the demands for political autonomy to match the economic independence will catch up even with London.

Scotland's Hard Fate

Two centuries after James Watt, who built a better steam engine and ushered in the Industrial Revolution, left his hometown of Greenock, twenty-five miles west of Glasgow on the Firth of Clyde, IBM established one of its first European factories there, in the 1950s. Today, the Greenock plant supplies IBM's personal and laptop computers to European, Middle East, and African markets. The U.S. computer maker calls Greenock its "most productive plant in Europe."[12] Perhaps that is the reason 140 electronics manufacturers have invested in Scotland in the past decade, bringing the total to 300 firms, employing 50,000 people, with an additional 4,000 working for 250 software firms. Scotland claims to produce 35 percent of the personal computers sold in Europe, and 10 percent worldwide.

Scotland's efforts to attract the electronics industry, many of whom come to the "Silicon Glen" between Glasgow, the country's biggest city, and Edinburgh, the capital, forty-five miles to the east on the Firth of Forth, are part of an attempt to counter the decline in those traditional industries—steel, textiles, machinery, ship-building—that made Glasgow "the Second City of the Empire" during Britain's heyday at the turn of the century. Economic planners are trying to tap the tradition of Scottish inventiveness, distinguished by its emphasis on practical application. For instance, the Scot John McAdam invented the modern road asphalting process (giving us terms like tar*mac* and macadamize), and another, James Chalmers, produced the first adhesive postage stamp.

Scotland has had a hard fate since its king, James VI, ascended to the English throne as James I in 1603, moving the Scottish court to London, where political control remains to this day. Since then, Scotland has been an integral part of Britain, with the loss of identity that entails. Whatever is normal or modern in Scotland is lost in the greatness of Britain, leaving only a few familiar caricatures to define what is "Scottish"—kilts and cabbage patch, Brigadoon and bagpipes.

So completely has Scotland been coopted into the British system—the Queen holds court every spring in Edinburgh's Holy-rood Castle and takes her summer holiday at Balmoral in the Highlands—that in a 1979 referendum the Scots could not muster enough votes for a separate Scottish parliament and are skimping in their support for the Scottish National Party, which is calling for independence, or at least autonomy. But Britain's gain has been Scotland's loss. Gross domestic product, according to the government index where 100 represents the U.K. average, was 92.7 in Scotland at the beginning of the 1990s, compared to 102.4 in England. The difference is more egregious between Greater London at 148.0 and Strathclyde, the region including Glasgow, at 88.8.

Glasgow is a graphic example. The "second city" saw its population decline from a peak 1.1 million in 1939 to an expected 650,000 by 1996. The city has worked hard to clear away slums, redevelop run-down sectors, clean up its sandstone buildings, and give itself a new image, with the result that it was named European City of Culture in 1990, putting it in the company of laureates like

Paris, Berlin, Athens, Florence, and other more prominent tourist destinations. While Edinburgh, with its castles and Georgian facades and summer arts festival, remains the main tourist draw, Glasgow is at least on the map now. Most important, though, the city has developed a far more diversified economic base—activities include food and drink, engineering, construction, printing and publishing, clothing and textiles, financial services, crafts—built a conference center on the banks of the Clyde, expanded the airport, and done whatever else it could to live up to the famous slogan launched in 1983, "Glasgow's Miles Better" (than before? than Edinburgh? London?).

Atlantic Spirits

The Normans eventually extended their rule throughout the British Isles, driving out the Vikings. The Plantaganet dynasty which came to the English throne in 1154 retained vast holdings in France, extending at one time or another virtually along the entire western coast—Normandy, Brittany, Anjou, Poitou, Guyenne (Aquitaine), Gascony. Two English kings prominent in history, Henry II and his son, Richard the Lion-Hearted, spent far more time in France, where they were nominally vassals of the French king, than in England, where they were sovereigns. Richard, whose triumphal return to England after the Crusades has been celebrated in countless Robin Hood films, may not even have spoken English!

When Eleanor of Aquitaine married Henry Plantagenet, the future Henry II of England, in 1152, she ushered in three centuries of prosperity for the region around Bordeaux. The earliest surviving document granting municipal privileges to the port city in southwest France dates from 1199 and is signed by King John of England, Eleanor's son. It was that same King John, the infamous brother of Richard the Lion-Hearted forced to sign the Magna Carta in 1215, who promoted consumption of the dry red wine from Bordeaux's vineyards, fostering what is to this day the region's most important industry. The French victory in 1453 at Castillon, a village just outside Bordeaux, ended the Hundred Years' War and English control of Aquitaine. It also put an end temporarily to Bordeaux's prosperity, because its wine, previously traded by sea routes with merchants from England, Flanders, and the Hanseatic League, now had to trundle over the bad roads to Paris.

Throughout its history, Bordeaux resisted control from the French capital, earning for itself long periods of repression. The city, whose Latin name Burdigala may be derived from the Celtic for "port city," enjoyed its best times when it was free to pursue its fortunes at sea. Bordeaux actually is set forty-five miles inland, at the tip of the Gironde estuary, so called (the name means "swallow" in French) because the two rivers flowing into the estuary, the Garonne and the Dordogne, look on a map like a swallow's tail. Bordeaux reached its zenith in the eighteenth century, when trade with England flourished again and the United States opened up a big new market for its wine. The magnificent facades of the Place de la Bourse and Old Bordeaux date from this time. The grace and harmony of these edifices prompted the nineteenth-century French novelist Stendhal to acclaim that "Bordeaux is, without any argument, the most beautiful city in France."[13]

The city bears other traces of its history in commerce. Robert Mitchell, an Irish immigrant who designed the bottle that distinguishes Bordeaux wine, has two streets named after him. Numerous Irish-English names—Barton, Lawton, Johnston, Cruze—are common in Bordeaux. The wine usually travels now by road to Marseilles, Le Havre, or Rotterdam for shipment, but Bordeaux, which produces 10 percent of French wine, worth $2.4 billion, still accounts for half of France's wine exports.

With great fanfare, the city in early 1992 opened the elegant Wine and Spirits International Business Center, the heart of a redevelopment of the Chartrons quay area, the historic site of the wine trade. The new center is part of a belated effort by the city to keep pace with some of its more dynamic neighbors, like Toulouse and Montpellier, in attracting new investment. The Bordeaux area relies heavily on aerospace production, particularly for the French military—a sector that faces a period of retrenchment. Like other Atlantic Coast cities, Bordeaux is worried that the opening of eastern Europe will push it to the periphery. The city was proud of landing an investment in 1990 from the Norwegian energy concern, Norsk Hydro, against competition from Nantes and Hamburg, two other Atlantic Coast cities.

As with Bordeaux, Atlantic connections have played an important role in the economic development of the Charentes region north of the Gironde, and in northern Portugal. In the Middle Ages, North Sea merchants coming to La Rochelle, the west coast port, to buy salt were reluctant to take the sour Charentes wine. So the vintners boiled it down, distilled it, to make it easier to transport. The idea was to mix it later with water again and reconstitute the wine. To their surprise, and that of their clients, the vintners discovered that the distilled alcohol actually tasted much better in its own right, and the region's brandy began to get a reputation. It was when the distillers started to store the brandy in oak casks from neighboring Limousin, however, that it attained a unique flavor which made it a global hit as Cognac. The region nowadays exports 95 percent of its Cognac production, valued at about $2 billion, earning more foreign exchange for France than Airbus.

Atlantic immigrants played a major role in developing the markets for Cognac, as they had for Bordeaux wines. Two of the leading Cognac brands today, Hennessy and Remy-*Martin,* betray the Irish origins of their founders. It was English traders, in the main, who developed a fortified dessert wine in northern Portugal. Named port wine, after the harbor town of Oporto (or because it was set aside for export at the port—both stories are told), the distinctive taste came when vintners began doctoring the coarse Douro wines with grape brandy. The brandy not only strengthened the wine, but arrested fermentation, leaving a sweetness that made the wine more palatable. Port became a big tradition in England, and, as wine expert Alexis Lichine comments, "it is still easier to get vintage Port in England than in a good restaurant in Lisbon."[14]

The Atlantic Arc

At the tip of an island in the Loire river, not far from where it flows into the Bay of Biscay on France's west coast, stands a new structure outlined in pillars of cement tinted pink to resemble granite, walled by gleaming windowpanes and crowned by a cupola of darkened glass. The building, completed in 1987 as part of the development of the Ile Beaulieu in Nantes, is the administrative headquarters for the Pays de la Loire, one of the twenty-two regions in France.

Across the branch of the river toward the center of town is a much older palace, started in the fifteenth century by the powerful dukes of Brittany to establish their capital in Nantes. It was Duchess Anne of Brittany who, by marrying the king of France (actually, two kings of France, after the first one left her a widow) at the end of the century, brought Brittany under the control of the French crown after centuries of independence.

The ministries in Paris, when they carved France into regions in the mid-1950s to promote postwar recovery of the economy, somehow neglected to put Nantes, the capital of historic Brittany, in the new region of Brittany, including it instead in another region pieced together from surrounding territories. When the regions became political units through the decentralization measures of 1972 and 1982, though, Nantes became the capital of the new creation, Pays de la Loire. After the first direct elections for a regional council in 1986, Olivier Guichard, a longtime Gaullist and a pioneer in regional economic development in France, became the first president of the region, and started building his gleaming *Hotel de la Region* (as in *"Hotel de Ville"*—city hall) on the Ile Beaulieu.

In 1989, Guichard, a large, imposing man people have trouble saying no to, proposed the creation of an Atlantic Arc Commission to counter the shift of Europe's center of gravity toward the east after communism began to collapse there. The proposal was accepted by the Conference of Peripheral Maritime Regions, a body set up in 1973 to promote development along the entire seaboard of the EC. Guichard became the first president of the new commission and housed the Atlantic Arc's secretariat in Nantes' *Hotel de la Region*.

The Atlantic Arc groups twenty-three EC regions in Scotland, Ireland, Wales, southwest England, western France, northern Spain, Portugal, and southwestern Spain. The territory included loosely traces an arc along the western coast of Europe. Following its constitutive assembly in 1990 in Rennes, the capital of modern Brittany, the group levied modest dues, obtained matching funds from the EC, and embarked on several pilot projects, some of which received additional money from Brussels. One was to computerize operations at six ports—Plymouth in southwest England, Bordeaux in southwest France, Vigo in northwest Spain, Viana do Castello in northwest Portugal, Lisbon in west Portugal—with a view to facilitating short-haul trade, or "cabotage." Once developed, the computer linkage could be extended to other ports in the region. In another project, twenty-seven university and business training centers studied the possibility of joint programs of formation; Saint-Nazaire, the port thirty-three miles downriver from Nantes at the mouth of the Loire, began with a common training program for the shipping trade. A third project brought together experts from financial markets in Glasgow, Dublin, Nantes, Bordeaux, Bilbao, and Lisbon to talk about how to reinforce financial services. Other groups looked at standards for shellfish farming and ways to coordinate investments for tourism.

The Atlantic Arc hopes that such nuts-and-bolts projects will make the coastal region competitive in a world economy less dependent on natural resources and more interested in intelligence and innovation, demanding "new forms of international and interregional division of labor," in the words of the group's brochure.[15]

The notion of the interlinking chain seems increasingly apt to describe development in the region. When specialty steel producer Altos Hornos ran out of space in Bilbao, on Spain's northern coast, it expanded in the dock area of Bayonne, along the coast across the French border, about sixty miles south of Bordeaux. Biarritz airport, outside the French resort near Bayonne, caters increasingly to a Spanish clientele in the Basque Country. In Plymouth, from which the Mayflower set out in 1620, new port facilities originally designed for freight have been converted to ferry ports to meet the demand for travelers from the southwest English port to Brest in France and Santander in Spain. Bordeaux has taken the initiative to organize a closer cooperation in the southern half of the Atlantic Arc, grouping Poitou-Charentes to the north, the Basque Country, Asturias, Galicia, Castile and Leon, and North and Central Portugal to the south and west.

Atlantic Destinies

Following the flurry of Spanish celebrations in 1992—Sevilla Expo, Barcelona Olympics, Madrid as European City of Culture—a more modest, but nonetheless ambitious, fete was set for 1993 in Spain's northwestern corner, Galicia. That year, as every year when July 25 falls on a Sunday, was a Holy Year for Santiago de Compostella, the destination that ranked with Jerusalem and Rome in the Middle Ages as a goal for pilgrims from Christian Europe. The reputed burial place of the Apostle St. James the Greater, discovered in the ninth century when most of Spain was under Moslem control, became a symbol for Christendom's resistance to Islam.

It was far to go then—the route is five hundred miles along the northern coast of Spain once across the Pyrenees—and it is still out of the way. Cape Finisterre, the "end of the world," juts out into the Atlantic from the coast west of Santiago. The holiness of the site did not keep Galicia from being marginalized even in the Middle Ages. As the Reconquista driving the "Moors" out of Spain proceeded southward, the region's political center of gravity followed the drift—Asturias grew into Leon which grew into Castile. The marriage of Ferdinand of Aragon and Isabella of Castile in the fifteenth century further shifted the weight of activity to the east and the south. When Madrid became the capital of an increasingly unified Spanish kingdom in the sixteenth century, and Portugal definitively gained its independence in the seventeenth century, Galicia's isolation was complete.

The Galicians have many things in common with their Celtic cousins. John Hooper writes, "Whether because they share with the Irish, Welsh and Bretons a common ancestry or because they live in a similarly windswept, rain-sodden land on the edge of the Atlantic, the Galicians have many of the characteristics associated with Celtic races—a genius for poetry, a love of music, a fascination with death and a tendency towards melancholy."[16]

The other Atlantic Coast regions which bear the full brunt of the ocean's fury share Galicia's isolation and underdevelopment. Northern Portugal, Ireland, western Scotland, and Norway are all thinly populated regions with barren soil and bad weather, despite their glorious scenery. All of them have a history of emigration. Ireland's population declined by half in the century following the famines of the 1840s, from 8 million to less than 4 million, where it remains today. Per capita income in the Republic of Ireland is two-thirds of the average EC level, putting it, with other peripheral regions like Greece and Portugal, among the poorest members of the Community.

A British geographer, Gordon Neil Minshull, describes the situation in northwestern Ireland in words that would fit northwestern Spain or Norway, too: "These north-western coastlands lie on the remotest fringes of Europe and illustrate both the worst extremes of the Atlantic mountain environment and some of the most marginal economic conditions in the whole of the European Community."[17] While light industry like electronics assembly has come to the industrial zone near Shannon airport in western Ireland, Donegal county in the northwest has to be content with low-tech manufactures like textiles and ball-bearings that exploit the reserves of the low-paid, underemployed female work force in the region.

These are the nightmares that haunt Atlantic Coast politicians. The French launched the Atlantic Arc because they were worried that their own "Atlantic facade," from Le Havre to Bordeaux, would succumb to the same fate. Their answer, as detailed in a collection of studies entitled *Atlantic Destinies,* is to reinforce the local economies of cities along the coast and to create an infrastructure linking them into a network of "Atlanticities."[18] The key to success in this strategy is to strengthen the identification of the residents with their cities and regions, these experts feel.

Europe is recomposing itself beneath our eyes. In the west, and recently in the east, ancient ethnic communities, stifled for so long by an administration at times totalitarian, are taking on new life. The states are de-concentrating, decentralizing, delocalizing and regionalizing functions that were centralized up till now. Spontaneously, cities are regrouping in networks, crossing regional and national frontiers. Everywhere, the desire for a new citizenship is being asserted.[19]

In this way, they hope to turn their peripheral position to their advantage, to be a bridgehead and not just a "Cape Finisterre."

CHAPTER SEVEN

MITTELEUROPA: EUROPE'S HEARTLAND

When the Berlin Wall fell on the night of November 9, 1989, a shudder ran through Europe.

It came in part from the sheer emotional thrill of the moment. Here was the symbol of terror and division that had split up families and killed dozens of people striving for freedom rendered suddenly harmless at the stroke of a pen. Images of weeping, laughing, astonished people crossing the Wall in both directions—broadcast live —moved television audiences around the world. In person, the emotion was all but overwhelming.

The shudder came also from fear. Fear of the unknown as the familiar political accommodations of four decades collapsed and left a yawning void. Fear of the all too well known—the military juggernaut that was Germany had been conquered and divided after starting two horrific wars in living memory, and now that division was gone. All the comfortable calculations of the previous day— the Single Market of Europe, the security of NATO, the threat of communism—no longer added up the same way.

Less than a year later, on October 3, 1990, the German Democratic Republic ceased to exist and became part of the Federal Republic of Germany, a forty-one-year-old state that marked the longest experience the German nation had ever had of representative democracy.

The removal of the Wall and the ugly border down the middle of the truncated Germany that had come out of World War II marked for many the end of the twentieth century, which began in historical terms with the outbreak of World War I in 1914. The reunification of Germany, capping the liberation of eastern Europe from communist dictatorship and preparing the way for the disintegration of the mighty Soviet Union itself, ushered in a new era for Europe and the world.

Its significance can hardly be overstated. Even as Europe moved into the 1990s, the semblance of continuity misled politicians and public alike. European integration continued on the road mapped out for it, and unification Chancellor Helmut Kohl, reelected by a reunited Germany, was the most eager to sign the Treaty of Maastricht, calling for political and economic union of the European Community by the end of the (calendar) century. Soon enough, though, Europeans once again began asking "the German Question": What to do with a restless nation in the middle of Europe that has no natural borders, that is too small to control all of Europe but too big to live quietly in it?

The debate in western Europe on ratification of the Maastricht treaty often seemed to turn on this German question. Both those for and those against the treaty worried about Germany. Those in favor wanted to "bind" Germany into a bigger whole, to contain it and control it. Those opposed to the treaty feared it would be more dangerous to be trapped in a cage at the mercy of this ravaging lion than to be out in the jungle with it running free. The French argued openly about the German menace in the runup to their September 1992 referendum on the treaty. In that same month, currency speculation disrupted the European Monetary System, forcing several weaker currencies, including Britain's pound sterling, out of the fixed exchange rate scheme. The German central bank, the Bundesbank, stubbornly ignored any calls to lower its interest rates because it feared inflation at home. This obliged other European central banks to keep their rates high despite sluggish economic conditions. Europe felt crushed under the power of the deutsche mark, the German currency, and the British, in particular, bitterly blamed Germany for humiliating their currency, and thus their country.

The term "Fourth Reich" leapt easily to the lips of those skeptical about Germany's latter-day conversion to peace and democracy. Heleno Sana, a Spanish journalist who has lived in Germany for many years, wrote a polemical book entitled *The Fourth Reich: Germany's Delayed Victory*. He claimed that Germany would accomplish with its economic prowess what Kaiser Wilhelm and Hitler had failed to do through military force: conquer and rule most of Europe. Obviously, writes Sana, Germany will move in to fill the void left in eastern Europe by the collapse of communism. "The FRG [Federal Republic of Germany], or the Fourth Reich, will not tolerate any alternative to its authoritarian capitalist system. In the long term, there will be de facto hardly any sovereign states left; all of them will have to bow more or less to the dictates of the German Leviathan." And that's not all. "The Germanization process will by no means be limited to eastern Europe, however, it will also take in the western and southern parts of the continent. Countries like Switzerland, Belgium, the Netherlands, Denmark are already tightly bound into the West German system of business and vested interests."[1]

A British journalist, Robert Harris, wrote a novel called *Fatherland*, set in a Europe of 1964 after Hitler had won the war. The book, which portrayed the European Community as an association of weak satellite countries around a victorious and dominant Germany, became a bestseller in Britain partly because it seemed to many that this was Germany's role in contemporary Europe, even without Hitler.

French historian Pierre Behar, although more optimistic about the constructive role of Germany in late twentieth-century Europe, nonetheless could not resist calling his book on Germany *From the First to the Fourth Reich*. He argues that Germany's pursuit of the chimera "Reich" through the centuries has hurt the Germans most of all by keeping them from finding a suitable political regime to benefit their own people. The new Germany is westward oriented, Behar writes. "If it is true that Germany unity will be achieved *at* Berlin, it will not be fashioned *around* Berlin, but around Rhenish and southern Germany, which, economically and culturally, anchors the ensemble in the world of Western values."[2]

The emergence of the superregion Mitteleuropa supports this view. The strong bond between Germany and France, harking back to the time when Charlemagne's empire embraced the two, is at the heart of contemporary Europe. The *Drang nach Osten* still tugs at the German soul, but the integration with the West has firmly anchored the country. The current German push into the lands on its eastern borders rounds out Mitteleuropa, but the core remains the swath of territory around the Rhine.

The Core of Europe

Mitteleuropa, by definition, lies in the center of Europe. It is in the middle, along both the north-south axis and the east-west axis. Mitteleuropa borders on all other superregions except the hapless Balkan Peninsula; it contains the capital district. With approximately 140 million inhabitants, it is the most populous superregion, aside from Slavic Federation, and the most prosperous, the economic heart of Europe. Two rivers bracket the region—the Seine, which runs through Paris, and the Vistula, which runs through Warsaw. Two other rivers are its principal arteries, the Rhine and the Elbe.

Starting at Hamburg, at the juncture of three superregions, the Mitteleuropa border goes west along the coast, sharing the border with Atlantic Coast as it reaches the Seine and turns due south, passing Tours and Poitiers to arrive at the Garonne River, where it meets the Latin Crescent border. The Mitteleuropa boundary follows the curve of the Latin Crescent eastward to the Rhone River, where it meets the Alpine Arc border at Valence. There it turns to follow the Alpine Arc border to the northeast, tracing the curve of the Jura Mountains west of Geneva and Lausanne, south of Basel, north of Zurich to Munich, where it meets the Danube Basin border. Mitteleuropa's border continues east, passing north of Linz, Vienna, and Bratislava, turning northeast to follow the White Carpathian Mountains, which separate the Czech lands from Slovakia. It passes through Cracow, which sits at the juncture of Mitteleuropa, Danube Basin, and Slavic Federation, and follows the Vistula northward, along Mitteleuropa's shared border with Slavic Federation, through Warsaw to meet the Baltic League border just north of Torun. There it turns west, following the Baltic League border along the coast to Hamburg.

Mitteleuropa includes all of Germany, except the northern coastal strip and the southeast corner, all of Luxembourg, and all of Netherlands and Belgium, except for a narrow strip along the North Sea. It also embraces the central and eastern part of northern

France, the Basel region in northwestern Switzerland, all of the Czech Republic (Slovakia belongs to the Danube Basin), and the western two-thirds of Poland.

For better or worse, these borders largely duplicate those of the territory ruled directly by Nazi Germany during World War II. It is important to emphasize at this point that the borders of the superregions represent an area of cooperation for peace and prosperity in contemporary Europe, whatever nationalistic territorial ambitions they may have served in the past. Unquestionably, the same economic and geographic factors are at play now as then, but the declared goals of most political leaders in late twentieth-century Europe, happily, are to live and work together in peace and mutual respect; the former Yugoslavia forms the tragic exception to this rule.

This reminder applies most particularly to Poland, not only because of its bitter experience in World War II, but because of the traumatic partition at the end of the eighteenth century which wiped Poland off the map and kept it from being a sovereign nation for more than a century. The superregion borders decidedly do *not* represent a new partition of Poland, any more than they represent a political division of the proud nation-state France. Rather, they reflect, in the contemporary context of peaceful cooperation, the historic cohesion of the superregions in question.

"Mitteleuropa"

Although not as menacing as the Fourth Reich, Mitteleuropa itself has meant many things in history. From the time the term came into use at the beginning of the nineteenth century, it defined various territories in Europe. In the twentieth century, Mitteleuropa came to be a code word for German geographers to describe the Reich's territorial ambitions. Early users of the word tended to refer to the part of Europe between north and south as "mittel" or "central." Thus, August Zeune, in 1808, had Mitteleuropa stretching from the Atlantic Ocean to the Black Sea, incorporating all of France to the west and the entire Danube basin in the east. "Natural Germany" was at the center of this middle Europe, between the Rhine and Oder rivers.[3]

Later, "middle" took on an east-west orientation, and referred to the territory between France in the west and Russia in the east, often reaching into Scandinavia in the north and down to the Adriatic in the south. Friedrich List, an economist writing in the middle of the nineteenth century, focused on Germany, Austria-Hungary, Switzerland, and the Low Countries (Belgium, Netherlands, Luxembourg).

In the twentieth century, the concept of Mitteleuropa became increasingly politicized to serve as a theoretical justification for Germany's imperial aims. The borders shifted farther east and south to accommodate political realities. Economist Friedrich Naumann, whose 1915 book *Mitteleuropa* became the standard reference on the subject, described Mitteleuropa as the German-Austrian hegemony over all the peoples of Europe between the Russians and the English. During World War I, Mitteleuropa, the area of German overlordship, was seen as extending from the Meuse River, the border between Germany and the Netherlands, to the Bosporus, on the Black Sea, just as the German Reich itself extended "from the Meuse to the Memel," the river now called the Neman that runs through Belarus and Lithuania.

After that war, many writers tended to identify Mitteleuropa with the vanished Austro-Hungarian empire, the territory between Germany and Russia, including southeastern Europe and eventually taking in Poland. This is by now the normal meaning of Central Europe in English.

In the last years of the Cold War, as perestroika in the Soviet Union led to a thaw in Eastern Europe, some German writers began to hanker for a return of Mitteleuropa. For many, this was simply nostalgia, a yearning for a culture and a way of life that had vanished forever. This prewar Central Europe, an easterly Mitteleuropa, depended on the large Jewish population to hold it together. The Nazi genocide, killing 6 million Jews and driving most others away from the vast territories controlled by Germany, wiped out that Central Europe irretrievably.

Other writers, though, eschewed nostalgia and looked to a new type of Mitteleuropa, including Germany, as a Third Way between the superpowers. Karl Schlogel, a German specialist on eastern Europe, wrote feelingly of the mobility in Central Europe before the war, with frequent, direct train connections, informal border controls, easy telephoning. "This density and fast pace of life are explained, not by—measured according to contemporary standards—

the short distance between Vienna and Berlin, Munich and Dresden, Prague and Copenhagen, Budapest and Amsterdam, Trieste and Warsaw, but alone by the homogeneity of the cultural space. . . ."[4]

Ideally, Schlogel hoped, a resurgent Mitteleuropa would not be an exercise in nostalgia, but a genuine, modern alternative to the models offered by the superpowers. "A Mitteleuropa that shows that it could be a form of civilization more likely to cope with the unsolved problems and dynamite that the super nation-states of the western and eastern hemispheres have piled up, would have a very good chance to become a center of attraction in its own right or even an influence for reform in East and West."[5]

Other writers were more overtly political. Bernard Willms, a West German sociologist who favored German neutrality, suggested a Central European Federation made up of both German states, Czechoslovakia, and Austria. Otto Schily, a leftist politician, called for a Mitteleuropean Peace Union from Denmark to Austria, Belgium to Poland.[6] As German historian Hagen Schulze observes, these later views of Mitteleuropa generally were anti-Western in tone, excluding France and Britain as representatives of Western values and parliamentary democracy.

> Mitteleuropa, in this context, means giving up the laboriously won commitment of West Germany to the Atlantic West and its constitutional standards, giving up the special German-French relationship, encapsulation in an intellectual nostalgia province and a return to a seesaw policy between West and East, whose unhealthy effects have been sufficiently illustrated by German history in the past two hundred years.[7]

The Iron Curtain divided Mitteleuropa in two, cutting off the traditional economic, cultural, and social flows across the northern European plain, skewing developments on each side for four decades. Its removal allows that lifeblood to renew its flow between the two parts. French writer Alain Minc describes it this way: "Europe was half-paralyzed in three ways: the West vis-à-vis the East, West Germany vis-à-vis East Germany, and Germany as a whole vis-à-vis the center. Looking at it this way, Mitteleuropa is on its way back: it is taking on life again because Germany has recovered its rightful place."[8]

Minc, like the latter-day German commentators, would not draw the boundaries of Mitteleuropa in the same way as the superregion described here. Although their comments still seem appropriate, they are looking at the more easterly Mitteleuropa. The superregion Mitteleuropa shown here goes back to earlier boundaries, taking in a wider territory in the middle of Europe. It falls back on much older borders, namely the core territories of the Frankish empire in late antiquity—Neustria, comprising northern France, and Austrasia, including the Low Countries and western Germany. By the time of Charlemagne, the Franks had extended their rule farther south, into Aquitania and Burgundy. Later, in the Middle Ages, Germany began its push toward the east, across the Elbe, the Oder, the Vistula, even across the Memel, with settlements as far east as Tallinn, the capital of present-day Estonia.

The superregion Mitteleuropa, although rooted in this more profound history, draws its present cohesion from a much more contemporary phenomenon—namely, the special bond between France and Germany that has grown so strong in the postwar period. That bond has been the motivating force for European integration in the half-century since the war; that bond is also the base for Europe's most powerful superregion.

The central geographical feature of Mitteleuropa is the north European plain, described by Harvard geographer Raoul Blanchard in these terms: "South of the Baltic Arc, from Poland to the North Sea, extends a vast depression, probably tectonic in origin, but which has had its forms changed by the passage of the glaciers."[9] French historian Pierre Behar shows the effect of this geography on the history of the region. "This depression offers no natural frontiers. The only breaks are those made by the rivers. Desperately parallel, these rivers—Dvina, Neman, Vistula, Oder, Elbe, Weser, Rhine, Schelde—are powerless to impose borders on men."[10] Germany's eastern border shifted from the Oder west to the Elbe, from there much farther east to the Neman, then returned to the Oder, where it is now. Poland also has shuttled back and forth between these rivers, sometimes disappearing altogether.

One of the main contests in European history has been that of Germany and France to establish the border between them. The Roman Empire extended to the Rhine; beyond the strongly fortified border along that river was the barbarian wilderness known as "Free Germany" by the Romans. But it was a Free German tribe, the Franks, that penetrated the growingly porous border and even-

tually inherited all of Roman Gaul, corresponding, except for Brittany on the west coast, to today's France. This territory was united with Frankish conquests in the east under Charlemagne, whose ninth-century empire reached from the Elbe River in the east to the Atlantic in the west, and stretched down to Rome in the south. After his death, Charlemagne's empire was split into three—West Francia, which became France; East Francia, which became Germany; and, between the two, the choicest part, the "filet cut" in the middle, which is known in history as Lotharingia, a name that survives in vestigial form in today's French region of Lorraine. East Francia quickly acquired Lotharingia, so that for a long period what came to be known as Germania included not only the Benelux countries, but much of northern and eastern France, as far south as Provence and northern Italy.

Through the subsequent centuries, the French kings pushed that border eastward, eventually conquering most of today's France, and then some, but it was left to Napoleon to extend France up to the Rhine and beyond. In the nineteenth and twentieth centuries, Germany pushed the border back, culminating in Hitler's occupation of northern and western France early in World War II, leaving only the southeast briefly as a separate entity with a puppet government in Vichy. The energies of postwar Europe have been directed at keeping France and Germany peacefully united. This has been the motor of West European integration, from the foundation of the European Coal and Steel Community in 1952, to the signing of the Treaty on European Union in 1992.

In that benevolent and peaceful half-century between the defeat of Napoleon in 1815 and the rise of Bismarck, who forged a unified Germany in the heat of a war against France in 1870, there was a surge of brotherhood between the two peoples, which, Spanish writer Heleno Sana observes, led already then to the emergence of "the idea of a German-French idyll."[11] The French nationalist historian Jules Michelet in that nineteenth-century period of calm deplored the "cruel separation" of the two peoples and suggested a close cooperation between France and Germany as the core for the Europe of the future. Victor Hugo, the novelist, wrote of his love and respect for Germany, and felt himself to be a native son of this "holy fatherland of all thinkers." If he were not French, he would like to be German, he said.[12]

The historic forces forging the superregion Mitteleuropa are the same ones at work to integrate Europe, because Mitteleuropa is the cultural and economic core of Europe, the center that holds the rest together. This is the real significance of the French-German rapprochement since the war. The EC is an institutional expression of it, and the Europe of the next century will reflect that fundamental unity at the core.

This trend has emerged only slowly in the perceptions of a world fixated on the ideological rivalry between the superpowers. One geopolitical analyst and consultant, Michael M. White, was able to describe the fundamental movement in his 1985 book, *Opportunity in Crisis*. He boldly predicted that, by the end of 1980s, "France and Germany will have begun the process of merging into one superstate, from which a single power will emerge, changing the face of both international and European politics."[13]

Writing at the nadir of the EC's institutional evolution, before Jacques Delors relaunched the Community with the Single European Act, White misjudged the timing. Also, of course, he could not take account of the collapse of communism, which no one anticipated at that time. Nonetheless, he identified the underlying dynamic at work in European integration—the forging of a cohesive unit at the center of Europe through the union of France and Germany.

In the turbulent days of September 1992, as the French debated whether to ratify the Treaty of Maastricht and speculators drove several currencies out of the European Monetary System, this naked reality emerged more clearly. The French, in a finely nuanced referendum vote, approved the treaty by a slim margin. But that, given the tenor and substance of the debate, was not a sufficient mandate for the sweeping changes of the Maastricht treaty. German chancellor Helmut Kohl visited French president Francois Mitterrand immediately after the vote, and the two reportedly drew up contingency plans for a narrower monetary union between their two countries, that others could join later on, depending on their political will and financial discipline.

This alternative followed White's 1985 prediction in remarkable detail. In a somewhat different scenario, White had forecast that a conservative German government in a crisis situation would opt for a "two-track" Europe, favoring closer union with France and leaving other countries behind. "In monetary terms this would at first entail a much closer currency relationship between the French franc and the German mark, and ultimately this would imply a joint central bank."[14] This joint money would not come into existence smoothly, White continued, but would become a reality in the course of the 1990s. "After this," he concludes, "Franco-German unity in a Carolingian state will only be a matter of time. As this new nation thrives and prospers it will geonomically [sic] and geopolitically change the world's balance of power as we know it today."[15]

This French-German unity at the heart of Europe may take the form of the superregion Mitteleuropa, rather than a new "superstate." The western and southern regions of France are following their own historic patterns in drifting toward Atlantic and Mediterranean groupings, while the historical core of the country joins with a reunited Germany, whose economic influence extends into western Poland and the Czech lands. The Benelux countries wedged in between France and Germany remain an integral part of the new entity.

The Rhine

The most profound impact of French-German rapprochement after the war, starting with the European Coal and Steel Community, was on the Rhineland. After a millennium of disputing control of the river basin, of looking at the great waterway as a border instead a grand unifying bond, France and Germany made it possible for the Rhine to realize its full economic potential for the first time in the modern era. The Schuman Declaration of 1950, which called for establishment of the ECSC, aimed for the economic unity of the Rhine, "always prescribed by geography, always prevented by history." Achieving that goal has been one of the main accomplishments of European integration. As British geographer Gordon Neil Minshull comments, "In place of the unstable Rhinelands of nineteenth-century Europe, a 'super-core' region on a continental scale has emerged."[16]

The Rhineland forms the core of Europe's "heavy industrial triangle," based on the coalfields stretching from northern France, through southern Belgium to western Germany, across the Rhine along the Ruhr River valley. In the coal- and steel-based boom of the Industrial Revolution, the triangle from Dunkirk on France's west coast, to Munster at the northern end of the Ruhr area, to Metz in the Lorraine region of eastern France, became the heart of Europe's continental production. A comparable center grew up in England's Midlands, and a smaller version in northern Italy. National frontiers between France, Belgium, and Germany kept the heavy industrial triangle from realizing the economies of scale and rationalization that would have permitted more efficient production. The ECSC, the beginning of the French-German economic integration, freed the way for improved performance.

Depletion of iron and coal reserves, the rise of new, more efficient industrial centers around the world, and global shifts in the terms of trade led to a sharp decline of the European steel industry, entailing difficult adjustments in the heavy industrial triangle. But the region had accumulated enough capital, entrepreneurial expertise, labor skills, and sheer population through its decades of prosperity that it adapted by developing new industries with more technology input and a higher service component that increased the value added and kept the region competitive on world markets.

The Ruhr area, with its high concentration in coal and steel, faced the most difficult challenge as these industries declined continuously through the 1970s and 1980s. "And yet," the *Financial Times* wrote in December 1991, "what local headline writers persist in calling the 'dying heart' of Germany has so far demonstrated a curious reluctance to stop beating."[17] North Rhine-Westphalia, the province that includes the Rhine-Ruhr industrial area, accounted for one-fourth of Germany's 47,000 new companies in the first half of 1991. The region was creating 130,000 new jobs annually to make up for lost employment in coal and steel, as the percentage of jobs in that sector went from 60 percent at their postwar peak to 30 percent. The province employs 450,000 in more modern electronics and electrical goods activities, while 3 million, 51 percent of those employed, are in services. The accumulated resources of the past sustain this economic vitality. As the *Financial Times* noted, "Forty percent of all the consumers in the European Community (the richest, at that) live just one day's journey away along some of the best communications networks in the world."[18]

The Rhine-Ruhr conurbation alone—including cities like Duisburg, Dusseldorf, Cologne, and Bonn along the north-south axis of the Rhine River and Essen, Bochum, and Dortmund along the east-west axis of the Ruhr River—represents a population of 10 million people, united by one of the densest highway networks in the world. The resurgence in the Rhine cities has given them a new élan. Dusseldorf, headquarters for the big industrial companies and government center for the province, has reinforced its reputation as Germany's capital of chic—it was no accident that world-class photo model Claudia Schiffer was discovered in a Dusseldorf disco. Cologne, most famous for the twin spires of its Gothic cathedral and *eau de cologne* toilet water, has become a magnet for radio and television broadcasting and vies with New York for the global lead in contemporary art. Even though the capital of reunified Germany is supposed to move to Berlin, Bonn continues to build like there is no tomorrow, confident of keeping much of the federal government's "back-office" activities and landing new European Community institutions.

Farther south along the Rhine, at the confluence with the Main River, lies a much smaller conurbation, with "only" 1.5 million people, consisting of Mainz and Wiesbaden on the Rhine and Frankfurt, a scant twenty miles east on the Main. Frankfurt is one of Europe's main transportation hubs, with the largest airport on the continent and the largest railway station in Germany. The city also houses the headquarters of Germany's leading banks and biggest stock exchange, making it the main financial center for the country.

Even though coal and steel industries have shrunk, the Rhine harbors other major industries that have continued to expand. The river connects an unequaled concentration of chemical manufacturers. The three largest chemical companies in the world are the German multinationals Bayer, Hoechst, and BASF, all of which have their headquarters and main factory complexes along the Rhine. Farther south still along the Rhine, at Basel, three big Swiss chemical companies—Sandoz, Hoffmann-La Roche, and Ciba-Geigy—have their headquarters.

Ford Motor's German subsidiary has its headquarters and main manufacturing facility at Cologne. General Motors' German unit, Adam Opel, is located near the Main-Rhine confluence. And Daimler-Benz, maker of Mercedes cars and trucks, has important facilities at Gaggenau and Mannheim.

The Rhine's capacity for navigation makes it desirable as a site for heavy industry. Oceangoing vessels can go as far as Cologne, while barges of 5,000 tons get as far south as Mannheim. Smaller barges, but still carrying 2,500 tons, can navigate the river to Basel. This means that large bulk cargoes, like iron ore imports for the Ruhr steel industry or bulk chemical exports from the Big Three, can be loaded or unloaded at Rotterdam, the biggest port in the world, at the mouth of the Rhine. For its part, Duisburg claims to be the biggest inland port in the world, with a 1992 volume of 45 million tons.

This resurgence of prosperity harks back to the previous eras of affluence in the region, due to its role as a crossroads for commerce. The Romans already made considerable use of the Rhine for trade and transport of bulk goods. In the tenth century, the Rhineland was the first northern European territory to pull out of the "Dark Ages" following the ravages of the Vikings and the Magyars. In the eleventh and twelfth centuries, the Rhine remained the focus of artistic and intellectual life as well as economic activity until the Capetian dynasty consolidated its control of Ile-de-France and Paris took over that role. By the end of the twelfth century, Cologne, already a prosperous city under the Romans, was the largest German city.

"With the development of commerce between the south and the north of Europe, the Rhineland became the chief avenue of trade and also one of the most highly urbanized areas of Europe," historical geographer Norman J. G. Pounds writes of this early medieval period. Long before the smokestacks and collieries of the Industrial Revolution, the Ruhr valley was prominent, too, as the main trade route between Flanders and eastern Europe. "At the same time," Pounds continues, "the natural routeway, variously known as the loess belt and as the Hellweg, from the Low Countries and lower Rhineland eastward through Germany to Poland, developed a chain of cities which reached from northern France to Silesia."[19] The *Hellweg*—literally "the road to hell," according to one interpretation—paralleled the Ruhr River from Duisburg via Dortmund to Paderborn. Germany's present-day Federal Highway 1, the express thoroughfare for the Ruhr area, follows the route of the Hellweg.

The Burgundy Model

The French campaign in support of the Treaty on European Union was launched at Selestat, a small town in Alsace thirty-five miles southwest of Strasbourg, not far from the Rhine River. Former French president Valery Giscard d'Estaing, a political conservative, and Elizabeth Gigou, minister for Europe in the Socialist cabinet, mounted the same tribune in June 1992 to rally French opinion in support of ratifying the treaty in the forthcoming referendum. Alsace responded with an overwhelmingly positive vote—nearly two-thirds in favor of the Maastricht treaty.

Selestat was a cradle of Renaissance humanism, home to the felicitously named Beatus Rhenanus, a disciple of the peripatetic Desiderius Erasmus, a Dutch scholar who spent most of his later years in nearby Basel, where he died in 1536, after long sojourns in Paris, Oxford, and Louvain. Among other things, Rhenanus had his hand in the early dissemination of the name America to describe the New World discovered by Columbus. These liberal humanist intellectuals of the Renaissance are held up today as inspirations for a borderless Europe—the "Republic of Letters" that they created across Europe had no frontiers except ignorance and intolerance. The highly successful EC program for university student exchange is called Erasmus, a pseudo-acronym standing for European Community Action Scheme for the Mobility of University Students.

Alsace was part of the Holy Roman Empire of the German Nation until the seventeenth century, when Louis XIV made it part of France. Bismarck's new Reich won it back in the nineteenth century, along with part of Lorraine, and kept it until the end of World War I, when France reclaimed it as part of the spoils of war. The Germans occupied it again for four years during World War II, but of course lost it again. Now, 57,000 workers from French Alsace commute to work in Germany across a border that exists only on maps. Thirty thousand cars cross the Pont de l'Europe in Strasbourg every day, across the Rhine, the official border; but as an Alsatian high school student in favor of European union told *Le Monde,* "it's not the Rhine that's going to separate France from Germany."[20]

French workers in Germany, benefiting from higher wages and a generous tax treaty, take home up to twice as much pay as those working in French companies. As a result of the large number of commuters who take advantage of this situation, the unemployment rate in Alsace runs about half the French national average, while the region is the most prosperous in France after Paris. Commuters are not the only source of prosperity, though. Five hundred foreign companies have subsidiaries in Alsace, including multinationals like E.I. Lilley, General Motors, Dow Chemical, W.R. Grace of the U.S.; Siemens and Daimler-Benz of Germany; and Sony, Ricoh, and Sharp of Japan, who like not only the central location but the high return on Alsace's productive and modestly paid workers. German and Swiss citizens are buying property in Alsace for half the price of land at home.

Cross-border cooperation is taking on an institutional character. There are several regional cooperations, including the *Regio basiliensis,* one of the oldest in Europe, originally taking in the cantons around Basel, and now joined by the Mulhouse region of France, and southwest Baden-Wurttemberg in Germany; other cross-border regions are grouped around Freiburg and Karlsruhe northward along the Rhine. The *Regio Freiburg* talks of a *"Provincia Alamanica,"* because local German dialects in Alsace, Switzerland, and Baden-Wurttemberg trace their roots to the language spoken by the Alamanni tribe. Universities of Basel in Switzerland, Mulhouse and Strasbourg in France, Freiburg and Karlsruhe in Germany have banded together in a "European Confederation of Universities of the Upper Rhine," to promote joint programs not only in cultural studies but in fields like biotechnology. The regional Chamber of Commerce in Strasbourg claims that the territories of Alsace, Baden-Wurttemberg, Rhineland-Palatinate—the German province just north of Alsace—and northern Switzerland represent the greatest concentration of academics, researchers, and technological and industrial resources in Europe.

The number of commuters from the French region of Lorraine traveling north every day to work in Luxembourg doubled in the ten years to 1992, to 31,000, creating jams on roads not really designed for that much cross-border traffic. The president of a football team in Forbach, a town on the French border with Saarland in Germany, told one visiting journalist, "The people from the Saar are not really German, and the Lorrains are not really French." Many Germans have moved across the border to Lorraine to escape higher German taxes. The head of a German cable company in the Forbach industrial zone said, "For us Europe is already united—there is no France, there is no Germany."[21]

This propensity for coadunation has a long history in the region, dating back to the golden age of the dukes of Burgundy. Like a landlocked Atlantis, Burgundy is a land that has vanished in history but left a haunting memory. Today's Burgundy, the administrative region in eastern France, is only a shadow of the realm that once seemed on the verge of becoming one of the great powers in Europe. In the fifteenth century, the duke of Burgundy was the most powerful ruler in Europe, and his realm the most prosperous, a swath of territory from Amsterdam to the Alps. As much as in Florence and Rome, the Renaissance was born in the court of these dukes, who were more powerful than their nominal liege lords, the king of France and the Holy Roman Emperor.

The original Burgundians were a German tribe settled east of the Rhine who moved first to the Champagne region and then to eastern Gaul in the fifth century. There they founded a kingdom between that of the Ostrogoths and Visigoths. A Burgundian princess, Clothilde, married Clovis, king of the Franks, and usually gets the credit for converting him to Christianity, an event of paramount significance for the future of Europe. The kingdom of Burgundy became the third major component of the Franks' growing empire, along with Neustria and Austrasia. The region became the southern part of Lotharingia when the empire was divided after Charle-

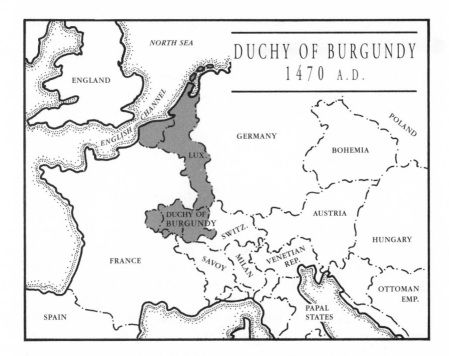

magne's death. Subsequent wars and alliances parceled out the territory.

It was a branch of France's Valois dynasty that brought new dynamism to Burgundy. Through inheritance, marriage, and conquest, the dukes of Burgundy in the fourteenth and fifteenth centuries extended their rule to Artois and Picardy in northern France, to Flanders, Hainault, and Brabant in Belgium, and to Holland. Rotterdam, Amsterdam, Brussels, Antwerp, Bruges, Amiens, Nancy, and Macon were among the cities making up this wealthy federation. The last of the Valois dukes, Charles the Bold, too audaciously tried to recreate Lotharingia to its full extent, from the North Sea to the Mediterranean. The Swiss defeated him in two major battles, and he perished in another battle at Nancy. The French king annexed the duchy of Burgundy itself and the other French fiefs, and the Habsburgs inherited most of the rest, partitioning a powerful entity out of existence.

Historians sigh at the thought of what might have been had Charles been less bold. But Burgundy has left indelible traces in the texture of Mitteleuropa, in the faded grandeur of an Arras or Dijon, the fine wine cellars of Brussels, that touch of style and refinement throughout the region. Renaissance Burgundy beckons as a model across the centuries, as the region recomposes itself. On the one hand, Belgium is breaking into its component parts, Flanders and Wallonia, while on the other hand, Lorraine and Luxembourg, Alsace and Baden-Wurttemberg are creating new forms of cooperation. Burgundy, "divided into various governing bodies, respectful of local traditions and local liberties,"[22] resurfaces to show a way to preserve autonomy in unity.

"Rhenish" Capitalism

As the Single Market became a reality, French business and government leaders, spurred two decades previously by the "American challenge" to adopt U.S. business methods, began to look toward Germany as a more appropriate model than the United States. Edith Cresson, the French prime minister who sharply attacked Japanese business practices, had only praise for German methods, and urged French businessmen to imitate Germany's sophisticated training programs. The commitment of German firms to formation struck Michel Albert, chief executive of France's second largest insurance group, as one of the distinctive features of German business ideology. In his 1991 book, *Capitalism Versus Capitalism*, Albert maintained that the new ideological struggle, now that communism has collapsed, is between two fundamentally different approaches to capitalism, the "Anglo-Saxon" type as practiced in the United States and the "Rhenish" version practiced not only in those countries bordering the Rhine, but in Japan as well.[23] Albert leaves no doubt that the latter type, with its emphasis on consensus and long-term planning instead of short-term profits, is the preferable model for French companies.

Taking the example of human resources, Albert contrasts the approach of the two capitalisms.

> According to the Anglo-Saxon model, in order to maximize competitivity, you have to maximize the competitivity of each one of your employees. And so you must, everywhere and at all times, recruit the best and, to keep from losing them, pay them every moment according to their market value. The salary is essentially individual and precarious, like the job itself. In the Rhenish-

Nippon concept, on the contrary, the essential is not considered to be that. The enterprise does not have the right to treat its employees as a simple production factor, that it buys and sells on the open market like a raw material. It has, on the contrary, a certain obligation toward security, fidelity, and professional formation that is expensive. As a result, rather than pay everyone according to his current value on the market, the enterprise should prepare career paths, smooth out the curves, avoid destructive rivalries.[24]

Albert's book found considerable resonance in France. The French had trouble anyway reconciling their generous state-sponsored health insurance and pension schemes, not to mention the tradition of government intervention in industry, with the American model of capitalism. Although French industry up to the 1980s was still hampered by archaic paternalistic structures, the challenges of the Single Market brought changes quickly, and the French began to realize they had more in common with German attitudes toward work and profit and their role in society than with American. Nothing illustrated this more than the success of Socialist Pierre Beregovoy, first as finance minister and then as prime minister, in keeping France on such an orthodox course in fiscal and monetary policy that the country actually bettered Germany on inflation and made the French franc for a time at least virtually as hard a currency as the German mark. The new admiration for the German example was neither servile nor defensive; the unspoken belief of many French leaders was that they could actually improve on the German models with a dash of Latin creativity.

None other than Friedrich Naumann, the author of *Mitteleuropa,* described the secret of German success in business as the ability of the individual to submit to the organized work of the collectivity. "This insertion of the individual ego into the collective ego, that is what we are capable of and through which we achieve a greater diversity of products and stronger world-market qualities in trade. Individualism is fully developed, but then taken up into the next highest form of economic communal existence."[25] While these words, written early in the twentieth century and infused with a certain Wilhelmine triumphalism, presage a dangerous vulnerability to the temptations of fascism, they unquestionably describe the underlying attitudes that have made German industry so successful in the postwar period as well.

It continued to make converts in France. Bernard Collomb, chairman of Lafarge Coppee, a French multinational in the construction materials sector, says that he had revised his own thinking, which used to reflect U.S. methods. "I have always favored mobility and flexibility. But I must note that the people doing the best in the world today—the Germans and the Japanese—are the least flexible people. There is something to learn in that: People need mobility, but they also need some underlying stability."[26]

A Mitteleuropean Company

The exchange of business expertise between France and Germany is not always in a single direction, however, as the story of one French manager demonstrates. When he was writing to his pen pal in Dortmund in the 1950s to practice his German, teen-age Daniel Goeudevert, a native of Reims in the Champagne region of northern France, probably did not expect he would marry this German girl three decades later, shortly before he became a top executive in one of Germany's biggest and best-known companies, Volkswagen.

Like any good French provincial of his generation, Goeudevert went first to Paris to make his career. He quickly abandoned schoolteaching to become a door-to-door salesman, a potentially more lucrative profession. He sold cars, Citroens, and was so good at it that he soon was back in the classroom, teaching other Citroen salesmen the secrets of his success. In February 1969, Citroen sent Goeudevert to the Geneva Auto Show to train the hostesses hired for the occasion, and the Swiss subsidiary, pleased to have a Frenchman who spoke German, held on to him and made him commercial director. From there he rose rapidly, becoming head of Citroen's Swiss and German subsidiaries in quick succession. When another French carmaker, Renault, hired him away to head their German operations, Goeudevert did not enjoy his usual success. But a headhunter offered him a top post with Ford Motor's big subsidiary in Cologne and by 1981 he was the head of that company. In 1989, finding the way to a higher post in Detroit blocked by his nationality, Goeudevert quit and mulled over various job offers in Germany until Volkswagen called him up and implied there would be no obstacles to advancement in Wolfsburg, the small town in Germany where VW has its headquarters.

Wolfsburg, for decades only ten miles from the barbed-wire border between East and West Germany, suffered for a long time from its isolated location on the edge of Western Europe. When Hitler established the company to realize his vision of a People's Car, the location in Lower Saxony was at the geographical center of his Reich, on the main road from the Rhineland to Berlin. But the new factory had to produce military vehicles during the war, so the funny-looking car designed by Ferdinand Porsche came into mass production only afterward. The VW Beetle, so well-suited to the modest means of postwar Germany, puttered into first place in car sales, and became one of West Germany's most successful exports as Americans made it the fashionable second car in their two-car garages.

VW was slow to realize that increasingly affluent Germans had outgrown the Beetle by the end of the 1960s, so the company had some anxious years until it began in 1973 bringing out a new generation of bigger cars with the engines mounted in the front. The compact Golf, called Rabbit when it was introduced in the U.S., quickly took the relay from the Beetle, enabling VW to become the biggest automaker in Europe and the fifth biggest in the world by the 1990s. In 1992, VW was producing 3.5 million cars in Wolfsburg and elsewhere in Europe and the world.

As Daniel Goeudevert was acclimating himself to his new company, VW found itself in the middle of new Europe. The barbed wire and minefields between Wolfsburg and eastern Europe were removed. VW entered a bidding contest against Renault and Volvo to take control of Czechoslovakia's state-owned automaker, Skoda, located at Mlada Boleslav, thirty miles northeast of Prague in the Czech Republic. The German company won the bid against the French-Swedish duo largely because VW convinced labor representatives that its corporate culture gave a much bigger voice to workers than did that of Renault or Volvo.

This commitment to dialogue with labor is characteristic of big German companies, where workers make up to half the board of directors. Not coincidentally, labor relations are a forte of Daniel Goeudevert, a big, bluff man with reddish-blond hair and a charming manner, who says he talked individually to 2,500 VW employees in his first three years at the company. In 1992, VW became the first European company to establish a European-wide works council to give labor a forum for discussing the carmaker's overall strategy for the continent.

In the meantime, VW faced tough times again, running big operating losses on its car manufacturing. The company successfully developed new models, steadily increased its market share in Europe, and invested billions of dollars in new capacity, but neglected under chief executive Carl Hahn to keep costs under control, so that profits came under increasing pressure. As the situation grew urgent—operating losses in 1991 reportedly neared half a billion dollars—VW turned not to communicator and manager Goeudevert, but to an engineer, Ferdinand Piech, to succeed Hahn as chief executive, with the assignment to cut costs and restore profitability. Goeudevert became deputy chief executive. Piech, an Austrian, is the grandson of that same Ferdinand Porsche who designed not only the first Beetle, but also the first Porsche. Independently wealthy from his family holdings in the sports car company, Piech had worked his way up in the VW hierarchy by making Audi, a brand acquired by VW in 1965, a serious competitor of Mercedes and BMW in the market for bigger cars.

Although Goeudevert was disappointed, he consoled himself by realizing a project he had been dreaming of already at Ford—to set up a management school to train executives for VW and other multinationals. With direct responsibility for VW brand cars, which account for 80 percent of the group's sales, Goeudevert remained true to his dual vocation of salesman and schoolteacher. As Germany's recession deepened, however, CEO Piech reorganized top management and forced out the Frenchman in 1993.

Volkswagen's ambitious investment program called for more than $3 billion in new production capacity in Saxony, in former East Germany, and up to $6 billion in Skoda's auto works. VW planned to raise overall car production capacity to 4.5 million units a year, while reducing employment in Germany by 10 percent, or 12,000 persons. One stock market analyst commented sarcastically that VW seemed to have entered an age of "profitless prosperity" under Hahn's management. Worse even, VW reported a loss of nearly $800 million for the first quarter of 1993 alone, prompting Piech to lay off further thousands of workers and cut back investment spending.

Besides the new acquisitions and investments in Saxony and the Czech Republic, VW increased capacity at SEAT, a Spanish carmaker acquired in the 1980s. Volkswagen also has production sites in South Africa, Argentina, Brazil, and Mexico, but decided to close its loss-making U.S. plant in 1988. As a consequence, VW's sales in the United States fell to 70,000 units in 1992, compared with 570,000 in 1970, in the Beetle era.

In little less than a year, Volkswagen hired a Frenchman as a potential chief executive and embarked on investments of billions of dollars in the former East Germany and Czechoslovakia. VW hardly limits itself to the territory of Mitteleuropa, but in its culture and worldview it is quintessentially Mitteleuropean, which inclined it more than some other companies to make these moves. Daniel Goeudevert's approach to labor relations—"listen, convince, agree" is the way he described it to German television—fits right in with the company's corporate culture. VW has a reputation of setting standards in worker representation and dialogue, and typifies the consensual approach to management found throughout northern Europe.

Eastward Expansion

Many of the dissidents who led the demonstrations against communist rule in East Germany were not seeking reunification with West Germany. Rather, they wanted a separate state that could live up to the high ideals always proclaimed for the German Democratic Republic but never realized. They were pushed aside by their compatriots who wanted the good life they had envied on the other side of the Wall, and by the West German political parties eager to cater to those desires.

Many Germans referred to the "unification" of Germany, rather than the "reunification." The Germany that came into existence on October 3, 1990, in fact had never existed before. The border changes following World War II deprived Germany of much historic territory, particularly in the east, that predated Hitler's conquests. Nearly half of today's Poland belonged to Germany before the war (while the Soviet Union acquired a third of prewar Poland).

Poland has been a victim, but also a beneficiary of northern Europe's sweeping lack of geographic barriers. At its apogee in the

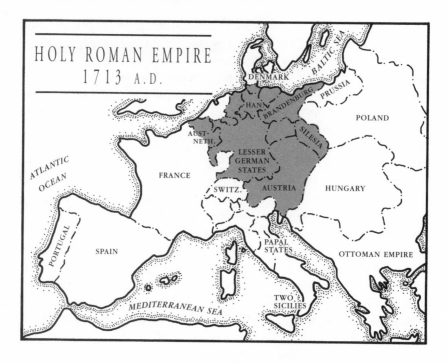

fifteenth and sixteenth centuries, Poland, united peacefully with a powerful Lithuania, extended from the Baltic Sea to the Black Sea, as far east as Kiev, including all of what is today Belarus and much of Ukraine. The nadir came in 1795, when Prussia, Russia, and Austria completed their three-way partition of the country, and it ceased to exist politically. At that point, Prussia reached its zenith, encompassing most of northern Germany and present-day Poland.

To the south, historical links go back even further. The original territory of Bohemia, enclosed by small to medium mountain ranges, appears clearly on any relief map of Europe as a diamond shape in the middle of the continent. At its height in the fourteenth century, the kingdom of Bohemia incorporated Moravia to the southeast (the other main part of today's Czech Republic), Silesia to the north (now in Poland), and reached northward via Lusatia (now the eastern part of Saxony) to include Brandenburg itself, the territory around Berlin and future heart of the German empire. When Czechoslovakia was formed in 1918, more than one-fifth of the population had German as a mother tongue, and most of them were in the Czech lands (Bohemia, Moravia, and part of Silesia).

Part of the cultural glue holding these territories together is the long-shared history in the Holy Roman Empire. For instance, that boundary, which held for centuries, separated the Czech lands from Slovakia. The seventy-four-year existence of Czechoslovakia, broken up by the Nazis' seven-year division of the country, pales by comparison. Bohemia came under Habsburg rule in the fifteenth century, but the German-speaking population dated to a time even earlier, to the massive eastward colonization of Germans in the Middle Ages. The deep roots of these Sudeten Germans formed the basis of Hitler's claim on the territory.

It is not surprising, then, that in the wake of communism's fall in eastern Europe, former cultural and economic patterns are reasserting themselves. As capitalist West Germany incorporates the former East Germany and draws the border territories in Poland and the Czech Republic into its economic sphere, the superregion Mitteleuropa is being filled out to the east. This economic expansion has led to some friction in the former communist countries. The tension between the need of foreign capital for economic recovery and the fear of losing the national patrimony characterized the relationship between a unified Germany and its eastern neighbors, but need gradually overcame fear.

The Reclus geographers in Montpellier predicted in September 1991 that the arc running through Hamburg, Hannover, Berlin, Leipzig, Dresden, and Prague, then fanning out through the Danube basin, "has every chance to count for something in the future."[27] Loosely following the Elbe River, this arc parallels the Rhine as an axis of economic development, mirroring the Paris-Lyons-Marseilles axis to the west.

The Elbe never played the same role in transport that the Rhine has. It is not as easy to navigate, it freezes over more often, and it never had the iron and coal cargoes to support growth. When the border was drawn between the two Germanies just thirty miles east of Hamburg, cutting the river off from its access to the sea, barge traffic virtually ceased. After the reunification of Germany, Hamburg began improving facilities to transfer goods arriving by sea for transport on inland waterways. The Elbe runs southeast through Magdeburg and Dresden into Bohemia, passing within twenty miles of Prague, which is joined to it by the Vltava River tributary.

The express highways radiating from the Berlin Ring in the directions of Hamburg, Hannover, Leipzig, and Dresden were quickly built up after reunification but are dreadfully congested with the increase in truck traffic. The hundred miles between Dresden and Prague has been served in the early 1990s only by a single-lane highway, so that fluvial transport of freight was expected to play a bigger role.

The glacier that created the northern European plain made the river valleys shallow, and so it was easy to build canals on an east-west axis to link the rivers flowing north-south. Large-capacity canals connect the Rhine to the Elbe, and the German government decided in July 1992 to spend $2.5 billion expanding the canals linking the Elbe to the Berlin waterways, so that big barges carrying up to 3,500 metric tons can use them.

The Future of Berlin

The Berlin Wall was 100 miles long, 12 feet high on average, fronting a 30-foot wide "death strip" with mines and dogs, 252 watchtowers, 136 bunkers, and 14,000 soldiers patrolling it, reputedly with orders to shoot anyone trying to cross. Seventy-nine people were killed trying to cross from the time the Wall started to go up on August 13, 1961, until the time it started to go down on November 9, 1989. Small sections of the Wall, colorfully spray-painted on the western side, were preserved as art, while the rest was torn down. The West German firm in charge of recycling the massive cement blocks making up the Wall hired the East German officer responsible for maintaining it for the last ten years of its existence, so that after a training course in Bavaria he could supervise the crushing of the concrete into rubble.

Berlin has been a capital city for much of its history. Founded sometime in the 1230s by Germans migrating eastward into Slavic territory, the city became a trading center and member of the Hanseatic League in the fourteenth century, seat of the Elector of Brandenburg in 1470, capital of the kingdom of Prussia in 1701, capital of the German Reich in 1871, capital of the Third Reich in 1933, capital of the German Democratic Republic in 1949, and, in name at least, capital of the Federal Republic of Germany in 1991.

During its forty years as a divided city, Berlin was kept alive artificially through subsidies designed to make each half of the city a showcase for its respective ideology. Nonetheless, West Berlin became a political and economic backwater. Bright young people desiring a career left the city, and so did anyone with any money. Old people stayed; draft dodgers, dropouts, and other counterculturists came. East Berlin became the home of the sprawling East German government bureaucracy and Communist Party apparatus.

In June 1991, the German federal parliament in Bonn held a bitter debate about moving the country's capital back to Berlin. Those in favor of the shift to Berlin said that history and the explicit commitment through the decades of the Cold War to Berlin as capital of a to-be-reunified Germany obliged them to make the move. Also, it was necessary to make East Germans feel like part of the reunified Germany, and, in practical terms, to foster reconstruction and create employment in the East. Those opposed to Berlin said it was identified with the authoritarian regimes of the Prussians, the Nazis, and the communists; that it would become a centralizing force at odds with Germany's postwar federal structure; that, only fifty miles from the postwar Polish border, it was too much on the edge, the wrong edge, of the country; that it would cost too much to move the entire government to Berlin and it would be better to spend the money on the economic reconstruction of East Germany.

Those in favor of Berlin carried the vote, but only barely. Those opposed and the entrenched federal bureaucracy in Bonn began a rear-guard action to delay and sabotage the move. They insisted that certain ministries, particularly those that employed large numbers of people, remain in Bonn. They calculated that the earliest possible time to move the real decision-makers would be a good ten years away, in the next century. They decided that all the federal government buildings under construction in Bonn should be completed. They questioned whether the parliamentary resolution mandating the move was legally enforceable.

Robbed of most of its subsidies, reunited Berlin began to sink to the standard of living of the poorer eastern Germany surrounding it, dragging down the spoiled West Berliners accustomed to a more tranquil and prosperous existence. Shortages developed in consumer goods as people came from all over eastern Germany to shop in West Berlin. The gap in living standards between the old West Germany and the old East Germany was most visible in the new Berlin. The city, famous for its people having a big mouth but lots of heart, lost its soul and earned a reputation for being aggressive and unfriendly. The Western politicians who took over administration of the whole city had risen through the party ranks when West

Berlin was a marginal, provincial satrapy, and lacked both the vision and charisma to meet the challenge of uniting the city and making it the vibrant capital of western Europe's biggest country.

The largest city in Europe between Paris and Moscow, Berlin had a total of 3.3 million people when the Wall fell, compared with 4.3 million at the outbreak of World War II. But it had no company headquarters of any note. Electrical multinational AEG moved its head offices to Frankfurt after Germany was divided; Siemens went to Munich, the Big Three commercial banks—Deutsche, Dresdner, and Commerzbank—to Frankfurt. There were no decision-makers and no big money left in the former capital. Nor, after an initial flurry when it looked like the government would move quickly, was anyone in a hurry to come back. Western media that opened new bureaus in Berlin started to drift away again; the government, and the news, remained in Bonn. Britain downgraded its Berlin consular office, transferring all visa and passport activities to Dusseldorf, forty miles down the Rhine from Bonn.

For better or worse, the time of mighty imperial capitals has passed, and the power of national capitals in Europe is fading. As capital of a federal Germany in an integrated Europe, Berlin cannot hope to recapture its former preeminence. It can and will remain a major European city—it is the size of Barcelona and has the charm and fascination of a genuine metropolis. It is a major hub in Mittel-europa, a potential counterweight in the east to the Rhine cities and Paris in the west. But it must share commercial and financial prosperity with Hamburg and Frankfurt, industrial power with Hannover, Chemnitz, and Dresden, cultural magnetism with Munich and Prague. The capital, even if the government really does move there finally, cannot regain the central role in Germany that it has in France or in Britain, no more than Paris or London can maintain that kind of hegemony in a changing Europe.

Rebuilding Regions

Kurt Biedenkopf turned out to be a happy choice as prime minister of Saxony. The maverick Christian Democratic politician from Westphalia matched well the untamed Free State carved out of the former East Germany. The industrial powerhouse of eastern Germany, Saxony lost its northern sector to a voracious Prussia early in the nineteenth century, but the rump territory entered Bismarck's empire as a kingdom in its own right, like Bavaria, and a free state. Saxony had to give up its autonomy after Hitler's rise to power in 1933, and lost its regional identity when the new state of East Germany divided up the country into administrative districts. German reunification in 1990 saw Saxony reinstated in the Federal Republic. Relatively small in area, Saxony retained the strongest industrial base in eastern Germany, in the triangle formed by three vigorous cities—Dresden, Leipzig, and Chemnitz. A restored Saxony set about reconstruction with a will. As French historian Pierre Behar observes, Saxony was one province where "the freedom of spirit was never stifled by Prussia; it's hardly by chance that the liberation movement for East Germany started in Leipzig and Dresden."[28]

Biedenkopf, a short, tough law professor, entertained notions in the 1970s of leading the Christian Democrats to power and becoming chancellor of West Germany. But Helmut Kohl prevailed and banished his would-be rival from any high political positions. Biedenkopf was never able to mobilize the masses and was not equal to the back-room intrigue of political parties. When East Germany collapsed, though, virtually the entire political class was too compromised by its involvement with the communist regime to remain in office. To fill the vacuum, the cities and reconstituted provinces turned to churchmen who had resisted the regime or imported political talent from West Germany. Biedenkopf saw his chance, and volunteered to head the Christian Democratic ticket in Saxony's first elections. He won overwhelmingly and at last gained a popular following.

He had his work cut out for him when he arrived in the provincial capital of Dresden. The firebombing of Saxony's glorious baroque city was one of the tragedies of World War II. The British and American attack in the closing days of the war has been criticized as militarily useless, killing thousands of civilians and destroying a priceless European heritage. Biedenkopf, not glossing over the difficulties of the transition after decades of communist neglect, tirelessly preached optimism for the longer term. Many beautiful monuments survived, and now others are being rebuilt, so that Dresden still offers a striking view across the Elbe River. As in Leipzig, a commercial center less damaged in the war, building cranes dominated the skyline in Dresden in the months following reunification.

Saxony benefited from an influx of outside capital. Volkswagen led the way with an investment program of $3 billion in Zwickau, near Chemnitz. Although the downturn in the automobile industry forced VW to stretch out its investments from 1994 to 1997, the company was already producing 400 Golfs a day in the first half of 1993, and would manufacture 1,200 units a day once the plant was completed. In keeping with modern production strategy, VW subcontracted up to 70 percent of the manufacture to suppliers, many of them in the surrounding region.

Other West German companies followed. Mail-order house Quelle laid out $650 million for a gigantic facility near Leipzig, capable of sending out 25 million packages a year. Siemens invested $265 million in diverse manufacturing facilities in the province. Chemicals firm Degussa spent $215 million on a pharmaceutical plant. The Kempinski hotel chain rescued a historic Dresden palace by putting up $165 million to convert it into a luxury hotel. Foreign investors came, too. A Finnish paper company, Enso, sank $535 million in a factory to supply east Germany's exploding newspaper market. Coca-Cola invested $135 million in various subsidiaries. Philips, the Dutch electricals giant, which already has substantial operations in west Germany, spent $50 million upgrading a Saxon company to capture some of the $35 billion Deutsche Telekom planned to spend by 1997 to modernize east Germany's telephone system.

Like many other prime ministers in the German provinces, Biedenkopf quickly became a champion of regional autonomy and cooperation. An integrated Europe is too broad a territory to do justice to the continent's diversity in language and culture, Biedenkopf argued in an April 1992 speech in Berlin. "As the nation-states lose their central function in the wake of political integration in Western Europe, however, the regions have to take their place as a source of identity."[29] Regions are the political unities that permit the most direct participation by citizens, Biedenkopf said, with the best overview of how to regulate society to everyone's benefit.

In keeping with this policy, Biedenkopf promoted cross-border regional cooperation. An initial effort was the *Regio Egrensis*— cross-border regional cooperation in Europe often falls back on Latin names for the organizations, so that it can be used uniformly in all languages involved. This targeted the Egerland, a territory at the juncture of Bavaria, Saxony, and Bohemia, near Bayreuth. At the eastern end of Saxony, talks began for a "three-country corner" that would include Silesia in Poland and northern Bohemia in the Czech Republic.

Biedenkopf sees a balanced growth in the whole region as critical for long-term prosperity. "We have to find our way as quickly as possible to an industrial development through which the people in Bohemia and Silesia also have the feeling that things are going ahead and that sooner or later they can also become a part of the European Community," he says. "Our goal is a Euro-region Bohemia-Saxony-Silesia."[30]

Such cross-border efforts won the quick approval of national leaders hopeful that nuts-and-bolts regional cooperation on infrastructure and environment could help heal wounds left from the war. The part of the Czech lands bordering on Saxony belongs to the Sudetenland that Hitler claimed in the 1930s because of the large German population there. The attempt of West European leaders to appease Germany in the Munich agreement of 1938, of course, is now seen as a fatal mistake that encouraged him to embark on further aggression.

For its part, Silesia represented one of Prussia's first great military conquests when the rising nation wrested it from Austrian control in the eighteenth century. After World War II, Silesia was given to Poland to help make up for territory that country lost in the east to the Soviet Union. In the bitter aftermath of Germany's defeat, Poland expelled 9 million German nationals from Silesia and other formerly German territories and Czechoslovakia drove out 3 million Germans from the Sudetenland, often brutally, with much loss of life, and no compensation.

The survivors of this forced migration and their heirs maintain a well-organized lobby in Germany, which caused chancellor Helmut Kohl to waver in his recognition of the postwar Polish border when Germany was reunified. The public apology of Czechoslovak president Vaclav Havel for the German expulsions annoyed his own countrymen without satisfying the claims of Sudeten Germans.

Against this historical background, Czech public opinion grew increasingly alarmed over the threat of "Germanization" as the country moved to a free market economy. Through 1991, as much as three-quarters of new foreign investment in Czechoslovakia, the bulk of it in the Czech Republic, came from Germany. Volkswagen led the way with its commitment to invest $6 billion in the Skoda auto company by the end of the decade. A spokesman for the

German Chamber of Commerce in Prague stated, "Culturally speaking, we are much closer to the Czechs than to the Slovaks."[31]

But the Czechs began to feel smothered by the German invasion. A Berlin newspaper reported in December 1991, "In Czechoslovakia, especially in the western half of the Czech Republic, in Bohemia, the displeasure with Germans is growing."[32] Their annoyance had many sources—from former East Germans who flashed wads of deutsche marks in local pubs along the border to know-it-all middle managers of German subsidiaries in Prague.

Some German investments were scaled back. Siemens' plan to invest $230 million in the Skoda Pilsen engineering company (separate from the auto company) ran into objections from the Czechs, who were not happy with Siemens' initial marketing efforts. A similar investment by Daimler-Benz in two Czech truckmakers was cancelled, largely because of the plunge in European truck sales. The Czechs deliberately sought other foreign investors to counterbalance the German influence. As a result, Germany slipped to third place in 1992, behind the U.S. and France, accounting for only one-sixth of the $1.2 billion invested in the country. Still, Germany remained in first place for the entire period from 1989, with two-fifths of overall investment.

At the same time, however, the Berlin office of the Czech embassy complained that too few German teachers were being sent to Czechoslovakia. German became the number-one foreign language in Prague, where advertising posters often were in German, and half the high school students picked German as first foreign language. Parents signed their children up for bilingual kindergartens, and plans were made to set up bilingual institutions through high school. The number of visitors from Germany doubled in one year, to 24 million (!), and an additional 6.5 million German-speaking Austrians flooded into the country. Czechoslovakia announced it would switch to the PAL color television system so that residents could receive programs from Germany; the communist regime had imposed the French Secam system precisely to prevent cross-border viewing.

Brandenburg, the reconstituted east German province to the north of Saxony, also moved to counteract border tensions by promoting regional cooperation. The historic university in Frankfurt an der Oder, the border city fifty miles east of Berlin, was rechartered under its old name Viadrina as a "European university," and plans were made to create Euroregions along the Oder, at Frankfurt, and farther north in the coastal region of Szcecin. More than half a million ethnic Germans still remained in Poland, mostly in the west of the country, and many Poles in Silesia still spoke German.

Siemens, AEG, Henkel, and MAN were among the big German companies who quickly set up subsidiaries in Poland, although the investments were relatively small. Medium-sized firms were eager to follow as soon as the government drew up clear rules about taking capital in and out of the country. But public opinion in Poland, too, feared a sellout to German interests. There were reports of Germans illegally buying land through straw men in former German provinces of Silesia, Pomerania, Western Prussia, and Eastern Prussia—all now in Poland. A fifty-acre Polish farm was going for $26,000, a fortune in Poland but dirt cheap for a German.

At the beginning of 1992, on the highway from Berlin to Poznan, an old Hanseatic city in central Poland that belonged to Prussia for a couple of centuries, there were fourteen motels, twelve restaurants, forty-two fast food outlets, and fourteen service stations to cater to German motorists. Signs were in German and prices often in deutsche marks. "In the end, the only thing left to do will be to move the border markers," grumbled the head of a local village to a Polish newspaper.[33]

Other Polish regions welcomed the prospect of regional cooperation as a way to gain greater independence from central control. As in other countries, communist authorities in Poland had divided up the historical regions to suppress local patriotism and formed forty-nine administrative districts to facilitate centralized government. Poland's democratic government, fearful that centrifugal regional forces might weaken Polish nationalism and central government authority, kept these districts intact.

One of them, however, Katowice, began to assert its regional identity. The district, which derives its name from the regional capital, a mining and industrial town located in the former Upper Silesia on the border with the Czech Republic, contains 3.6 million people, nearly 10 percent of Poland's overall population, making it the most populous district in the country. Katowice, under its first noncommunist district administrator, appropriately named Wojciech Czech, declared itself in favor of a "Europe of the Regions," and established relations with the "Four Motors" regions in western Europe—Baden-Wurttemberg, Rhone-Alpes, Lombardy, and Catalonia. When

Katowice established an Upper Silesian Business Bank and an Upper Silesian Publishing Company, neighboring districts began to worry about its "territorial" ambitions. They feared Katowice would try to reconstitute Upper Silesia, or even try to form a Greater Silesia by regrouping the entire southwestern region of Poland. Katowice administrator Czech, however, defended his policies by arguing that regionalism is a "consequence of modern thinking about the state and its structure, that allows the citizen the greatest possible participation."[34]

Mitteleuropa's Bond

The surge of right-wing extremism and xenophobia that rippled through Germany after its reunification, especially among young people in the former East Germany reacting against the repression of the earlier regime and the frustrations of the new free-market society, alarmed people both inside and outside Germany. It was perhaps a temporary phenomenon, arising from the special circumstance of Germany's partition and reunification. Or, who can say, it may have been the beginning of a dangerous new nationalism in Germany that can lead, as it has in the past, to hegemonial aspirations.

The antidote, in any case, is to keep Germany tied to France. German nationalism, from the time of Napoleon's conquest of much of German territory early in the nineteenth century, was defined in opposition to France. Bismarck forged German unity on the anvil of war with France and sustained it with the threat of France. The primary antagonists in World Wars I and II were Germany and France.

Historian Golo Mann recalls that France, prior to Bismarck, did not usually consider Germany its enemy. The French blamed the Russians and English for Napoleon's defeat, and looked to German intellectuals like Kant and Hegel, Goethe and Schiller to replenish their own exhausted store of inspiration. "Germany was seen as the country which had produced these great men, a philosophical, poetical, musical, non-political country. And as these were good qualities which France was conscious of having sacrificed to politics and the activity of the intellect, the French were not at all anti-German."[35] Even the prospect of a united German state did not frighten the French. "On the contrary, were not the two nations really meant for each other? Was it not their common task to be Europe's most powerful force . . . ?"[36]

The two nations complement each other: Germany, land of energy and emotion, a nation of poets and philosophers, builders and inventors, capable of massive solidarity; France, nation of intellect and debate, free thinking and individualism, with its revolutionary experience and republican ideals. In contemporary terms, the effect has been to give Germany a dominant economy, and France the political ascendancy. The political disarray in Germany following its 1990 reunification, and the lack of leadership in those first crucial years, underscored again the country's deficiency in political culture. As Heleno Sana comments, "Germany lacks a political tradition in the full, classical sense. . . . The Germans lack what Montesquieu called the *'vertu politique'* [politcal virtue], which he understood as the nerve of the republican system, and which was only the semantic paraphrase of the Aristotelian *'zoon politikon'* [political animal]."[37] The lack of political maturity, this critic maintains, is what makes Germans prone to accept the dictates of mediocre and incompetent politicians, or worse. He urges Germans to learn the virtues of disobedience so they can finally attain their proper spiritual level.

What better teachers could the Germans find in this endeavor than the French, who storm prisons, behead kings, and descend into the streets to get their way? The French often need a dose of German discipline, and the Germans certainly need a large measure of French revolutionary fervor. Together they can make united Europe a reality by giving it the strong center it needs.

CHAPTER EIGHT

THE SPECIAL DISTRICTS: MONEY AND POWER

Two and a half centuries before Baron Haussmann fashioned the Paris of wide avenues and broad carrefours that we know today, King Henry IV, sometimes called "the Great," made the first effort to transform a crowded medieval city into a true capital. The founder of the Bourbon dynasty in France, Henry IV, king of Navarre, a small territory along the western Pyrenees, acceded to the French throne at the end of the sixteenth century, when he abjured his Protestant faith and became a Catholic—"Paris is worth a Mass," he reportedly said. France had been torn apart by decades of religious wars, and the transformation of Paris became a symbol of healing and reunification. "[W]hen Henry IV was accepted as king of a united nation in 1594, he presided over a burst of new building, and pushed his schemes through with superabundant energy," one historian writes.[1] Henry's wife, Marie de Medici, came from Florence, and Italian architects and artisans directed much of the new construction. Henry IV straightened streets and created squares, expanded the city on all sides, built housing, fountains, and waterworks. The popular king completed the "New Bridge," Pont Neuf, across the Seine, the widest avenue in the city. He commissioned the Place Royale, now known as the Place des Vosges, which became home to the cream of Parisian society and a much admired model for its symmetry and harmony.

Besides his architectural plans for Paris, Henry had another "Great Design" in mind—a scheme for unifying Europe in a Christian republic of fifteen states. The plan, described by Henry's prime minister, the Duc de Sully, provided for a general council made up of delegates from all member nations to regulate affairs between states, as well as a system of regional councils. The idea, which Sully himself considered rather utopian, inspired many future champions of European unification—Frenchmen such as Rousseau, Saint-Simon, Hugo, but also other Europeans such as Leibniz, Kant, and Bentham. A week before France's September 1992 referendum on the Maastricht treaty, the leading national daily, *Le Monde,* reminded its readers of the heritage of Henry IV and his Great Design.[2]

This early notion of a European community that could preserve the peace was appealing. The religious wars in France during the sixteenth century had traumatized that country, and the Thirty Years War between Protestants and Catholics ravaged northern Europe. The same desire for peace motivated Jean Monnet, director of France's economic planning office, and Robert Schuman, the Luxembourg-born foreign minister of France, to urge the foundation after World War II of a European Coal and Steel Community as the first step in unifying postwar Europe. Schuman presented his plan in 1950 in the gilded Hall of Clocks in France's foreign ministry on the Quai d'Orsay. The Treaty of Paris establishing the ECSC was signed less than a year later.

From its beginnings, the ideal of a federal Europe joining free nations together has been largely a French inspiration, and Paris has provided the intellectual and political impetus for European integration in the postwar period. From Monnet and Schuman to Mitterrand and Delors, the major initiatives for European unification have come from France. This widely acknowledged fact explains the antagonism of former British prime minister Margaret Thatcher to the EC and Jacques Delors, who incarnated for her the centralizing and planifying tendencies of a French-style bureaucracy so abhorrent to her laissez-faire worldview.

Whatever direction Europe goes, chances are the way will be mapped out in Paris, which remains the intellectual font of Europe. The impulse for the Assembly of European Regions, the rallying point for "Europe of the Regions," came from Edgar Faure, a former prime minister of France. Founded in 1985, the AER installed its secretariat in Strasbourg, which is not only the seat of the European Parliament, but also of the Council of Europe. Like the Council, the AER includes members beyond the frontiers of the EC.

Paris also constitutes the main forum for discussing the growing trend toward regional autonomy. For one thing, political devolution in France represents a big change from the strong centralization of the country. For another, the formation of superregions affects France more profoundly than other European countries, by pulling it apart through centrifugal force. And yet, by virtue of the "capital" resources of Paris, including the sophistication of its political discourse, the French influence continues to be dominant in shaping Europe.

Nowhere was the notion of Europe 1992 taken more seriously than in Paris. Jane Kramer, European correspondent for *The New Yorker,* based in Paris, described the atmosphere in July 1991:

> The place to look for 1992 is Paris. . . . Paris was an easy, agreeable, beautiful, and remarkably boring city for the last fifteen or twenty years, and then, a couple of years ago, it was an exciting city, and everybody wanted to be here, and people said that the time to move was now, the time to buy was now, the time to make a place for yourself was now, because by 1992 Paris would be "finished"—meaning there would be no room for anybody else. . . . It wasn't so much that Parisians were getting more interesting or more welcoming or more creative; it was that Paris "anticipated" Europe, and began to feel like a capital, and took up its old vocation, which was providing the *lieu*—the enchanting space where people came together and a scene "happened."[3]

But for an accident of history, many Frenchmen believe, Paris would have become the official capital of the European Community from the beginning. The first effort in postwar cooperation, the Organization for European Economic Cooperation, more or less automatically set up in Paris to administer Marshall Plan aid. Rechristened the Organization for Economic Cooperation and Development (OECD), it continues its work of analysis and consultation in extensive offices flanking the sumptuous Rothschild mansion in western Paris that it has occupied since 1948. Paris as capital of Europe was, Italian writer Luigi Barzini noted in his 1983 book *The*

Europeans, the logical consequence of French promotion of European unity and the role of Jean Monnet in launching the European Communities. "[I]t was tacitly understood that united Europe, created and inevitably led by France, would have its capital in Paris. . . . Where else?"[4]

In the 1950s, however, when the location of the first European Community institutions was being decided, Pierre Pfimlin, at various times prime minister of France and mayor of Strasbourg, blocked selection of Paris as a possible site in order not to undercut Strasbourg, which housed the Council of Europe and landed the European Parliament. A die-hard International Committee for a European Capital has lobbied to rectify this mishap, proposing to develop a European "federal district" in a loop of the Seine west of Paris, without any noticeable success.

Official or not, Paris appears to many to be the de facto capital of Europe. When Paris, which had seen real estate prices triple and quadruple in the 1980s, finally succumbed in the course of 1991 to the global property slump, the *International Herald Tribune* reported: "Several experts cited the unification of Germany as an event holding 'market psychology' significance for Paris real estate, insofar as Paris' status as the perceived 'capital' of Europe—and all of the social, political, and economic cachet that goes with the unofficial title—is being threatened by a free, growing Berlin."[5]

Home to intellectual refugees and émigrés from the nineteenth-century German poet Heinrich Heine to contemporary Czech novelist Milan Kundera, historic capital of art and fashion, indispensable second home for jet-setters from Arab sheikhs to American movie directors, Paris is rivaled only by London and New York as a cultural capital. With thirteen universities, including Europe's largest, the Sorbonne, one of the oldest and most prestigious on the continent, Paris has been a center of learning since the early Middle Ages, attracting luminaries like Thomas Aquinas and Erasmus. Miraculously spared the destruction of fires and bombs, Paris maintains the imperial magnificence of the three centuries France dominated European affairs. New achievements like the Centre Pompidou and the Grande Arche de la Defense add to its prestige. All roads, and now all TGV tracks, lead to Paris.

After Rome, Paris is the oldest political capital in Europe, since the Frankish king Clovis made it his principal residence in the sixth century. Historian Edward James writes, "By the time he fixed his residence at Paris, towards the end of his reign, his authority over most of that area must have been unquestioned, and the Seine basin was henceforth to be the center of Merovingian power. . . . To this day, except briefly under the Carolingians, Paris has remained the center, symbolic or actual, of French political power."[6] In a certain sense, the French, long possessed of the notion that they have a special mission to civilize the world, consider a united Europe the ultimate fulfillment of that destiny.

Capital Cities

The Special Districts represent, it must be said, a tale of two cities, and precisely the two Charles Dickens dramatized in his novel. London and Paris have an influence not only throughout Europe, but throughout the world. They are truly global cities, and increasingly their preeminence has less to do with the fortunes of Britain and France but depends more on what the rest of Europe and the world brings to them. London is not only the financial capital of Europe, but, along with New York and Tokyo, one of the main financial centers in the world, and in some ways the most important. Paris is an intellectual and cultural capital for the entire world, a mecca for writers, artists, and intellectuals from around the globe. It is a lasting tribute to the French, but now the property of humanity.

At the same time, of course, London and Paris remain the principal economic centers of Britain and France, as well as national capitals. As such, they belong to their respective superregions, Atlantic Coast and Mitteleuropa. Their designation as special districts takes account of their wider role, but does not remove them from their superregions.

London is the financial district for Europe. The institutions and expertise in the City of London influence the whole continent. There are other centers, of course—Frankfurt in Germany, Paris in France, Amsterdam in the Netherlands, Milan in Italy, Zurich in Switzerland—but they are primarily of local interest. London draws on a whole culture of financial services with unparalleled expertise in accounting, legal, advertising, and other businesses that support financial activity.

Paris, for its part, is the intellectual font of European integration, dating back to Henry IV. In the long and passionate debate about ratifying the Maastricht treaty, Paris publishing houses churned out volume after volume on the theme. Bookstores in the capital had special displays of new books devoted to the subject of European integration, each one with a red banner across the cover proclaiming "Yes to Maastricht" or "No to Maastricht." French is the language of Brussels, Luxembourg, and Strasbourg, and Paris is the inspiration for the francophone world.

The capital district in Europe is a triangle connecting Paris to Brussels, Brussels in a line through Luxembourg to Strasbourg, and Strasbourg to Paris. The territory in between is Mitteleuropa, overlapping in part with the heavy industrial triangle built on the coal and steel industries. In its 1991 report *Europe 2000,* the EC Commission's map of European superregions designates this area the "Capitals Center," extending it to include London, The Hague (official capital of the Netherlands), and Bonn as well.[7] For our purposes, the capital district is not a separate superregion, but a superstructure within Mitteleuropa made up of the institutions and people who play a European-wide role. In the narrow sense, this means specifically the EC agencies or other European institutions, but in a wider sense it embraces the culture of European integration nurtured in these places.

The Washington, D.C., of Europe?

For many people, of course, Brussels stands as *the* capital of Europe. The Belgian city houses the European Commission and its bureaucracy, the most active and most visible institution of the EC. Because the Commission, which initiates, codifies, and executes EC legislation, has genuine power, in contrast to the European Parliament, the lobbyists and the press focus their attentions on Brussels. For many years, before the Commission abandoned it because of harmful levels of asbestos, the curvaceous Berlaymont building in Brussels served as an optical trademark of the EC, the usual backdrop for a television correspondent's standup. Brussels has embarked on an extensive building program not only to provide new and bigger quarters for the Commission, but also an appropriate hall for the European Parliament, in an effort to lure that body away from Strasbourg.

In the "Europhoria" of Europe 1992, with the prospect of closer union coming through the Treaty of Maastricht, the dream of a United States of Europe, and with it a capital like Washington, became more tangible. American journalist Axel Krause leads off his 1991 book, *Inside the New Europe,* with a chapter entitled "Brussels: The Washington, D.C., of Western Europe," which describes the city's booming optimism as it gets ready to play an expanded role in a unified Europe.[8] Although the trappings of a central government in Brussels are not as extensive as in the U.S. capital—for instance, the EC accredits 550 journalists, compared to 4,700 in Washington—the operative phrase of the Commission bureaucrats who talked to Krause seemed to be "not yet." For them it seemed only a question of time before the EC would rival the United States as a world power, and the EC capital would compare with Washington.

The backlash against centralization that accompanied the process of ratifying the Maastricht treaty could dampen Brussels' hopes, however. A strong capital, by definition, signifies a strong central authority, which popular sentiment in the EC seemed to repudiate in 1992. The underlying resentment toward an impersonal group of faraway bureaucrats intent on regulating and codifying national characteristics out of existence came to the surface in the debates and referendums of the ratification process. Rightly or wrongly, the Commission became the whipping boy for this resentment. Politicians in some member nations quickly exploited the voter backlash to brake development of EC institutions. Countries leery of a centralized federal Europe—notably Britain among the Twelve, but also some of the candidates for EC membership—seized the chance to slow down the movement in that direction.

Defining the proper role of a capital for Europe is part of the debate on the nature of European unification. The notion of a "federal district" like the District of Columbia haunts the thinking of federalists like Jean Monnet and his spiritual heirs. Antifederalists have fought centralization of EC institutions. In a curious way, the interests of both parties dovetailed in the choice of sites for EC institutions—their profile was low enough to please the antifederalists, but their very neutrality made them suitable candidates for a later federal district in the minds of those who wanted a true capital. Thus, the High Authority of the European Coal and Steel Community, the predecessor of the European Commission, went to

Luxembourg, a country small enough to be a federal district itself. The parliamentary assembly, which became the European Parliament, divided its sessions between Luxembourg and Strasbourg, where it rented the home of the Council of Europe, the Palais de l'Europe. By 1984, the wasteful extravagance of trucking documents and equipment back and forth between the two locations forced the Parliament to restrict plenary sessions to Strasbourg, but the offices of the legislators remained in Luxembourg. Strasbourg, on the border between France and Germany, historically belonging as much to one as the other, appealed to postwar leaders for its symbolic value.

The location of the European Economic Community's Commission in Brussels, however, made the Belgian capital a magnet for further development. Midway between Bonn and Paris, big enough to provide a cultured environment for Commission employees, the erstwhile imperial capital, rich from its Burgundian heritage and the wealth of its Congo colony, had excess "capital capacity"—that partly intangible capability to rule and administer things—for such an international institution. The division of Belgium into autonomous federal regions, whereby Brussels became a region in its own right distinct from Flanders and Wallonia, reinforced the city's "federal district" status. If Belgium were to go the further step of splitting into two separate nations, Brussels, a French-speaking enclave in Flemish-speaking Flanders, would no longer have a nation to be capital of and might find its salvation as capital of Europe.

As the locus of EC decision-making, Brussels has drawn the diplomats, the lobbyists, and the press. Many countries have three ambassadors in Brussels—one to the EC, one to NATO, headquartered on the outskirts of the city, and one to Belgium. The European Parliament, too, holds its committee meetings in Brussels, where it has greater access to the Commission staff. More than eight hundred multinational companies have flocked to Brussels with subsidiaries, three-fourths of them from the United States, in testimony to American acceptance of the EC as a United States of Europe and Brussels as a Washington, D.C. *The Wall Street Journal* located the offices of its European edition in Brussels. The EC directly employs 16,000 people in Brussels, most of them from other member states, but creates jobs for another 100,000 Brussels residents, local authorities estimate.

The European Court of Justice, which adjudicates EC law, and the European Investment Bank, an EC institution that makes development loans, were set up in Luxembourg. The Court of Auditors, established to monitor EC budgets and accounts, much like the General Accounting Office in Washington, also went to Luxembourg. The Parliament's presence in Strasbourg remains contentious. Brussels may decide the issue by building the new quarters for the Parliament on spec, so to speak, in much the same way as Bonn overtook Frankfurt to become West Germany's capital after the war simply by getting the buildings ready while politicians debated. Strasbourg dared not embark on new facilities for the Parliament without a French government guarantee, and may end up forfeiting the Parliament for that reason.

The fate of Brussels and the capital district depends on the course of European integration in the coming years. If there were a strong trend to centralization and federal structures for Europe, which seems unlikely in the aftermath of the Maastricht ratification process, Brussels could well become more like Washington, with the appurtenances of a big capital. If, however, which seems more likely, centralization proceeds more slowly as "subsidiarity" truly takes hold, then Brussels may have to adopt a lower profile and continue to share its capital-city prerogatives.

London's High Repute

London was a leading center in trade and finance long before it became capital of the British empire. The Roman historian Tacitus even described Londinium as "a town of the highest repute and a busy emporium for trade and traders." In the Middle Ages, the port city housed one of the key trading posts of the Hanseatic League, making it a major entrepot for trade between northern and southern Europe.

London developed the expertise and institutions to finance this trade. By the time Daniel Defoe made his "Tour Through the Whole Island of Great Britain" in the eighteenth century, the city enjoyed a sophisticated financial apparatus. Defoe visited the young Bank of England, the country's first shareholder-owned bank.

Here business is dispatch'd with such exactness, and such expedition and so much of it too, that it is really prodigious; no confusion, nobody is either denied or delayed payment, the merchants who keep their cash there are sure to have their bills always paid, and even advances made on easy terms, if they have occasion. No accounts in the world are more exactly kept, no place in the world has so much business done, with so much ease.

London's dominance of global finance in the nineteenth century often is depicted as a consequence of Britain's powerful and far-flung empire. But it is really the other way around—it was London's financial skill that enabled Britain to emerge first as a European Great Power and then as an imperial power and the leading industrial nation in the world. In his book *The Rise and Fall of the Great Powers,* Paul Kennedy writes that at the end of the seventeenth century, France, with its far larger population, greater agricultural resources, and huge army was much better positioned than Britain to dominate Europe. "For all this," comments Kennedy, "the English system possessed key advantages in the financial realm which enhanced the country's power in wartime and buttressed its political stability and economic growth in peacetime."[9] In the series of wars between 1688 and 1815, Britain spent £2.3 million—a massive sum at that time—on its war efforts and was able to finance a third of that in London's sophisticated money markets.

The efficiency and reliability of London's financial markets enabled the City to put Britain's surplus capital to work around the world as the empire progressed to its zenith in the nineteenth century. In 1832, Nathan Rothschild—scion of the legendary Frankfurt family of financiers, who established a merchant bank in London that still bears his name—could boast that trade bills drawn on London financed trade that never neared British shores, and that "this country in general is the Bank for the whole world . . . all transactions in India, in China, in Germany, in Russia, and in the whole world, are all guided here and settled through this country."[10]

London's dominance in international finance preceded Britain's rise to imperial power, and has survived the country's postwar decline. As Hamish McRae and Frances Cairncross observe,

On most measures, the City of London is the world's leading international financial center. More international insurance passes through London than anywhere else. There are more foreign banks in London than in any other city. More international security business is done in London than any other center. If anything, in the 1960s and 1970s London's dominance increased. The City established itself as the center first of the new eurodollar market; and then of banking's greatest growth area, international medium-term lending. In the 1980s it became the main center for international equity trading. . . .[11]

This ascendancy is not necessarily the result of a particular English genius for finance, but of a cumulative expertise and tradition built up over centuries in this particular place. As McRae and Cairncross point out, all but one of the top fifteen merchant, or investment, banks in London were founded by immigrants, and that one "native" bank bears the name of a Scot (Robert Fleming). The most innovative and influential financier in London in the postwar period was Siegmund Warburg, member of a German Jewish banking family who fled Hitler's Germany in 1934 and started a new bank from scratch in London. It is likely that Siegmund, who was knighted and whose bank is still one of the leading forces in London, was one of the brightest Warburgs ever to go into banking, but it is worth noting that while S.G. Warburg and Co. flourished in London, the Warburg bank in Hamburg, once the family regained it after the war, could not gain the same prominence in Germany's more regimented market. In fact, it is improbable that Siegmund Warburg could have achieved the same degree of success in Germany that he did in London. Rather, the institutional framework in the City enabled his genius to attain its full potential.

When other European financial centers talk of "competing" with London, it is only in a relative sense. Each national center—Frankfurt, Paris, Milan—means to say it is competing with London *for its own national business*. London's system of computer screen-trading for international equities claims to handle up to one-half of all trading in French and Italian shares and one-third of German shares. Attempts to modernize and streamline the stock exchanges in the other financial centers are a defensive measure to keep from losing more of their own business to London. But none of them can pretend to rival London in foreign equities trading.

Because of the strength of the German currency and the size of the Germany economy, Frankfurt, the main German financial center, sometimes is seen as a serious contender to be the leading European financial center. And yet, when Deutsche Bank, Germany's leading commercial bank and one of the strongest financial institutions in the world, wanted to develop its corporate finance business, it was obliged to pay nearly $2 *billion* in 1989 to buy the London merchant bank Morgan Grenfell. The chief executive of Morgan Grenfell took a seat on the bank's main executive board, but remained in London. So towering is London's lead in corporate finance that all of Deutsche Bank's mergers and acquisitions staff in Germany were required to report to London.

In fact, just as Germany was long described as an economic giant but a political dwarf, it could equally be portrayed as an industrial giant but a financial dwarf, given the underdevelopment of its markets and financial institutions. London's superiority rests on the tradition of disclosure and accountability in the markets that are lacking in Frankfurt, as they are in most other European centers and in Tokyo as well. Like Tokyo, which has become a leading global financial center by virtue of Japan's huge surpluses in international trade and capital flows rather than any overwhelming skill in financial transactions, Frankfurt has considerable monetary muscle, but is kept by a lack of transparency and anticompetitive practices from becoming a truly international marketplace.

Germany managed only late in 1992 to centralize stock market trading in Frankfurt, finally overcoming the resistance of regional stock exchanges, who jealously guarded their market share and made securities trading in Germany more inefficient than it needed to be. But even if the centralized stock exchange develops a state-of-the-art clearance and settlements system (in painful contrast to London, where a costly effort failed), Germany still lacks the culture of individual stock market investment and institutional money management that supports London's liquid and efficient market.

Aside from tradition and history, London outdistances any conceivable European competitors in sheer size. Richard Brealey, a professor at the London Business School who conducted a survey of London's characteristics as a financial center for City authorities, pointed out that 600,000 people work in financial services in London—a number equal to the *total* population of Frankfurt!

The Financial Power of London

The amount of money handled in London is mind-boggling. Currency trading forms the biggest market in the world, with daily transactions amounting to an estimated $1 *trillion* in 1992. (The New York Stock Exchange, by way of comparison, has an average daily volume of about $12 billion.) Nearly one-third of those daily foreign exchange trades, or $300 billion, was attributed to London, the leading center for currency trading, followed by New York with $192 billion and Tokyo with $128 billion—these figures, based on central bank estimates, are obviously approximate, but indicate the relative market share of the leading centers.

London also remains the center of the Eurodollar market, or Eurocurrency market as it is often called now to reflect the rise of other currencies in this global market for offshore deposits and loans. A Eurodollar, or Eurocurrency, is simply money deposited outside its country of origin. This free-floating pool of liquidity was estimated at $6 trillion to $7 trillion at the beginning of the 1990s. The lowering of obstacles to cross-border financial transactions in the course of the 1980s led to closer links between domestic financial markets and made the offshore market relatively less important. Nonetheless, it is obviously still a big business for the banks involved and an important source of finance for institutional borrowers throughout the world.

The practice in Britain of vesting corporate pensions has made the money management business there the most significant in Europe. Corporate pension plans in other countries, to the extent they exist, usually take the form of liabilities on the company balance sheet rather than real funds set aside for investment. In Britain, as in the United States, pension funds represent a large proportion of the money under institutional management. The pressure on institutional investors to turn in a good performance also contributes to making securities markets more liquid and efficient. Because London has a culture of money management, many American and Japanese investment specialists have located offices there to manage European portfolios.

London also leads the continent in the most glamorous financial activity, mergers and acquisitions. Although New York, especially with the rise of leveraged transactions and junk-bond financing in the 1980s, holds all the records in the size of such deals, London's corporate finance specialists are just as professional and sophisticated. After the large sell-off of Britain's state-owned institutions in the Thatcher years, London's merchant banks have become world specialists in privatization and took an early lead in advising the emerging democracies in eastern Europe on how to transfer large nationalized industries into the private sector.

Some scandals in recent years have tarnished London's reputation. Critics have faulted the Bank of England for not catching on sooner to the criminal activities of Bank of Commerce and Credit International, which authorities closed in 1991, with the result that thousands of honest depositors lost billions of dollars. Media tycoon Robert Maxwell allegedly pilfered the pensions funds of his London companies of nearly half a billion dollars prior to his apparent suicide in 1991, robbing thousands of employees of their planned retirement benefits. The wealthy individuals who provide Lloyd's of London with its capital have been deserting the three-centuries-old insurance exchange after bad luck and possible fraud rendered it a far less attractive investment, casting some doubt on the institution's long-term survival, at least in its present form.

But London has hardly been alone. New York was rocked by its insider trading scandals, culminating in the conviction of junk-bond supremo Michael Milken and the closure of Drexel Burnham Lambert, one of Wall Street's leading firms. Even Frankfurt had an embarrassing insider trading scandal, touching all of the big banks. Germany, alone among major industrial countries, has no law against insider trading, but the abuses constituted such an ethical violation they could not be ignored.

London relied traditionally on self-regulation among banks and brokers, combined with the legendary "nods and winks" from the Bank of England, to maintain its ethical standards. Adapting to the growth of the market, the City has now implemented an extensive system of regulatory boards—so extensive it is criticized as clumsy and unwieldy—and is working to find the right balance between flexibility and control to ensure a smooth and fair functioning of financial markets.

Canary Wharf

The saga of a spectacular real estate failure shows how uncertain are the rewards of serving Mammon, however, and stands as a cautionary tale for London's financial district.

With its gleaming marble plazas, its massive granite skyscrapers, its glittering storefronts, Canary Wharf was an impressive place as it neared completion in 1992. But it was disconcertingly empty, not so much like a ghost town as an amusement park prior to opening day. The Canary Wharf Tower on One Canada Place rose majestically from the complex of twenty-six new buildings, some still under construction, beckoning to the City of London two and a half miles westward across the Thames.

But the City of London was staying where it was. Even if it wanted to come to the spanking new development in London's Docklands, there was no way for it to get there. In the euphoria of mounting the project in the latter half of the 1980s, the developers and local authorities had unwisely neglected to build the roads and subway lines connecting the business center to the rest of the city. When other problems deflated the euphoria, Canary Wharf stood on the Thames, cut off from the world, a financial crisis in its own right rather than the grand financial center envisioned by its backers.

As an unparalleled example of hubris, Canary Wharf is perhaps a fitting symbol of the financial excess of the 1980s. After the last vestiges of London's port activities were moved farther downstream to sites more appropriate for modern shipping, the London Docklands Development Corporation was launched in 1981 to transform the area in eastern London into an office and residential complex to balance the city's other business centers in the City and the West End. At the same time, the rapidly expanding financial services industry in London was feeling the need for more space. Located in the narrow and expensive confines of the Square Mile—the traditional financial district corresponding more or less to the original Roman town of Londinium—the burgeoning finance industry, profiting from deregulation and growth in international markets, was blocked from expansion by restrictive building codes. The prospect of millions of square feet of brand-new office space, custom-designed for the high technological requirements of global finance, appealed to many of the bigger institutions, especially American giants like Morgan Stanley and First Boston.

In 1987, a year after London's much-touted Big Bang streamlined and deregulated securities trading and financial institutions embarked on an investment binge to take advantage of it, Olympia and York, a closely held company based in Toronto and one of the biggest real estate developers in the world, decided to take on the Canary Wharf project as the main office development in the Docklands. Riding the success of its World Financial Center venture in lower Manhattan and believing too much itself in the mystique of infallibility the secretive company had cultivated, Olympia and York decided to undertake the project all by itself, not sharing any of the potential profit, or potential risk, with partners, and not even lining up a bank consortium to finance it.

But the City of London retaliated to keep financial institutions from leaving, easing the building codes and approving long-delayed projects for new office space. In the meantime, the Big Bang expansion gave way to a severe consolidation, costing tens of thousands of jobs and forcing many marginal players to withdraw. One-fifth of the office space in the City, more than 14 million square feet, was vacant as the finishing touches were going on Canary Wharf's 4.5 million square feet.

The worldwide property slump and the decline in bank liquidity at the beginning of the 1990s made it increasingly difficult for the real estate developer to get the financing it needed. In early 1992, 40 percent of Canary Wharf was not yet rented, and far less than half of the finished space was actually occupied. Banks began to balk at new loans for the project and several urgent financings fell through. By spring, Olympia and York had to seek court protection for the Canary Wharf project.

Just as the binge of bank lending to Third World countries in the 1970s led to the global debt crisis of the early 1980s, the worldwide real estate spree in the 1980s threatened serious consequences for banks everywhere at the beginning of the 1990s. The Canary Wharf saga captured it all too well—a spectacular real estate flop in one of the world's leading financial centers. Someday, somebody will probably make a lot of money on Canary Wharf—it *is* an impressive place—but it almost certainly will not be the Reichmann family, who brought their company Olympia and York to the brink of bankruptcy because they got caught up in the decade's excesses. For

London itself, the whole affair may end well once things are sorted out, because it will have a large quantity of moderately priced office space for future expansion of financial services.

Banking on Europe

In late October 1989, just days before the Berlin Wall fell, French president Francois Mitterrand suggested in a speech to the European Parliament in Strasbourg that a new multilateral development bank should be established to help eastern Europe recover from the decades of communist rule. The idea came from Mitterrand's adviser Jacques Attali, a controversial polymath who occupied the office next to the French president from the time Mitterrand moved into the Elysee Palace in 1981. Just seven months later, in May 1990, forty countries signed in Paris the statutes creating the European Bank for Reconstruction and Development.

The twelve EC countries held 51 percent of the new institution, but shareholders also included the former communist countries in eastern Europe and the Soviet Union, as well as other major industrialized and developing countries, from the United States to South Korea. Some critics questioned the need for another development agency, arguing that the World Bank and the European Investment Bank between them should be able to provide sufficient aid to eastern Europe. But Mitterrand and Attali felt that a specialized institution would be more effective and could accumulate experience in handling the unique transition from centrally planned to market economies. Moreover, Attali thought it was important to have the east European countries participate as shareholders—most of them did not belong to the World Bank and International Monetary Fund at that time. He saw the new institution as a forerunner of broader European-wide organizations, much like the European Coal and Steel Community was the precursor of the European Economic Community.

There was the usual scramble among the shareholders to secure the headquarters in their country, or to have one of their nationals take charge of the new bank. London was particularly keen to have the EBRD located in the City, and even persuaded prime minister Margaret Thatcher, who otherwise disliked European institutions and visionary Frenchmen, to lobby for bringing the bank to London.

The Netherlands pushed both for the headquarters and chief executive, proposing Amsterdam as the site. But Paris and London struck a deal to support each other in designating London as headquarters and Jacques Attali as director. This tandem won approval from the shareholders, despite bitter recriminations from the Dutch and their allies. (Attali's opponents may have derived some satisfaction from his forced departure in 1993 for excessive spending, but another Frenchman, Jacques de Larosiere, was appointed to take Attali's place.)

The glossy trilingual brochure that London produced to argue its case not only tallied the many attributes of the City as financial center, but went so far as to note that London has a Baltic Street, a Poland Street, and a Moscow Road, and to picture a "native Polish restaurant" called Wodka. Some of the East European shareholders would have preferred a site closer to the region, like Vienna, but Attali countered that the London location would enable the new bank to draw on the high-powered financiers in the City and was closer to the markets where the EBRD would seek the financing for its projects.

The Treaty of Maastricht launched a new competition among financial centers, this time to land the proposed European Central Bank. The first stage of such an institution, a European Monetary Institute, was to start work already in 1994, to help achieve full monetary union by the end of the century, at which time it would become the common central bank responsible for Europe's single currency. London again leaped into the fray, as did Amsterdam, along with Frankfurt, Luxembourg, and Lyons.

The question of where to locate the ECB risked becoming academic as monetary union itself grew more problematic. France, willing to do anything to move beyond the existing situation which subordinated the French franc to the deutsche mark and French monetary policy to that of the Bundesbank, was ready to locate the ECB in Germany. The paramount consideration for the French was to obtain a voice in the conduct of monetary policy. In the case that Germany and France proceeded to monetary union on their own, perhaps together with the Benelux countries, Britain's objections to a German location would no longer be considered.

The location of the central bank itself, however, is not decisive for making a financial center. The U.S. central bank, the Federal Reserve Board, is located in Washington, but New York, obviously, remains the country's financial center. The Italian central bank is located in Rome, where it enjoys a hard-won reputation for independence despite its proximity to the national government, but Milan remains the country's banking and financial center. The presence of a European Central Bank in Frankfurt would help the city rise above its exclusively regional role, but could not change the course of history except in the very long term. London would remain the dominant financial center in Europe for many decades.

A European Vocation

In spring 1993, Pasqual Maragall, the mayor of Barcelona widely acclaimed for his program of urban renewal in the Catalan capital, was invited to London to offer his comments on the city's quality of life. Maragall deplored the squalor of the South Bank and regretted the emptiness of Canary Wharf, but could not help marveling at the royal parks and Buckingham palace, reminders of Britain's imperial power and splendor. "When I see all this, I think, God it's beautiful. It is the summit of humanity, but I also think, how unfair. Why is that it is always capital cities that have the wealth of the nations to spend on themselves? What will happen to London when it is not the capital of a sovereign state, when the real nation is Europe?"[12]

Such remarks are like a red cape in the eyes of Tory backbenchers determined to prevent just such a European eventuality. But the very difficulty of contemporary London in matching its nineteenth-century achievements shows how much its "capital" role has already waned. Not by chance, the two new developments Maragall admired the most were Canary Wharf, the would-be extension of the financial district, and the international terminal at Victoria Station designed for the high-speed trains arriving from Paris via the Eurotunnel (which also has become something of a white elephant after the fast trains were rerouted to a more northerly course).

Despite the problems of organization and timing evidenced by these two projects, the import is clear: The future of London, like that of Paris and other national capitals, lies in its European vocation. London with its financial expertise and Paris with its political genius will have special roles in a united Europe and will continue to develop as the continent's two global metropolises.

CHAPTER NINE

ALPINE ARC: THE MICROCLIMATE

Alpine Arc, the smallest and least populous of the superregions, depends the most on geography for its definition. It is unquestionably a region in its own right. The peculiar culture and economy of the region represent in distilled and pure form the interaction of society and geography.

Experts collaborating on a 1991 book, *The Real World*, which advocates a new approach to geography, consider the region a microcosm of the real world, exemplary of the concepts that modern geographers use as their paradigms. They see a region centered on Switzerland, but extending roughly from Stuttgart and Munich through Zurich, to Milan in the south and Lyons in the west as the "business heart of the new Europe, the center of the richest area"—an area that roughly corresponds to the Alpine Arc superregion.[1]

The Real World sums it up as follows: "Switzerland owes its existence to the Alps, the great arc of mountains that separates Mediterranean Italy from cooler, wetter northern Europe. . . . The Swiss have entered into a dynamic partnership with their geography. They have been challenged and changed by it—and in the process once again have subtly changed themselves."[2] Although great respecters of the environment, the Swiss have not hesitated to modify it for their own purposes, canalizing the Rhone River to prevent flooding, damming other waterways for hydroelectric energy, building roads and boring tunnels to improve access to the outside world.

The Alpine Arc superregion follows the broad curve of mountains across Europe. It takes in more than Switzerland, though it does not include the Alpine ranges in their extremities. Beginning at Valence, on the Rhone River south of Lyons, the Alpine Arc border shadows the Alpine foothills in a northeasterly curve, following the line of the Jura Mountains to the west of Geneva, south of Basel, north of Zurich to Munich. From there, it follows the shared border with Danube Basin southeast to Klagenfurt, in southern Austria, along the path of the Tauern highway between Salzburg and Klagenfurt. There it turns southwest, along the edge of the Alpine range, through Trent in a line to Milan, where it heads west and slightly south, north of Turin, across the mountains, south of Grenoble, back to Valence.

So Alpine Arc includes a small corner of eastern France, virtually all of Switzerland except the Basel region, a wedge of southern Germany, the western third of Austria, and part of northern Italy. Its residents number about 14 million.

A Mountain Society

The Swiss historically have been at the crossroads of Europe. Controlling the mountain passes essential for trade between Italy and northern Europe led to a flourishing service sector specializing, as *The Real World* authors put it, in "guides, guards, carriers, and accommodation." To this day, some of the best schools and strictest standards in hotel management are Swiss; one of the biggest European travel agencies, Kuoni, is Swiss; the Swiss national airline, Swissair, is not only one of the biggest in the world but consistently ranks as one of the top airlines in surveys of business travelers; the Swiss guards at the Vatican hark back to a long mercenary tradition that now also takes more modern forms like providing trained customs officers and surveillance personnel for countries around the world.

Banking and financial services also grew out of this crossroads function, although in recent times the mountain fastness and political neutrality of the Swiss banking industry have made it a specialist of dubious ethics—harboring the money not only of Jews fleeing Nazi persecution, but also of Nazi leaders who hedged their bets about the Third Reich's lasting a thousand years; taking large cash deposits from French and Italian residents across the border who are eager to evade taxes; stashing away billions of dollars of diverted public monies from corrupt Third World dictators like Marcos of the Philippines, Duvalier of Haiti, and Mobutu of Zaire; and laundering the large cash flows of illegal organizations.

The mountainous terrain has determined the rest of the Swiss economy as well. Isolation encouraged the famous watch industry and the manufacture of other precision tools and instruments as cottage industries among peasants in the mountain valleys, who thus kept their hands busy during the long winter months. Agriculture took the form of dairy farming that led not only to Swiss cheese, but to condensed milk and milk chocolate. Again, though, the Swiss seem to prosper through practices that meet ethical opposition elsewhere—Nestle has faced long periods of boycott for its marketing of infant formula in poor Third World countries, and the big Swiss pharmaceutical firms often come under attack by animal rights groups in campaigns against experimentation with animals.

The Swiss have a talent for arousing visceral enmity, particularly, it seems, in literary types. In a veritable frenzy of animadversion, D. H. Lawrence lashed out at the Swiss. On a walking tour to Italy before World War I, Lawrence wrote: "There is something very dead about this country. . . . [T]here was mile after mile of dead, uninspired country—uninspired, so neutral and ordinary that it was almost destructive. One gets this feeling always in Switzerland, except high up: this feeling of average, of utter soulless ordinariness, something intolerable." Zurich, too, was "soul-killing," and the young Englishman quickly hopped a lake steamer to take him away. On the other bank, he wound up in a "very rough inn" where the only meal was boiled ham. "[S]o I ate boiled ham and drank beer, and tried to digest the utter cold materialism of Switzerland." The evening was saved by the appearance of a group of Italians who lived nearby. Their bright, gay banter only made the Swiss customers, who "smoked on and talked in their ugly dialect," seem coarser.[3]

Just after World War II, a film, *The Third Man,* scripted by British novelist Graham Greene, had Orson Welles drawing another comparison between Italians and Swiss, blaming the boring nature of the latter for their lack of cultural achievement. Welles' Harry Lime character concludes a memorable scene in Vienna's Prater amusement park by observing: "In Italy for thirty years under the Borgias they had terror, murder, bloodshed—but they produced Michelangelo, Leonardo da Vinci and the Renaissance. In Switzerland, they have brotherly love, five hundred years of peace and democracy, and what did they produce? The cuckoo clock."

Of course, millions of visitors who have come to Switzerland on vacation have had a somewhat more positive impression than Lawrence did, and cherish precisely the tranquility that Welles so deplores; many of them buy a cuckoo clock as a souvenir. Prosperity, which is relatively recent in Switzerland, has probably made the Swiss more pleasant and amenable, and even more cultured. It is difficult to picture the Switzerland Lawrence encountered, accustomed as we are to the country's wealth nowadays. University of Grenoble economist Claude Courlet recalls, though, that Switzerland before World War I had a lower per capita income than Argentina. World War II, when Switzerland remained neutral, marked the turning point in its fortunes.

No one would actually refer to the Swiss as hillbillies, but some of their customs are so backward that they would be considered reactionary in an American or West European context. Women were finally allowed to vote only in 1971, and some cantons enforced laws against men and women living together outside of wedlock well into the 1980s. The thinly populated mountain regions never developed big cities, and the country's tradition of peasant democracy made it one of the few nations in Europe never to have an aristocracy. As a result, Switzerland missed out on the two main sources of intellectual and political enlightenment on the continent.

The Swiss Canton

These same geographical facts have contributed to a tradition of decentralization. Small settlements separated by lofty peaks hindered the development of a larger political unit with a strong central authority.

Celtic tribes, notably one called the Helvetii, occupied the Alpine lands until the Romans conquered the territory just prior to the Christian era. The Latin name for the region, Helvetia, survives in the official name of the country, Confederatio Helvetica, giving the CH abbreviation for its postal codes and auto emblems. As Roman rule waned, German tribes trickled into the mountain valleys, Alamani and Burgundians in particular. The Franks incorporated these tribal territories in their empire, and they remained part of it as the Holy Roman Empire evolved. But control was diffuse; geography kept manageable territories quite small.

The Swiss Confederation was born in 1291 when three forest districts, or cantons, in the Alps—Schwyz (which gives its name to Switzerland), Uri (home of William Tell), and Unterwalden—formed a league to oppose Habsburg rule. Although the confederation remained part of the Holy Roman Empire until the seventeenth century, the cantons, growing steadily in number as new mountain regions joined, fought ferociously to preserve their autonomy. Napoleon briefly held Switzerland, recasting it as the Helvetic Republic, but after his defeat the country was granted its independence and perpetual neutrality by the Congress of Vienna, becoming a small zone of silence in the Concert of Europe.

The Swiss model of confederation, a loose association of cantons with wide-ranging autonomy, permitting peoples of four different languages to live together peacefully over centuries and develop a common culture of sorts, appeals to many as a solution for unity in Europe as a whole. The Swiss cantons have practiced "subsidiarity"—the watchword in Brussels for maximum devolution of power—with a vengeance since their founding. Political decisions are taken at the lowest level practicable; town and canton governments leave as little as possible for the federal government to do, and resent even that.

Military preparedness remains one of the hallmarks of Swiss neutrality, heir to a long history of siege mentality resulting from the ambitions of powerful neighbors surrounding the landlocked mountain fortress. In modern times, the mountains are honeycombed with jet hangars and missile silos. All Swiss men perform military service and remain reservists until the age of fifty, taking part in annual training exercises. In most banks and companies, there is a double hierarchy among executives—one for their titles and roles in the enterprise, and the other taking account of their military rank.

Switzerland has a policy of building nuclear shelters, with the goal of having one for every inhabitant by the year 2000. It is no coincidence that the most widespread artifact of Swiss culture, combining this military tradition with instrumental precision, is the Swiss Army knife.

This obsession with independence—two of the leaders of the Reformation, Zwingli and Calvin, were based in Zurich and Geneva—has taken a curious turn recently: The country has started to attract a new type of "independent" central management for multinational companies. One pioneer was Asea Brown Boveri, an international company formed by the merger of two giant machinery and power plant makers from Sweden and Switzerland. The innovative Swedish chief executive, Percy Barnevik, located the headquarters of the merged company in Zurich, but set it up as a small, lean coordination center rather than a large bureaucracy with direct responsibility for the network of operating subsidiaries. General Motors followed ABB's lead and in 1986 located its European headquarters in Zurich, on the same model. The innovation met with such success that in 1992 Detroit made John F. Smith, Jr., the former head of the Zurich subsidiary and architect of the company's turnaround in Europe, president and then chief executive of the parent company in a desperate scramble to stem heavy losses in its American operations.

But if ardent independence is one aspect of Swiss character, the other is an equally determined faithfulness to one's comrades. This is the basis of confederation, appearing even more clearly in the German designation of Switzerland as an "oath-fellowship" (*Eidgenossenschaft*), whose citizens are "oath-comrades." Michel Albert, the French insurance manager who prefers Rhineland capitalism to the Anglo-Saxon variety, believes this Alpine mentality has had a profound impact on insurance. Here it is undertaken to spread, or "mutualize," risk out of solidarity with the community. Anglo-Saxon insurance, following the maritime tradition born in Venice and continued in London, "tends on the contrary to dilute solidarity through the precariousness of contracts."[4] Thus, he notes, European countries following the mutualist tradition have a mandatory uniform auto liability insurance, whereas those following the Anglo-Saxon tradition leave these rates entirely free, allowing a segmentation of the market that favors some customers at the expense of others. "It's not by chance," Albert continues, "that the reinsurance industry—an activity that requires a maximum of security and continuity—has chosen as its capital two cities of the Alps, Munich and Zurich,'' home of the two biggest reinsurance firms, Munich Re and Swiss Re.[5] Albert contrasts the success of the mutualist, Alpine approach with the crisis of the maritime tradition, aiming to provide short-term profit to the individual investor, as exemplified by the difficulties at Lloyd's, the London insurance market where poor risk judgment has damaged its credibility and viability.

Crossing the Alps

The completion of the Simplon Tunnel in southwest Switzerland in 1905 enabled the Orient Express, the legendary luxury train that connected Paris to Constantinople, to develop an alternate route through the Alps to complement the original line via Munich and the Danube basin. The ravages of war and politics soon made the Simplon route via Milan and Venice the preferable one for the train, such a powerful symbol in its time of European integration. It was the Simplon Orient Express that James Bond rode in *From Russia With Love,* and that in real life made its final scheduled run in May 1977; the revived package-tour Orient Express also took this route in the 1980s.

Since time immemorial, the Alps have been both a barrier and a bridge between northwestern Europe and the southern Italian and Balkan peninsulas. The mountains, divided into seventeen major ranges, run in a crescent 660 miles long from the French Mediterranean coast into present-day Slovenia and north nearly to Vienna. There are thirty-four road passes above an altitude of 3,300 feet, including the Brenner, the Great Saint Bernhard, and the Saint Gotthard passes as well as the Simplon. The Mont Cenis pass between Savoy in France and Piedmont in Italy may have been the one used by Hannibal when he crossed the Alps in the third century B.C. to invade Italy. Napoleon constructed the first carriage road across the pass at the beginning of the nineteenth century, and the Mont Cenis Tunnel, opened in 1871, was the first of the great tunnels through the Alps. The Simplon Tunnel, at 12½ miles, is the longest.

But not for much longer. In September 1992, Swiss voters approved a massive project to dig two new rail tunnels, one of 17½ miles at Lotschberg, just west of the Simplon Tunnel, south of Bern, and another of 30½ miles at the Saint Gotthard pass, farther east, on the line from Zurich to Lugano. The two tunnels, along with feeder lines requiring smaller tunnels, are budgeted to cost $11.5 billion; but with inflation, add-ons, and financing costs that figure is expected to double before the construction is completed in 2015. There is already a 9½-mile rail tunnel at Gotthard, built in the nineteenth century, but the new one will be at a lower elevation, avoiding the slow climb up and down the mountain to the present one.

Above all, the tunnels are designed to increase freight capacity transiting Switzerland from 20 million tons to 70 million tons. The Swiss were under severe pressure from their European neighbors to do something. The vote on the new rail tunnels was unofficially linked to Swiss participation in the European Economic Area and later EC membership; the surprisingly positive result, with two-thirds voting for the tunnels, was taken as a sign of strong Swiss feeling in favor of taking part in European integration.

To protect the Alpine environment, the Swiss had banned the big forty-ton trailer trucks from Swiss roads, setting a maximum of twenty-eight tons. They wanted the bigger trailers to be loaded onto trains for the trip through the Alps. But existing rail capacity was not sufficient to meet the rapid increase in intra-EC trade between Greece and Italy in the south and the rest of the EC members on the other side of the Alps. As a result, much traffic was diverted to Austria and France, who resented the Swiss stubbornness.

This transit role, an advantage in earlier times of slower travel, has become increasingly onerous for Switzerland. Travelers on modern express highways do not often stop overnight on their way through tiny Switzerland, and provide little income for local hotels, restaurants, and shops. Transit goods are not made in Switzerland or sold there, but exclusively benefit other countries while their passage through the country pollutes the Swiss environment with noise, noxious gases, and congestion, particularly from truck transport. The Swiss will finance the new tunnels while their neighbors will invest in new facilities for loading and unloading truck trailers onto trains. In general, such combination transport is seen throughout Europe as the best possible solution to highway congestion.

After decades of avoiding any foreign entanglements—the Swiss never joined the United Nations, even though some U.N. agencies are located in Geneva—Switzerland seemed ready to adapt to the late twentieth century and take part in more international organizations. But it showed little sign of becoming less prickly about its prerogatives. Switzerland's obdurate resistance on the tonnage limit for trucks nearly torpedoed the EEA negotiations in 1991. When Switzerland finally joined the International Monetary Fund and World Bank in 1992, it immediately insisted on having a seat on the board, even if that meant displacing some Third World members. As in the case of the trucks, it was difficult to oppose the Swiss on the validity of their argument—the Swiss franc is one of the strongest currencies in the world—but such unyielding singlemindedness is rare among nations more accustomed to the give and take of international relations.

The "Alpine Furrow"

The Swiss are not the only ones in the region with a reputation for independence. Neighboring territories in France and Italy demonstrate some of the same rugged qualities.

Grenoble nestles in an Alpine valley, surrounded by tall peaks. With 400,000 people in the city and suburbs, it is a mountain metropolis, capital of the French Alps, and one of the largest cities actually in the mountains. The site of the 1968 Winter Olympics, Grenoble has become a magnet for high-technology industry, the southern terminus for the *sillon alpin*, "Alpine furrow," of manufacturing and research that extends northward to Geneva. A clean, comfortable town with crisp air and overcast skies, Grenoble has been designated as one of four government-sponsored "poles of attraction" in France—the others are Strasbourg, Toulouse, and Orsay, a Paris suburb—benefiting from special incentives to lure high-tech industry.

The cradle of hydroelectric energy, baptized "white coal" after the melting snow that produced it, the *sillon alpin* has become a center for nuclear research since Nobel Prize–winning physicist Louis Neel left German-occupied Strasbourg during the war to continue his research in Grenoble. In 1956, the French government established the Grenoble Center for Nuclear Research, which now employs 2,000 people. The Laue-Langevin Institute, founded in 1967 as a joint project by France and Germany and since joined by Britain and Spain, has one of the world's most powerful neutron generators. The number of scientific and research establishments in the region has snowballed since then, with more than 30,000 new firms coming to the Isere district surrounding Grenoble in the ten years to 1992, many of them in electronics and computer technology. The European Synchotron Research Facility, due to open in 1994 in Grenoble, represents an investment of half a billion dollars and will be the world's biggest source of X-rays. Grenoble researchers participate not only in EC research programs like Eureka, which sponsors cutting-edge projects promising innovative breakthroughs, and Esprit, supporting efforts in industrial computer applications, but also in specialized projects on artificial intelligence, telecommunications, composite materials, and new manufacturing technologies.

Grenoble is home to Europe's largest software engineering firm, Cap Gemini Sogeti, and the European research center for Open Software Foundation, a joint venture of IBM and other global producers to develop interface software. It was a Grenoble firm, Aptor, that engineered the software and communications network for the interconnected technology of the Grande Arche in Paris, regulating everything from electricity supply, to air-conditioning, to door opening and alarm systems, over the 1.1 million square feet of the massive structure, site of the 1991 summit of the G-7 industrial countries.

Farther up the "furrow," in Annecy, France's National Center for Scientific Research has another facility for nuclear experimentation. And it was at CERN, the European Laboratory for Particle Physics in Geneva, that the winner of the 1992 Nobel Prize in Physics, Georges Charpak, a Polish-born French citizen, developed the particle detector cited in the award. His multiwire proportional chamber had enabled some CERN colleagues to win the 1984 Nobel Prize for research on the innermost structure of matter.

This western corner of the Alps never joined the Swiss Confederation—except for Geneva itself in 1815—but has displayed the same strain of independence throughout its history. At the beginning of the fifteenth century, Savoy, under Duke Amadeus VIII, was a considerable power, and the court at Chambery one of the finest in Europe. The Savoy region, which grew to embrace Piedmont in Italy, remained independent until 1858, when the Italians, rather than incorporate it into the kingdom of Italy being formed, offered it to the French as a reward for helping them repulse the Austrians; the Savoyards assented to the transfer in a plebiscite.

Another historic province, the Dauphine, taking in Grenoble and Valence in the south, came under the French crown by the fourteenth century, when its leader, destitute after taking part in the Crusades, sold it to Philip VI. The territory became a perquisite for the heir to the throne, who henceforth bore the title of Dauphin, much like the heir to the British throne automatically becomes the Prince of Wales. Nonetheless, the territory was among the first to rebel against royal authority in the prelude to the French Revolution. Grenoble's resistance to infringement of local authority, culminating in an attack on the city in June 1788 that the citizens repelled by hurling roof tiles at the soldiers, marks for many French historians the first violent clash of the Revolution.

History and geography both have worked against the Paris-devised region of Rhone-Alpes, which combines the Alpine furrow and the Rhone corridor even though these regions have no tradition of cooperation together. The French government wants to reinforce the link between Lyons and Grenoble to consolidate the region, but Grenoble generally has greater affinity for the mountain valley to the northeast. The Grenoble district and the two *departments* of Savoy decided at the beginning of the 1990s to launch a 5,000-acre industrial park southeast of Chambery, strengthening the axis of development between Grenoble and Geneva. In 1992, Annecy and Chambery announced a wide-ranging cooperation between the two cities in communications, urban development, business, education, and culture. The two cities also want to lobby together for a TGV line running the length the *sillon* from Geneva to Valence.

Grenoble economist Jean-Paul Laurencin sees all this fitting into a centrifugal scenario for the French region as European integration progresses. "A cross-border scenario establishes the dominance of centrifugal forces tending to accentuate the frontier dimension of the region with a brisk development of synergies with the border regions, Geneva in Switzerland and Piedmont in Italy," he writes in a book on the future of Rhone-Alpes.[6] Regional cohesion is too feeble for Lyons to exert any attraction on the Alpine territory. Lyons seems too firmly embedded in its north-south axis along the Rhone, like Grenoble in the *sillon,* for the east-west connection between them to function well, this economist suggests, even though the national government continues to pursue its program of amalgamating the region into a working whole. The mountains marking the boundary of the Alpine Arc superregion seem to have more influence than the decisions of Paris bureaucrats, however.

"Austrians in Italy"

In 1959, Bruno Kreisky, the longtime chancellor of Austria who at that time was foreign minister, told the United Nations that Austria was unhappy with the way Italy was treating ethnic Austrians in South Tirol, a region on the border between the two countries. His action came forty years after South Tirol was annexed by Italy as a reward for entering World War I on the side of the Allies against Germany and Austria-Hungary. But it was only thirty-three years after Kreisky's appeal, in 1992, that the dispute between Austria and Italy was finally settled. Kreisky intervened because the Treaty of Paris following World War II, when Italy was on the losing side, had appointed Austria as protector of the national rights of German speakers in South Tirol. Mussolini had brutally suppressed all manifestations of German language and culture in the region, and settled many southern Italians there to dilute the ethnic makeup of the region. Hitler conceded Mussolini's right to keep the territory, historically a part of Austria, but in 1939 offered ethnic Austrians the possibility of migrating to Germany. The majority of South Tiroleans were ready to do so, but the outbreak of war cut short the resettlements.

Although Italy agreed after World War II to restore the region's linguistic and cultural autonomy, they dragged their feet in implementing reforms. Also, they lumped South Tirol together with the neighboring Italian province of Trentino, and said autonomy applied to the combined region, which now had a majority of Italian speakers. This made the Tiroleans suspicious that Rome might revoke its concessions whenever it wanted, and prompted the province to insist on international recognition of its autonomous rights. When communism collapsed in eastern Europe, as Yugoslavian republics began declaring their independence and Germany sought reunification, there was new talk in Bozen, the capital of South Tirol, that the province should perhaps seek full independence from Italy or reunification with the other Tirolean provinces, which remained in Austria. The Italian government quickly acceded to Tirolean demands on autonomy and Austria formally dropped its complaint at the U.N.

Even so, Tiroleans still discuss the notion of a cross-border "European region" with their erstwhile compatriots. Tirol, like other

Alpine regions, has a tradition of fierce independence. In the sixteenth century, when Tirol was part of the Habsburg empire, it was the scene of a peasant uprising. And in the nineteenth century, when Napoleon won control of the region and attached it to Bavaria, the Tiroleans revolted.

Beyond the narrow confines of Tirol itself, though, the Alpine influence extends into northern Italy, at least as far as Milan. While the northern Adriatic coast has a nostalgia for the Habsburgs, Milan and Lombardy, and even Piedmont identify more readily with the efficiency and reliability of the Alpine regions. *The New Yorker* writer Jane Kramer reports that many Milanese, disaffected with the corruption that was so typically "Italian," prefer to say that they are "Austrians in Italy" or "Swiss in Italy."[7] A corruption scandal in the Milan city government, implicating many high-ranking local politicians, indicated they were perhaps more "Italian" than they realized. Still, Vittorio Feltri, who runs the *Independente* newspaper in Milan that champions northern separatism, told Kramer that Italy is "a country in name only," that "the south is the Third World and the north is Bavaria."[8] Whatever the actual state of affairs, they clearly hankered after that Alpine integrity.

Alpine Fissures

Jean Ziegler, a Social Democratic member of the Swiss parliament, is one of the few outspoken critics of his own country. In 1976, he published a book, which appeared in English under the titles *Switzerland: The Awful Truth* (U.S.) and *Switzerland Exposed* (Britain), that described in detail the hypocrisy of Swiss foreign policy and the activities of the Swiss financial Establishment in exploiting Third World countries and abetting corrupt dictators. The book was translated into fifteen languages and was a factor in bringing international pressure to bear on the Swiss Confederation to find and return the billions stolen by Haiti's Duvalier and the Philippines' Marcos.

In a 1990 book, *Switzerland Washes Whiter,* Ziegler accuses his own country of being the main mechanism for laundering hundreds of billions of dollars of illegal profits from the global drug trade. This activity takes place with the cynical compliance and support of the "emirs" of Swiss business, Ziegler contends. The husband of the justice minister herself, Elisabeth Kopp, was implicated in the activities of one "trading" company accused of money-laundering, forcing her resignation. "On our planet, Switzerland is today the principal place for the laundering, the recycling of the money of death. For generations, it has been the symbol of hygiene, of health, of cleanliness. Today it is the home of infection," Ziegler writes. "I don't know a social formation in the world more ignorant of itself, more set in place, more secret, more inimical to self-criticism, more fiercely determined to organize its own opacity than the Swiss Confederation."[9]

Increasingly, in Ziegler's view, Switzerland's preference for isolation was making it an outlaw in European society rather than just an outsider.

> By its own choice and against all logic—historical, cultural, political, geographic—Switzerland remains excluded from the EEC. The emirs fear like the plague any supranational legislation or authority. A European tax system, an international supervision of banking, an efficacious control of drug traffic, of capital flight, of speculative operations? That would be the end of the Emirate. The emirs of Zurich, Geneva, Lugano not being suicidal, Switzerland won't be part of Europe.[10]

Following the Kopp scandal, the Swiss did place new constraints on banks with regard to money that might come from criminal activities like drug trafficking. The Swiss government negotiated access to the European Economic Area as a preliminary step to joining the EC as a full member. But in a referendum in December 1992, Swiss voters rejected membership in the EEA by a narrow margin, 50.3 percent to 49.7 percent. However, the vote was not really as close as it seemed, because the bulk of those in favor of "Europe" were in the French-speaking cantons. The measure needed the approval of the majority of the cantons, and there the vote against membership was more decisive. Out of twenty-three cantons, only seven—the six francophone cantons and Basel—approved the proposition.

Although supporters of the measure hastened to say that rejection of the EEA did not necessarily entail a refusal to join the EC at a later date, the vote was seen as a major setback to Swiss integration in Europe. In particular, it widened the gap between the

French-speaking minority in the country and the German-speaking majority. Some of the French cantons studied the notion of a separate agreement with the EC, and there was loose talk of secession.

The EEA referendum exposed an underlying fragility that was always there. For Jean Ziegler, the very tentativeness of the Swiss political structure accounts for its immobility. "A unique case in Europe: as a national state, the Swiss state is a social formation of a great and permanent fragility. The specter of splitting up prowls like a phantom in the offices of Berne [the national capital]."[11] For this reason, the national government is rigidly apportioned among the main political parties, forestalling all political debate. Any criticism of the Swiss state is treated like high treason, Ziegler contends. (The parliamentarian has had to fend off numerous legal attacks for his outspokenness.)

The split on the EEA vote further accentuated the differences between the French- and German-speaking cantons. Jacques Pilet, editor in chief of the francophone newspaper *Nouveau Quotidien,* felt that the referendum strengthened the cultural identity in *Romandie,* as French-speaking Switzerland is called. "The feeling of belonging to *Romandie* is winning ground socially and politically."[12] Other commentators contend, however, that it is the very loss of cultural identity in a mass consumer society that makes the francophones yearn for EC membership.

Even in Switzerland, with its tradition of solidarity, the integrative forces in Europe are forcing a closer examination of regional values. The Swiss Confederation is often cited as a model for structuring Europe, but its own debate over Europe shows the dangers of preserving unity through political immobility.

CHAPTER TEN

DANUBE BASIN: THE EMPIRE STRIKES BACK

Europe is a watery place. Bristling with large peninsulas—Italian, Iberian, Balkan, Scandinavian—it is often called a peninsula itself, surrounded as it is on three sides by water. Some go so far, stretching geographical terminology, as to call it an isthmus, a narrow strip of land between two bodies of water. The completion of the canal between the Main River, a tributary of the Rhine, and the Danube in 1992, even if its commercial merits are dubious, created an historic water link across the continent—from the mouth of the Rhine in the North Sea to the mouth of the Danube in the Black Sea—like those across the isthmuses of Panama and Suez, only much longer.

However fanciful, such terms testify to the impact of water on the continent. Its thousands of miles of coastline are indented, corrugated, by myriad bays, gulfs, lagoons, estuaries, fjords, and firths, each with a long history of its own. A galaxy of islands, from Britain to Malta, cluster around it, separated by channels, straits, sounds, and seas. Wide navigable rivers snaking through the continent are so important to commerce that a city such as Duisburg, which from a quick glance at the map looks as landlocked as any, is one of Europe's largest ports, sitting as it does at the strategic confluence of the Rhine and the Ruhr rivers.

On September 25, 1992, German president Richard von Weizsacker officially opened the canal connecting the Main River to the Danube, 1,199 years after Charlemagne gave the first order for digging it. The 106-mile-long canal, running from Bamberg via Nuremberg to Kelheim in Bavaria, provides the missing link in Europe's waterways to connect the North Sea with the Black Sea, a 2,100-mile route along the Rhine, the Main, and the Danube.

Charlemagne abandoned the project—traces of his trench can still be seen—because he had, literally, other worlds to conquer. Napoleon was tempted to build the canal for strategic reasons, to circumvent any possible British blockades on the sea route, but found the cost prohibitive. No such temporal considerations worried King Ludwig I of Bavaria, who commissioned a smaller canal along a shorter route in the nineteenth century. By the time it was finished, in 1845, a new form of transport, the railroad, had rendered it obsolete, and it was never used.

In 1921, the Rhine-Main-Danube Company was formed to build the current canal. The work languished until the postwar Bavarian government relaunched it in the 1960s, over the protests of environmentalists concerned about its impact on the fragile ecology of river valleys. The government of chancellor Helmut Schmidt suspended federal subsidies in the late 1970s—a Schmidt aide said the canal was the most useless construction project since the Tower of Babel—but it was relaunched again on the somewhat specious argument that it would cost more to take care of an unfinished ruin than to complete it.

For the 1992 opening, von Weizsacker sailed in a small convoy of riverboats to the continental divide, 1,322 feet above sea level, in a ceremony that started with a concert in Nuremberg's Meistersinger Hall. The festivities alone cost $1.4 million, after construction costs estimated at $4 billion—not counting the subsidies implied in financing the project through interest-free government loans. In the final stages, considerable effort and expense, in response to environmental protests, went to recreate natural conditions supportive of wildlife, to design picturesque bridges incorporating the canal in the scenic villages along the way, to build bicycle paths and boat docks for residents and tourists. Still, a local pastor condemned the canal as "a monument to godlessness," and environmentalists called it monstrous because the potential economic benefit was dubious and the damage to wetlands irreparable.

Barges carrying 1,350 metric tons, or 3,300 when they go piggy-back, can use the canal. But one fifty-mile stretch on the Danube itself, between Regensburg and Passau, is often too low for the biggest ships, and dredging to bring it up to standard will not be finished until some time early next century. Many bridges on the Main are so low that containers can only be stacked two deep, instead of the four deep that makes barge transport economical. So many locks are needed to raise the traffic over the continental divide—there are fifty locks between Frankfurt and Passau—that a trip the full length of the waterway could take twenty-five to thirty days, compared with eleven days for the sea route. Thus, Rotterdam shippers estimated that the canal would carry only 3 million tons of traffic a year, not the 10 million predicted by the operating company, nor the 18 million tons it is technically capable of handling. But most of the trade will not be the full length of the route; rather, dry bulk cargos like coal, iron ore, fertilizers, animal feed, and sand will shuttle between Germany, Austria, and Hungary, eventually as far as the seaport in Rotterdam. The canal's partisans argue that each barge means eighty to ninety fewer trucks on Europe's congested highways.

National Geographic writer Bill Bryson, trying to balance the impressiveness of the achievement with the arguments of its critics, finally concluded that he could not decide whether the canal was a good idea or not. The question is moot, however, as Bryson realized one evening when he was gazing reflectively upon the canal: "As the sun tracked its way toward the hills to my left and the day's last tractors labored home across the neat fields, I couldn't help reflecting that it looked as if it had been there forever. Which is, of course, a merciful thing because, for better or worse, it will be there forever now."[1]

The canal itself lies in Mitteleuropa, but its main impact will be on the territories of the Danube Basin superregion. Perhaps the canal's worth as a symbol is greater than its commercial value—the Danube Basin needs a link to western Europe to revive its economy and even to establish its identity.

The Danube River's basin is a crossroads of the continent and a patchwork of diverse nationalities. Pluriethnic for centuries, the region exploded with the rise of nationalism in the nineteenth century. Because of the numerous distinct nationalities dispersed throughout the region, no national borders can be drawn without reducing some group to a minority that must, on the basis of historical experience in the region, fear for its political and cultural rights. The Danube basin geographic region urgently needs to develop cross-border cooperation to become the Danube Basin superregion. More than anywhere else, the ability to look beyond national borders for the welfare of the entire region is critical to the future of the Danube Basin. And the ability of the region to surmount nationalist rivalries, to pursue a mutual economic and cultural development, is crucial for the future of Europe.

In book after book, including one called *Austria-Hungary: An Idea for the Future,* French historian Pierre Behar has drummed home the urgency of a Danubian federation to replace the Austro-Hungarian empire dismembered after World War I. He cites the famous remark of Frantisek Palacky, a nineteenth-century Czech nationalist, who said that if the Austro-Hungarian empire of the Habsburgs did not exist, it would be necessary to invent it. "Because it no longer exists, the only thing for us to do is to reinvent it," Behar argues repeatedly in his works on the new geopolitics of Europe.[2]

Behar and many others see the need for a Danubian federation for two reasons: to enable the many different nationalities to live side by side in peace, and to counterbalance Germany, really to block the extension of German influence into eastern and southeastern Europe, which could destroy any chance of a lasting equilibrium in the continent. This was the main motivation, unspoken but clearly understood by the participants, of the attempt by Italian foreign minister Gianni de Michelis in 1989–91 to promote cooperation among former Habsburg territories—Italy's northern Adriatic region and South Tirol belonged to the empire—in a group first called the Quadrangular, after the four original members (Italy, Austria, Hungary, and Yugoslavia), and then Pentagonal and Hexagonal when the fifth (Czechoslovakia) and sixth (Poland) members joined. But the breakup of Yugoslavia torpedoed cooperation, and in 1992 De Michelis lost his cabinet seat as a new government in Rome turned its attention to Italy's urgent domestic problems.

Other efforts at regional cooperation continue, though. In May 1990, several Danube regional governments from Germany, Austria, Czechoslovakia, Hungary, Yugoslavia, Romania, Bulgaria, and the Soviet Union formed an Association of Danube Lands. They established a secretariat at Vienna and set up working groups to tackle questions of planning and environment, business and tourism, culture, research, and sport, and the World Expo initially planned jointly by Vienna and Budapest for 1995, and set by Budapest alone for 1996 after Vienna withdrew. The group was modeled on and partly overlapped with an older organization, the Alpine-Adriatic Regional Association, grouping regions in Germany, Austria, Italy, Yugoslavia, and Hungary, established in 1978. The Council of Europe and the Ford Foundation cosponsored the foundation in early 1993 of an East Carpathian Euroregion at the juncture of Polish, Slovakian, Hungarian, and Romanian borders, to promote cooperation between these historically linked regions.

A Weak Center

Like Mitteleuropa, Danube Basin is a central region. For many writers and historians, this region *is* Mitteleuropa, the Central Europe between Germany and Russia. In postcommunist Europe, though, this region makes a feeble center. Despite its long common history under the Habsburgs, the cohesion in contemporary Danube Basin is so weak that, of all the superregions, it has the greatest chance of splitting apart and disappearing. Austria, Slovakia, even Hungary, could be drawn into the German orbit, becoming part of a swollen Mitteleuropa. Slovenia and Croatia, perhaps Bulgaria, could sink into the morass of Balkan Peninsula. Romania and Bulgaria could come under the sway of Slavic Federation, especially if a nationalistic Russia becomes dominant and expansionist, overrunning the Ukraine and menacing the former Soviet satellites. The northern Adriatic region would remain the marginal backwater it is today, divided among Latin Crescent, Mitteleuropa, and Balkan Peninsula.

Given these alternatives, the consolidation of Danube Basin and its emergence as a strong and vital superregion takes on a critical importance for equilibrium in Europe and a peaceful future. It would not take much for the ethnic animosities that have ravaged the Balkan peninsula to spread to the national checkerboard of the Danube basin. Worse, it could become a region where Germany and Russia vie for influence, an even more dangerous threat to peace.

The hope, born of the Habsburg history, would be that strong cooperation between Vienna and Budapest would make for a stable superregion. Like the bond between France and Germany that holds

Mitteleuropa together, this link would constitute the core of the superregion. The other capital cities—Bratislava in Slovakia, Ljubljana in Slovenia, Zagreb in Croatia, Sofia in Bulgaria, Bucharest in Romania—as well as Trieste, Venice, even Milan in Italy could create a network of economic and cultural exchange around this core.

The early signs for such cooperation were not good, however. Vienna, with its own comfort in mind, withdrew from the joint World Expo with Budapest, which Budapest had counted on to cement its link, literally, with Vienna and thus with the West. In addition, Bratislava and Budapest engaged in a bitter fight over the Slovakian project to dam and divert the Danube for a hydroelectric power plant. Budapest and Bucharest have continued their war of nerves over the rights of the Hungarian minority in Transylvania. Zagreb has joined Belgrade in dividing up Bosnia-Herzegovina to compensate for its loss of territory to an expansionist Serbia.

With more than 2 million people, Budapest is one of the largest cities in Danube Basin, along with Vienna and Bucharest. Hungary's 10.5 million people are less than half of Romania's 23 million, but more than any of the other countries in the region, following the breakup of Yugoslavia and Czechoslovakia. In addition, there are more than 3 million ethnic Hungarians living in the neighboring countries, including 2 million in Romania, half a million each in Slovakia and Serbia (in Vojvodina), and 170,000 in sub-Carpathian Ukraine, the former Ruthenia, that belongs to the Danube Basin superregion.

In short, the Hungarians are well-positioned to be the federating force in the region. Historically, they have been amenable to cooperation. In the six hundred-some years after the founding dynasty died out in 1301, Hungary elected only one king of Hungarian origin, Matthias Corvinus in the fifteenth century. For the rest of the time, they were content to take their rulers from the Angevin dynasty in France, the Luxembourg dynasty in the Low Countries, the Jagellon dynasty in Poland-Lithuania, and lastly, the Habsburg dynasty in Austria. By the same token, they stoutly defended their autonomy. Even when the Ottoman Turks occupied most of Hungarian territory in the sixteenth and seventeenth centuries, they preserved their own institutions, making Poszony, today's Bratislava, the royal capital. The Hungarians resisted the various attempts of the Habsburgs to suppress their autonomy, winning virtual independence from Vienna's control in 1867.

But that cooperative spirit faced severe challenge in the course of 1992 as nationalism surged in the region. The new constitution adopted in Slovakia in preparation for full independence offered few explicit guarantees for the large Hungarian minority. Romanian extremists in Cluj, the capital of Transylvania, adopted deliberately provocative measures against Hungarian language and culture. It was, ironically, the dispute over replacing a *Hungarian* pastor in Timisoara, in western Romania, that set in the motion the chain of events in late 1989 that brought down Romanian dictator Nicolae Ceausescu. The Serbians' ruthless policy of "ethnic cleansing" in Bosnia-Herzegovina and Croatia caused worry in Vojvodina, formerly an autonomous territory in northern Serbia, that Hungarians and other minorities there would face persecution.

These tensions, combined with the Hungarians' resentment over the loss of two-thirds of their territory after World War I, make it unlikely that Hungary alone can hold Danube Basin together. As in history, the Hungarians need the stabilizing influence of the Austrians to balance their own labile tendencies.

The Danube Basin superregion does not run the full length of the Danube River; from its source in the Black Forest in southwest Germany, through Ulm and Regensburg to Passau, the Danube flows through Mitteleuropa. The Danube Basin border, beginning at Munich, goes east and slightly north, crossing the Danube between Passau and Linz, continuing east to the north of Vienna and Bratislava, where it turns northeast, following the line of the White Carpathian Mountains, between the Czech and Slovak republics, to Cracow. There it turns east again, skirting the Carpathian mountains until it meets the Dniester River, coming out of the mountains from its source. The superregion border follows the Dniester then southeast to the Black Sea. This corresponds to Romania's northern border between the wars, incorporating Ruthenia, now part of Ukraine, and Bessarabia, the former Soviet Republic of Moldava, now independent.

In the west, the Danube Basin border, starting in Munich, shares the Alpine Arc border to Klagenfurt, where it turns southwest, following the Alpine range through Trent in a line to Milan. There it meets the Latin Crescent border, which it follows east to Chioggia, a town just south of Venice. The superregion border follows the Adriatic coastline around through Trieste, south to Dubrovnik. Then it follows the Croatian border with Bosnia-Herzegovina north, then east to Belgrade and the Danube. The border continues along the Danube, turning south to follow the frontier between Serbia and Bulgaria in the West Balkan mountains, to Sofia, where it turns due east, following European Route 772 across Bulgaria to Burgas on the Black Sea coast. That coastline, running north along the vast delta of the Danube to the mouth of the Dniester, forms the eastern border of the superregion.

Thus the Danube Basin includes the southeast corner of Germany, the eastern two-thirds of Austria, Hungary, Slovakia, a sliver of southeast Poland, the southwestern corner of Ukraine, Romania, the northern half of Bulgaria, the former autonomous region of Vojvodina in Serbia, Slovenia, Croatia, and the northeastern corner of Italy. Within the borders described here, the Danube Basin superregion has a population of about 75 million.

As a result of the war in the former Yugoslavia, the superregion border running through that territory may change. In principle, Bosnia-Herzegovina, Serbia, Montenegro, and Kosovo belong by history and mentality to Balkan Peninsula, while Slovenia, Croatia, and the autonomous province of Vojvodina belong to Danube Basin. But Serbia's aggressive expansion and pernicious policy of "ethnic cleansing" may result in permanent changes in the region. Those parts of Croatia and Vojvodina that remain under direct control of Serbia would belong willy-nilly to Balkan Peninsula, unless a new Serbian regime adopts policies of democracy and cooperation.

"History Land Vienna"

Based on tradition, Vienna would seem to be the logical leader of this region. A grand and glorious city, the Habsburg capital draws millions of tourists every year to admire its majestic Ringstrasse, the Hofburg, St. Stephen's Cathedral, the parks and gardens of an imperial city, the cafés reminiscent of a flourishing intellectual scene that nurtured satirists and caricaturists, journalists and novelists, painters and psychologists. Gothic, baroque, art nouveau buildings blend in special harmony, a backdrop for visions of waltzes and wine gardens, opera and art, chocolate cake and whipped cream.

But this great monument to the past is just that, a museum of former glory that has little to do with the present. Only in Venice, perhaps, is the gap between the splendor of history and the city's modest contemporary role greater. Vienna is a city of nostalgia, not only for visitors but also for its residents.

It is tempting to believe that Vienna has slumped into the provincialism that characterizes it today because Austria was deprived of its empire and much of its own territory after World War I, leaving a landlocked rump of a nation with a corner of the Alps, a stretch of the Danube, and a monumental capital. But a closer reading of history provides evidence that the Austrians were always provincial and conservative, only fortunate enough to have a ruler whose dynasty over centuries acquired other nations as well. Austria's bureaucratic turn of mind served it well when the Habsburg emperors dispatched flocks of German-speaking pigeon-holers to administer their territories in the Danube basin, but appears today as a sterile exercise in paper-pushing that stifles a society not too lively to begin with. An amusing and mildly ridiculous vestige of imperial administration is the Austrian obsession with titles. Not only is the holder of a doctorate addressed as "Mr. Doctor Kramer," but even more modest achievements are acclaimed, as in "Mr. Bachelor-of-Arts Kramer," or "Mr. Assistant City Clerk Kramer."

Whatever greatness or renown the House of Austria gained in the centuries before its decline, the marginal territory that produced the dynasty has reverted to its geographical situation, a small border zone of mighty Germany. Most of Austrian industry not owned by the state belongs to German multinationals like Siemens and Daimler-Benz. German tourists overrun the hotels and villages of Austria for summer holidays and winter skiing.

In fact, the German princes chose Rudolph of Habsburg as their king in the thirteenth century because the ruler of this buffer territory on the edge of the Holy Roman Empire was so weak he would leave his betters free to rule their own territories as they pleased. But the Habsburgs did not remain weak. By the time of Charles V in the sixteenth century, after many marriages and battles, the dynasty controlled huge portions of Europe, ruling in Spain and Portugal, parts of Italy, Central Europe, and the Low Countries, as well as nominally heading the Holy Roman Empire itself. The Habsburgs encircled France, so that Louis XIV and then Napoleon fought to diminish their possessions. By the time Napoleon abolished the Holy Roman Empire, the Habsburgs were reduced to their Danube territories. Siding with Germany in World War I, the Habsburgs lost their empire, which was carved into several new kingdoms and republics, and their various thrones.

In its final stages and for most of its history, the Habsburg dynasty, the greatest ever seen in Europe, was conservative, even reactionary. The long reign of Francis Joseph, from 1848 to 1916, became a byword for incompetence and inertia. The Viennese novelist Robert Musil satirized the Austro-Hungarian empire (which he calls Kakania, after the German abbreviation K.u.K., for "imperial and royal") early in the twentieth century:

> There, in Kakania, that misunderstood state that has since vanished, there was speed too, of course, but not too much speed. . . . The conquest of the air had begun there too, but not too intensively. Now and then a ship was sent off to South America or the Far East; but not too often. . . . There was some display of luxury; but it was not, of course, as oversophisticated as that of the French. One went in for sport; but not in madly Anglo-Saxon fashion. One spent tremendous sums on the Army; but only just enough to assure one of remaining the second weakest among the great powers.[3]

The bubbly, glittery cultural life of turn-of-century Vienna arose precisely because the political structure was so rigid. Culture became the only outlet for liberal feeling. British historian Robin Okey explains that "the effervescent social world which has since come to be thought of as quintessentially Viennese" resulted from the repressiveness of the regime, which led the middle class to focus on its own pleasure and amusement. "It is no chance that the psychological theories of Sigmund Freud were first developed in this rather introverted milieu," Okey writes, "or that the leading objects of popular attention at the time were not statesmen or sportsmen but designers, actors or musicians, like Gustav Mahler, whose stormy artistic life as head of the Viennese opera mirrored the preoccupation of the Austro-German middle classes with cultural rather than political disputation."[4]

All of this produced an attitude toward life that characterizes Vienna and Austria to this day. In his book *Danube,* which he describes as "a sentimental journey from the source to the Black Sea," the Italian writer Claudio Magris says the essence of Austrian attitudes can be found in the works of Franz Grillparzer. The nineteenth-century Viennese poet and dramatist abhorred Napoleon and his concept of history for going straight to the main point and ignoring the "minute particulars," the marginal and secondary things in life that have their own dignity and should not always be sacrificed to the overall scheme of things. "Austrian culture defends what is marginal, transient, secondary," writes Magris, "the pause and respite from that mechanism which aims at burning up such things so as to attain more important results."[5]

The debate about whether Austria is a full-fledged ethnic nation continues to be topical. Hitler, himself an Austrian, argued that the country is German, and he brought it "home into the Reich." Today's right-wing Freedom Party of Austria under Jorg Haider takes over many of Hitler's themes and also wants to move Austria closer to what Haider sees as its German homeland. Austria lacks, of course, its own language, often the main criterion in establishing ethnic identity. There are many who worry that Austria's entry into the EC, effectively removing the border to Germany, would duplicate Hitler's annexation of the country in the 1938 *Anschluss*.

During the Cold War, Vienna carved out a small niche for itself as a neutral capital for United Nations agencies and a staging post for Western operations in the East Bloc. With the removal of the Iron Curtain in 1989, Vienna experienced a period of euphoria similar to that in Berlin. Ambitious plans were made for a joint World Expo with Budapest and ground was broken for new office developments to accommodate the expected influx of companies eager to exploit the opening to the east.

But Vienna quickly retreated into its more comfortable inertia. Viennese voters rejected the Expo in a referendum. Development projects were scaled down, and some of the more audacious proposals for modern structures, like the new Museum Quarter in central Vienna, were put on hold. The city resisted any innovations that might jeopardize its "his-touristic" identity, as an architecture correspondent for *Frankfurter Allgemeine Zeitung* put it, an identity that long since was only an image. "Thus the staging of the Vienna identity follows the lines of the Disney strategy. Without admitting it, 'History Land Vienna' in the long run has an edge over fresh, aggressive competitors like Berlin, Warsaw, Prague and Budapest," this correspondent comments with irony. "In the network of the new competition between cities, Vienna could create a new type of city: the 'Big City Museum,' historic and orderly, where the technical side of a big city camouflages itself and hides behind the stage of the performance. And the residents are the players, jealously watching out that no one dares disturb their eternal game by not filling the role assigned to him."[6]

Whether Austria can overcome its provincialism and rise to the challenge of helping to rebuild eastern Europe remains to be seen. An alliance with Hungary to spread capitalist expertise and wealth through the Danube region would be the best way to preserve a specifically Austrian identity. Otherwise, it is likely to become increasingly indistinguishable from Germany.

There are some hopeful signs, however. Austrian firms, often small and medium-sized manufacturers, represented nearly one-fourth of the 9,000 joint ventures in Hungary through the first half of 1992. Conversely, large Hungarian firms, like travel agency Ibusz, are listed on the Vienna Stock Exchange to encourage foreign shareholders. More than 700 foreign companies, including 130 from the U.S. and 70 from Japan, have offices in Vienna, usually for operations in eastern Europe. At the beginning of 1992, Coca-Cola moved its commercial office for eastern Europe from west Germany to Vienna. Siemens invested $100 million in a Budapest telecommunications factory via its Austrian subsidiary. Austria vied with Germany for the lead in investments in Slovakia: The two countries accounted for half of the $212 million invested in Slovakia through September 1992. In the end, it may be businessmen, and even foreign businessmen, who lead the way in bringing Austria and its eastern neighbors closer together.

Hungary's Head Start

The Danube River—wide, blue, serene—lends Budapest a dramatic majesty that the Seine cannot give to Paris, or the Tiber to Rome. The Danube, at 1,776 miles the longest river in Europe after the Volga, is also one of the widest, often forming a border between countries. Other large Danubian cities—like Vienna and Belgrade—lie to one side or the other of the massive waterway. Until 1872, when they merged into one, Buda and Pest faced each other across the river, first one, then the other serving as Hungarian capital.

No other country paid as a high a price for losing World War I as Hungary did. The 1920 Trianon treaty reduced it to less than one-third of its historic size, a territory Hungary had controlled for a thousand years from the time in the tenth century when the Magyars settled on the broad Hungarian plain. Vikings on horseback, the Magyars, a federation of Asian tribes from the Ural region, raided western Europe ruthlessly before the Germans defeated them decisively in 955 near Augsburg. Instead of retreating back into the Asian steppes like the Huns and Avars before them, the Magyars established themselves on the edge of German territory, assimilated local Slavic populations, and developed a distinctive culture that has resisted the vicissitudes of centuries, including dynastic alliances with Poland, Luxembourg, and Austria, and subjugation by Ottoman Turks and Soviet Russians. Even under the Habsburgs, Hungary remained technically intact and by 1867 wrested back full autonomy, so that the Austrian Empire became the Austro-Hungarian Empire, the Dual Monarchy.

Following World War I, Hungary lost Slovakia to the newly formed Czechoslovakia, Croatia to the newly formed Yugoslavia, and Transylvania to the lucky Romanians, who hardly fought in the war but had the good sense to choose the winning side. The Hungarians themselves were a minority in these regions, so there was no justification in strictly national terms to hold on to them. As a result of the partition, though, one-fourth of the Hungarian nationals found themselves living in another country after the war.

But Hungary kept alive its sense of sovereignty, even though the end of World War II brought Soviet domination. After the popular uprising in 1953 in East Germany, put down by Soviet tanks, Hungary was the first of the East European satellite nations to challenge Soviet rule, declaring neutrality in 1956. Again, Soviet tanks crushed the revolt, forcing many to flee the country.

In the 1970s and 1980s, Hungary tried a different form of resistance to the communist system. Remaining politically orthodox, the country began liberalizing the economy, moving away from strict central planning on the Soviet model. The government permitted private property and private sector business, a Western-style banking system, and state bonds. Hungary cultivated international financial markets, became a leading borrower of funds to modernize its economy, and earned high marks for its professionalism and sophistication.

The most potent symbol of the Iron Curtain, the Berlin Wall, was breached in November 1989. But its foundations were undermined in the weeks beforehand by Hungary, which cut down the barbed wire on its border with Austria, freeing the way for East Germans to seek refuge in the West via Hungary, which was accessible to them as tourists. On October 23, 1989, the anniversary of the uprising thirty-three years previously, a government of reform communists declared Hungary a simple "republic," dropping the adjective "People's" that branded it as a Soviet satellite.

The earlier liberalization gave Hungary a head start in making the transition to a market economy. It was the first of the east European countries to reopen a stock market and to trade shares in big industrial companies. Privately owned Hungarian companies, founded a decade earlier in the course of the economic reforms, were among the first East Bloc industries to expand abroad. One of the biggest of these was Muszertechnika, started in 1981 by Gabor Szeles. In launching his company, the electrical engineer took advantage of legislation allowing workers in state-owned factories to form their own "working groups" to take on special orders. Szeles wanted to augment his salary so that he could afford to buy gas for his Russian-made car. By 1991, Muszertechnika, manufacturing electronic instruments, employed four hundred people in Budapest and a dozen foreign subsidiaries—in Switzerland, Munich, Cleveland, Kazakhstan, and elsewhere—with annual sales of $100 million. Szeles himself started driving a Mercedes and imported one hundred Opels from General Motors' German subsidiary for his employees.

But Hungary's head start had disadvantages as well. Its success at borrowing on foreign markets exceeded its success at earning hard currency to pay off the loans, so that it was left with the highest per capita foreign debt in the East Bloc. The country had opened its doors to foreign investors even under the communist regime, but many of these—General Electric, General Motors, Ford—found all their calculations thrown awry by the collapse of the Soviet trading bloc. Instead of a foothold in a closed, stable economic system, they had factories of dubious strategic value in the new competitive situation. For instance, GM and its partners built a new car engine plant on the Austrian-Hungarian border, designed to earn enough foreign currency through exporting engines that GM could import automobile kits to be assembled for sale in the protected Hungarian market. After the fall of the Soviet bloc and the opening of Hungary's borders for trade with the West, it was much more efficient to import the manufactured cars directly from factories in Germany. Because of competition from other imports, and the recession that hit Hungary and all other east European countries making the change to a market economy, GM had to re-export the cars assembled in Hungary at high cost to the

West—turning the original idea on its head and making the whole operation much less profitable than planned.

Having led the East Bloc in economic liberalization under the communist regimes, Hungary became more cautious and complacent under a new conservative government. Countries like Poland and Czechoslovakia, making all their economic changes at once, soon overtook Hungary in privatizing state-owned industry, so that finally Hungary had to begin copying their methods for transferring ownership of state companies to the public.

Still, with its relatively stable government and democratic orientation, Hungary continues to attract foreign investment. In late 1992, Audi, a subsidiary of Volkswagen, chose Hungary over east Germany to build a new motor component factory for $215 million. Suzuki invested $250 million in a new car assembly plant near Budapest. In a much smaller investment, U.S. West, one of the Baby Bells, launched a successful cellular telephone operation in Hungary with only $15 million.

A major source of foreign investment are ethnic Hungarians living abroad. The Central European Development Corp., headed by Ronald Lauder, an heir to the Estee Lauder cosmetics fortune and great-grandson of a Hungarian emigre, channeled a good portion of CEDC's $80 million in capital into Hungary and acted as middleman for other foreign investments. Hungarian-American George Soros, a successful and well-known money manager, donated $100 million to east European ventures, many of them in Hungary. The Zwack family returned to Hungary in 1989 to retake control of their historic drinks company, which they took public in 1993. The creator of the trendy New York restaurants The Four Seasons and Cafe des Artistes, George Lang, returned to his native Hungary to revamp the historic Gundel restaurant in Budapest.

The food industry in general was a major target of investment. Multinationals like Kraft, Philip Morris, Tate & Lyle, Ferruzzi, and McDonald's were early investors in the sector. With some of the most fertile and productive farmland in Europe, Hungary also had considerable success in attracting foreign investors for 125 large state farms it put up for long-term leasing. Backed by U.K. investors, British farmer Mark Cherrington rescued 22,000 acres of crop and grazing land from bankruptcy and turned the rechristened Danube Farms into a thriving business.

This type of success gave Hungary some optimism about turning around the economy and coping with the foreign debt. A resurgent economy could help the country overcome nationalist sensibilities and encourage regional cooperation.

Slovakia's Poor Image

The Slovaks seem to have an image problem. When nationalists won 1992 elections in the Slovak Republic, the Czechs quickly tired of arguing about increased autonomy and proposed a "velvet divorce" that would permanently split up the country first put together in 1918, much as the "velvet revolution" had overthrown the communist regime. Vaclav Havel, the Czech playwright and dissident elected as the first postcommunist president of Czechoslovakia, who earned a global reputation for his expressions of tolerance and statesmanship, complained in public that seven decades of Czech efforts to civilize and westernize the Slovaks had been in vain.

This condescension demonstrated poignantly just why the Slovaks chafed under the forced partnership with the Czechs. Everything from the name of the country, which put the Czechs first, to the federal capital, the historic Czech capital of Prague, made the Slovaks feel like second-class citizens. Czechs outnumbered Slovaks two to one in population. The Czech lands, more advanced economically when the country was formed, increased their advantage during the communist years. After the fall of the communist regime in 1989, the bulk of new foreign investment, primarily from neighboring Germany, was in the Czech half of the country.

For nearly a thousand years, Slovakia was ruled by Hungary, and, because of its mountains, it was known as Upper Hungary. Magyars dominated the local administration, keeping most Slovaks subjugated as peasants. Today's Slovakian capital, Bratislava, was the seat of the Hungarian Diet, and the capital for the rump of Hungary left free during the period of Turkish occupation. But the cement wasteland that the Slovaks built up in Bratislava under communist rule has little in common with the discreet and charming Hungarian town of previous centuries.

One-fifth of the 5 million people in the proposed sovereign nation of Slovakia are not ethnically Slovakian, but Hungarian or gypsy. Yet the constitution adopted in 1992 recognized civil rights in the new state only for ethnic Slovaks. This worried the minority populations, because Slovakia does not have a good record in democracy. The only other time an independent Slovakia existed, from 1939 to 1945, it was a Nazi satellite under a ruthlessly fascist, nationalist government headed by the reactionary bishop Josef Tiso, who enjoyed widespread popular support.

Even before actual independence, in late 1992, Slovakia embroiled itself in a diplomatic dispute with Hungary over Bratislava's decision to divert the Danube to power a new hydroelectric plant. Although Hungary had signed a treaty approving the project in the 1970s, when Czechoslovakia and Hungary were communist allies, the democratically elected Hungarian government, after unsuccessful efforts to negotiate an end to the damming and diversion of the river, unilaterally renounced the agreement in 1992.

But Slovakia mulishly went ahead with it, arguing that it had spent more than a billion dollars on the project and needed the new generating capacity to replace environmentally dangerous coal and nuclear generators. The Hungarians made an eleventh-hour appeal to the European Community to block the diversion, which they claimed damaged the environment and shifted the border between the two countries, but were not able to stop the Slovaks, who proceeded with the damming and started operation of the power plant in November 1992. The dispute strained Bratislava's already difficult alliance with Prague and soured its relations with Budapest in a time when the new country needed as many friends as it could find.

These tensions made nearby Vienna the likeliest candidate as Slovakia's gateway to the West, despite the historic link to Hungary and the continuing cooperation with the Czech Republic. Austria accounts for two-fifths of 2,000-odd joint ventures in Slovakia. Vienna's international airport is only twenty-one miles from Bratislava. The Slovakian capital, which lies on the Danube, is just thirty miles east of Vienna—close enough to have lunch in Vienna and still make a 3 P.M. appointment in Bratislava, as one businessman put it. But potential foreign investors remained cautious about Slovakia until it became clearer what kind of regime nationalist leader Vladimir Meciar, who won the 1992 elections and negotiated the divorce from the Czech Republic, would conduct in the newly independent country.

Romanian Riddles

Best known as the home of Dracula, Romania remains for many westerners a mysterious and somewhat forbidding place. The name of the country, the origin of its inhabitants, the validity of its historical claims on territory are all mysteries, in fact. Yet these secrets are the subject of passionate debates today, and the source of differences that could flame up into conflict again.

Originally populated by Dacians, a non-Celtic, non-German tribe of uncertain origins, the territory in the western part of today's Romania was conquered by the Romans at the beginning of the second century A.D., who thus extended their empire north of the Danube for the first time. Did they exterminate the indigenous Dacians or assimilate them? No one knows for sure.

Only a century and a half later, the Romans, menaced by the Goths, retreated from Dacia back across the Danube. After that, there is no record of Dacians or Romans in the region for a full millennium. "What happened in the meantime?" asks French historian Andre Sellier. "Second—and considerable—mystery."[7] The Romanians maintain that the Latinized tribesmen remained in the region, hiding in the Carpathian mountains whenever hostile invaders appeared, and emerging afterward. They trace Romania's heritage, the country's name and its language, which is derived from Latin, to this uninterrupted habitation of the region by Romanized Dacians. The Hungarians contend that the territory was left empty when the Romans withdrew. Only much later, in the thirteenth century, after a Mongol invasion came and went, did descendants of Dacia's former inhabitants, by now mixed with other peoples from south of the Danube, come back across the river to settle in Walachia, a province between the Danube and the Carpathian Mountains. In the meantime, the Magyars had moved into the abandoned region. Neither side has conclusive evidence for its version of events, but both consider it important to establish a historical claim on the region, particularly to justify possession of the northern sector, now known as Transylvania. The Hungarians, at any rate, held Transylvania from 1003 to 1918, when the victorious allies of World War I awarded it to Romania.

The Hungarians also conquered other parts of Dacia that developed into two principalities—Walachia, in the south of present-day

Romania, and Moldavia, in eastern Romania and in the former Soviet republic of Moldava. A succession of Romanian princes and foreign suzerains—Hungarian, Polish, Turkish, Russian—took turns ruling the region. One particularly cruel Walachian leader in the fifteenth century, known as Vlad the Impaler for his favored method of punishing his enemies, is considered to be the source of the Dracula legend. By the eighteenth century, Walachia and Moldavia were known as the Danubian Principalities, and served as a skirmishing ground for the Russian and Ottoman empires. In 1861, the two principalities won recognition as a united country of Romania, imported a new prince from Germany, and achieved full sovereignty in 1878.

The postwar communist regime in Romania followed a cruelly repressive line domestically, while asserting its independence from Moscow in foreign affairs. Nicolae Ceausescu, who came to power in 1965, instigated forced industrialization of the agriculturally rich country, embarking on numerous ruinous and inefficient projects. He leveled many rural villages and much of old Bucharest in pursuit of his goals to collectivize and control the population. Finally, in a drama that gripped the world on Christmas Day 1989, Ceausescu was overthrown and executed, and the National Salvation Front took power, later legitimizing its position with elections of uncertain merit. The resounding victory of ex-communist Ion Iliescu in new presidential elections in 1992 did not fully remove Western doubts, but did shore up the country's political stability.

In his willingness to inflict suffering on his people, Ceausescu had ruthlessly deprived the populace of heat, light, food, and consumer goods to repay the country's foreign debt during the 1980s. At the cost of untold misery during that period, Romania had at least the benefit of that rigid policy—no foreign debt—as it haltingly made the transition from central planning to a market economy. However, continued Western skepticism about the country's commitment to democracy and capitalism under its government of former communists hindered the growth of trade and investment in the difficult years following Ceausescu's demise. Still, by 1992, 8,000 foreign companies had invested in Romanian enterprises. Most of these were small businesses in trade and tourism, but large multinationals like Minolta, Du Pont, Hewlett-Packard, Fiat, and Mitsubishi were exploring opportunities as well. The country expected $600 million in new direct investment during 1992, more than double the previous year. Exports, a critical indicator of international competitiveness, were also on the way back to prerevolution levels. Although it proceeded more slowly than Hungary or Czechoslovakia, Romania was also making progress in privatizing state-owned industry.

By bulldozing large sections of Bucharest to make way for Stalinist architecture like the monstrous, half-finished People's Palace, Ceausescu robbed the capital of most of its charm. The city had a reputation in the 1920s and 1930s of being a "small Paris," and was comfortable in a Latin indolence that prompted some visitors to compare it with Buenos Aires or Madrid. Postcommunist Romania would in fact like to imitate Spain's success in appealing to tourists, which contributed greatly to that country's economic surge in the 1980s. The beaches of the Black Sea coast and intact villages of the rural countryside are among the principal attractions. The television images of machine-gun fire during the struggle to topple Ceausescu remained vivid in the minds of potential visitors, though, and made tourism sluggish.

There is considerable sentiment in Romania for reunification with the newly independent Republic of Moldava, the former Soviet republic that originally was part of Moldavia and Romania. Russia had acquired the eastern half of Moldavia, known as Bessarabia after Walachia's medieval Bassarab dynasty, in the nineteenth century. Romania regained Bessarabia after World War I, but the Soviet Union won it back in World War II.

Moldava, where ethnic Romanians make up two-thirds of the country's 4.5 million inhabitants, shares that sentiment to a certain extent. But the presence of a million Russians and Ukrainians, imported by force into Moldava as part of the Soviet Union's "Sovietization" policy, complicates any eventual reunification. The ethnic Slavs are concentrated on the left bank of the Dniester River, along with much of the heavy industry built by the Soviets, in territory that never did belong to Romania. In 1990, Russian nationalists in the territory declared an independent "Trans-Niestrian Republic," a thin sliver of land uncomfortably squeezed in between Moldava and Ukraine.

Historically, Romania, except for Transylvania, had closer ties to the Russian and Ottoman empires than to the Habsburg domain in the west. Today, the Danube links it economically to the western region; the main seaport for the river is the Romanian harbor of

Constantsa. For better or worse, Transylvania, with its large Hungarian and German minorities, will tie its fate to other Danube Basin territories. Its best hope for prosperity, as for its neighbors to the west, is to work toward a coherent economic sphere in the superregion that will link it to the more advanced western Europe.

The Bulgarian Heartland

The same holds true for the northern half of Bulgaria. Cut in half by the Balkan mountain range running west to east, Bulgaria belongs in good part to the Balkan peninsula. Under Ottoman rule from the fourteenth century until its liberation by Russian troops in the nineteenth century, the country remained very much under the influence of Balkan events, and participated in the Balkan Wars of 1912 and 1913 to liberate and divide up Macedonia. But the northern half of the country, between the Balkan mountains and the Danube, has been the heartland of the Bulgars since the Turkish-speaking people first migrated from the region north of the Caspian Sea, intermingling with Slavic peoples along the lower Danube in the seventh century to the point that they were completely Slavicized. The Byzantine Empire authorized the Bulgars to settle the territory north of the Balkan Mountains.

In two golden periods, the Bulgars extended their empire westward and northward into neighboring regions, in the tenth century reaching to the Adriatic, and nearly as far again in the thirteenth century. For the rest of the time, though, they were subject to the Byzantine and then Ottoman empires. The superregion border between Danube Basin and Balkan Peninsula that runs through the center of Bulgaria corresponds loosely to the ancient border between Thrace—a Roman province that included today's southern Bulgaria, northeastern Greece, and European Turkey—and Lower Moesia, covering northern Bulgaria. When the Congress of Berlin, meeting in 1878, arbitrated a settlement between Russia and Turkey on the borders for a liberated Bulgaria, it settled on this one, designating the territory to the south as Eastern Rumelia and assigning it to the Turks. (Rumelia was the Turkish name for the original territory of the Eastern Roman Empire.)

In postcommunist Europe, the capital of Bulgaria, Sofia, will be facing both ways, northward to Danube Basin, and southward to

Balkan Peninsula, as Bulgaria makes its transition to democracy and a market economy. The country followed Moscow's lead so closely during the communist period that it was referred to as the sixteenth republic of the Soviet Union, as much a part of the union as the fifteen actual republics. Although it duly deposed its corrupt communist rulers in 1989, it actually gave a majority to the reformed Communist Party in 1990 elections. Constitutional reforms and new elections in 1991 brought the democratic opposition to power and made former dissident Zhelyu Zhelev the directly elected president, but Bulgaria lagged behind other former communist countries in changing its economic structures.

By the time the country of 9 million people began to negotiate an association treaty with the EC and EFTA to trade within the European Economic Area, the West had grown much less willing to make the same concessions it had in earlier treaties with Poland, Hungary, and Czechoslovakia, even though these could hardly be described as generous. Frustrated and bitter, one top Bulgarian official complained to a German interviewer, "We have had to grasp the fact that for the EC and EFTA we are simply not important."[8] The United States took up the slack to a certain extent, interested in Bulgaria because of its strategic location on the Black Sea. The Bulgarians reciprocated, picking Westinghouse Electric to dispose of nuclear wastes from its Soviet generators, and buying Boeing planes for the national airline. Deputy secretary of state Lawrence S. Eagleburger in early 1992 urged American companies at a conference in Washington to invest in Bulgaria. He said "the Bulgarian revolution has traveled the furthest distance" of any in eastern Europe.[9]

Nonetheless, the country proceeded slowly. It finally got its trade agreements with the EC and EFTA, although these left out several key sectors, including Bulgaria's important wine industry. But the accords will help draw the country into western Europe's economic sphere, via the Danube Basin superregion. Germany's Siemens and France's Alcatel were expected to invest in production facilities to take advantage of Bulgarian labor's skill in electronics.

The first big target for Bulgaria's privatization program was the national airline, Balkan Bulgarian Airlines, the second largest in the former East Bloc after Aeroflot. The tourism industry, including some attractive Black Sea resorts, was also slated for privatization. The two measures promised to open up the country, which could also lead to closer ties with the West. But Bulgaria could still opt for a strong Balkan or Black Sea orientation that would bring it closer to other superregions.

Slovenia and Croatia

Yugoslavia, which means "land of the South Slavs," was probably destined to fall victim to Serbian dreams of recreating the glory of their medieval empire, when Serbia spanned the Balkan peninsula from the Aegean to the Adriatic, from the Danube to the Gulf of Patras in present-day Greece, and had its own czar. The explosion of hatred and brutality that followed the collapse of communism nonetheless came as a shock to everyone outside the region. Bewildering as events seemed, though, they were dismayingly consistent with the history of the region, characterized as it is by an amazingly stable territorial makeup and a profound awareness of the past. Historian Robin Okey observes:

> Eastern Europe is a complicated place. Its complexity may seem daunting at first. But a thorough study of the ethnic map and geography of the area will pay great dividends, for its largely stable ethnic and physical inheritance has shaped many regularities of attitude and assumption which underlie the confused flux of events. Thus the details of Balkan politics have always been torturous but the basic objectives of the various Balkan peoples can be readily grasped. . . . People are aware of, and reflect, their past. Indeed, history dies hard in these parts.[10]

Europe had been spoiled for so long by the postwar period of peace that the war in Yugoslavia came as a numbing shock. As one observer commented, not at all facetiously, it was hard to imagine people with videorecorders and mobile telephones fighting in a bloody war, so much did such barbarism seem to belong to the past. Once again Europe had been lulled into thinking that the last war ended all wars, even though the prospect of violent conflict had been looming in Yugoslavia for years.

Yugoslavia, and particularly the northern republics Slovenia and Croatia, enjoyed the highest standard of living in the East Bloc, leaving aside East Germany. Although it remained communist, Yugoslavia's successful break with Moscow after the war enabled the federation to devise a more flexible, decentralized economic system and to develop more trade and cultural exchange with the West.

In February 1992, less than a month after gaining international recognition for the country's independence, representatives from the Republic of Slovenia mingled with the top-level business and political leaders attending the World Economic Forum in Davos, a ski resort in eastern Switzerland. The Slovenians handed out a glossy brochure with the inviting headline, "A new state on the sunny side of the Alps." At the eastern end of the Alpine range, where the mountains taper off into the Pannonian plain, the Slovenes voted at the end of 1990 to make the territory they had inhabited since the seventh century an independent country with their own name. After preferring to shelter behind bigger powers that whole time—the Bavarians, the Franks, the Holy Roman Empire, the Habsburgs, Napoleon, Yugoslavia—the Slovenes saw no alternative, in view of the political polarization in Yugoslavia, but to go their own way. When western Europeans warned nations in southeastern Europe against fragmentation into small countries, Slovenia replied that with 1.9 million inhabitants, it was six times the size of Luxembourg, an independent country and founding member of the European Community.

Slovenia, a constituent republic in the Yugoslav federation, had the highest per capita income and highest standard of living in the country. Industrious and relatively efficient, Slovenians accounted for one-fifth of Yugoslavia's gross domestic product, about the same as that of Serbia—not counting the autonomous provinces of Vojvodina and Kosovo—which had three times the population. Some of Yugoslavia's best-known exporters, like Gorenje, a maker of home appliances, were Slovenian.

In addition to distributing the brochures at Davos, the newly independent country paid for special supplements in the *Financial Times* and other business publications to attract foreign direct investment. Separated from Serbia by Croatia, Slovenia experienced only brief fighting in June 1991, quickly repulsing the Serbian-dominated federal army, which withdrew to concentrate its firepower on Croatia, and then Bosnia-Herzegovina, where Serbia had territorial claims. Nonetheless, of course, Slovenia had to struggle to convince foreign companies that the country was a safe and profitable investment. Likewise, although brochures were also distributed at London's tourism fair in December 1991, it was difficult to lure vacationers to the new country's Alpine ski slopes or its Mediterranean beaches.

Not to be discouraged, Slovenia issued its own currency, the "tolar"—a cognate of "dollar"—set up a central bank along Western lines, lobbied neighboring regions and countries, particularly the Austrian federal government in Vienna, and set out to make independence work. Because of Yugoslavia's half-capitalist economic system and Slovenia's own high standard of development, many experts reckon the new country, in spite of its size, has a good chance of making the transition to a Western-style market economy relatively quickly.

Historically part of the Holy Roman Empire and faithful adherents of the Roman Catholic Church, the Slovenes were the most westernized of the southern Slavs. Their active participation in the Austrian empire under the Habsburgs had earned them widespread acceptance, and they were known as "Slavic-speaking Austrians." Napoleon made the Slovenian city Ljubljana the capital of his short-lived Illyrian Provinces, which included part of Austria, the port of Trieste, western Croatia, and the Dalmatian coast, on the eastern shore of the Adriatic. The Slovenians later joined forces with the Croatians in an "Illyric" movement to unite the southern Slavs, and supported the formation of Yugoslavia to avoid being divided up between Italy and Austria after the collapse of the Habsburg empire in 1918. After the borders were drawn, significant Slovene minorities remained in those countries.

In the aftermath of independence, Slovenian-registered cars clogged the streets of nearby Klagenfurt, capital of Austria's Carinthia region. Slovenian bookstores in the center of this German-speaking city featured new works on cross-border cooperation. Slovenian carpenters and painters and plumbers bustled about, earning hard schillings to take back across the border at the end of the day. Amateur sports clubs straddled the border, drawing players from both sides. The osmosis was nearly as great, in miniature version, as that between East and West Germany after the Wall fell.

By the same token, some Italians remained in the Istrian Peninsula, which juts into the Adriatic south of Trieste. When borders started to be contested in Yugoslavia, the Italian right became vocal in reclaiming the peninsula, creating friction with the former Yugoslav republics there. Slovenia has a corridor to the sea in Istria, and Croatia controls the rest.

Croatia is more Western in attitudes and lifestyle than Serbia, and is more productive and efficient, but less so than Slovenia. Also Catholic, but never part of the Holy Roman Empire, Croatia came under Habsburg rule when Hungary did in the seventeenth century because it was joined in a perpetual dynastic alliance to Hungary in the eleventh century. For the most part, Croatia retained its own institutions under Hungarian rule; obviously, it had a different orientation throughout its history than did Slovenia. Croatia shares the same language with Serbia—Serbo-Croatian—but, because of its Catholic tradition, writes it with a Latin alphabet, while Serbia, Orthodox in its religion, uses the Cyrillic alphabet prevalent in Orthodox countries like Bulgaria and Russia. Their Catholic religion is one of the main factors distinguishing Slovenia and Croatia from other former republics of Yugoslavia.

In its borders as a constituent republic of Yugoslavia, Croatia also took in the Dalmatian coast, which was controlled by Venice for much of its history, and Dubrovnik, the historic Adriatic port city which, known by its Italian name of Ragusa, was an independent city-state for many centuries and a maritime rival to Venice. In the east, Croatia included Slavonia, a Croatian crownland from early times. To its sorrow, Croatia also had a large Serbian minority, the basis of the bloody fighting in the country in 1991–92. The total population before the fighting was 4.7 million. Croatia's borders and the composition of its population could emerge somewhat different from the conflicts. Zagreb, the capital, a city of 750,000— bigger than Frankfurt or Geneva—with a fair share of Western chic and verve, could attract new investment once peace is assured, and the long coast, with Dubrovnik still an attraction, could restore tourist revenues to the new country, too.

For all of its charm, however, Croatia inspired ambivalent feelings in the rest of Europe. The country fostered a particularly vicious brand of fascism during the 1930s and 1940s, and its postindependence government in 1992 did not enjoy the same reputation for democracy as Slovenia's. Its role as an aggressor in the Bosnian conflict also tarnished its image.

Somber Adriatic

Much is made of Trieste's Habsburg heritage. The port city in the northeast alcove of the Adriatic Sea, just barely part of Italy now on the Slovenian border, reached its zenith in the nineteenth century, when it was the main harbor for the Austro-Hungarian Empire, heir to the eastern Mediterranean's cosmopolitan merchant traditions, an exotic stop on the Orient Express. When the borders were redrawn after World War I, Italy obtained Trieste, and the city went from being a southern port for Austria with a big hinterland, to being an eastern port for Italy with no hinterland at all. It declined; much of the port grew derelict, the median age of the city's residents became quite advanced.

There were murmurs after the collapse of the Iron Curtain that Trieste could regain its hinterland and become the springboard for Italian involvement in eastern Europe. But Italian businessmen preferred to seek east European markets from their comfortable offices in Milan and Bologna, and war-torn Croatia had no immediate need for Trieste's port services. Besides, Croatia had Rijeka (also known in history by its Italian name, Fiume), a sizable seaport eighty miles southwest of Zagreb on a comfortable inlet of the northern Adriatic, while Slovenia, striving for autonomy even as part of Yugoslavia, had installed its own modest port facilities at Koper, virtually a suburb of Trieste. Austria and Hungary had developed well-oiled land supply routes, so that highly efficient northern ports like Rotterdam and Hamburg stood to gain more from their increased trade.

From the time the ancient Romans pushed northward to make the Danube the frontier of their empire, the river basin has had close ties to northern Italy. In medieval times, the Holy Roman Empire included the western Danube region and most of northern Italy. Although Venice subsequently rose as an independent power, the Habsburgs continued that tradition through their control of the Lombardy region and Milan. When the Venetian Republic was dissolved in 1797, Venice and its hinterland came under Austrian control, except for a brief period under Napoleon. Austria had to cede these territories as the nation-state of Italy came into being in the 1860s, but with Trieste and the Dalmatian coast kept a foothold on the Adriatic until World War I.

Because of this history, the northern Adriatic region retains a strong affinity for the former territory of the Danube monarchy. But unless a genuine cohesion and economic dynamism can develop in the Danube Basin superregion, this region is likely to continue as it has been through much of the postwar period, moribund and backward. The two marvelous jewels of maritime power, Venice and Dubrovnik, a longtime rival to the bigger and more powerful Venice, have been bypassed by shifts in trade. Like Vienna, they resemble Disney theme parks, monuments to historic glories. Italian foreign minister Gianni de Michelis, who came from Venice, tried to launch several schemes to give his home a more modern role, but they all foundered on opposition from people who felt the city's structure was too fragile and its historic heritage too important to jeopardize with new experiments.

Likewise, De Michelis's plan for regional cooperation among the Danube countries quickly ran out of steam. Nostalgia alone was not enough to keep his Pentagonal and Hexagonal going. (It may be that the somewhat abstruse names for the grouping also deflated enthusiasm.) The small, well-intentioned efforts of organizations like the Alpine-Adriatic Regional Association remain marginal in the absence of significant new economic ties. In the early 1990s, war and the threat of war in the former Yugoslavia have overshadowed all efforts at peaceful cooperation.

Danube Mists

Born in Trieste, Claudio Magris grew up with the ambiguity of the Danube basin. A literary critic and novelist, he is a contributor to the arts pages of Milan's *Corriere della Sera,* one of Italy's leading daily newspapers, but also an expert on literature of the Habsburg monarchy. In his book on the Danube, itself a quirky and often obscure narrative, he plumbs the murky writings of authors who, like himself, are caught in the ambiguity of the region.

The waters of the Danube, a river "cloudy, wise and great," for Attila Jozsef, with their monotonous flowing, meant old age and the contemporaneous presence of many centuries, the conflu- ence of the victors and the vanquished, the impact of races which then became mingled in time and in the waters, as the Cumaean [from an ancient Greek settlement in southwestern It- aly] blood of his mother mingled in his veins with the Rumanian Transylvanian blood of his father. His Danube was "past, present and future."[11]

This timelessness makes any effort to analyze the region seem ultimately futile. "It isn't easy to write about the Danube, because the river—as Franz Tumler said a few years ago in his *Propositions on the Danube*—flows on in a continuous and indistinct way, unaware of propositions and of language sewing and severing the fabric of its existence."[12]

But the hard economic realities of making the transition to a market economy are dispelling some of this Danubian mistiness. The challenge even seems to be breathing new life into Austria. An east European expert at Vienna's WIFO economic research institute, Jan Stankovsky, dreams of a "Central European" region within the framework of the EC, embracing the east and south of Austria, parts of Moravia and Slovakia, Hungary, and Slovenia. "The massive presence of Austria in east European markets is due first of all to geographic proximity, but also to a number of factors difficult to define that I would call 'cultural affinity,' " he says.[13]

Whether this affinity reaches farther down the Danube remains to be seen. But a functioning Danube Basin superregion is the way for these east European territories in transition to access the powerful economies of Mitteleuropa and Latin Crescent and achieve the economic growth they need to stabilize and reform their societies.

CHAPTER ELEVEN

BALKAN PENINSULA: THE BACKWATER

Western civilization reveres Greece as the cradle of democracy. Philosophy, man's quest to understand the meaning of his existence, is said to be a footnote to Plato. Greco-Roman culture refers to the classical models in architecture, sculpture, and literature created by the Greeks and propagated by the Romans. The golden age of Athens in the fifth century B.C. inspired the Renaissance in medieval Europe, and remains an inexhaustible source for modern thought and culture.

Greece disappeared as a separate entity when Rome conquered it in the second century B.C., subsumed into the Roman Empire, and then the Eastern Roman, or Byzantine, Empire from the fifth century, and then the Ottoman Empire from the fifteenth century. Conquest, immigration, time—all worked to change the complexion of Greek society, alter the language, replace democracy with tyranny and despotism. And yet, when the rise of nationalism in nineteenth-century Europe reawakened Greek patriotism, the British poet Lord Byron and other Romantics like him, in homage to the glories of Pericles' Athens, gave their lives in the struggle to liberate Greece from the Turks. In 1830, modern Greece was born on the southern tip of the Balkan peninsula.

Today, after bouts with military dictatorship, Greece has a parliamentary democracy, belongs to the European Community and NATO, and has become one of the world's favored tourist destinations. But the ruins of the Parthenon on top of Athens' Acropolis, trademark symbol for Greece's classical period, face their greatest menace in twenty-five centuries from the corrosive effect of uncontrolled pollution in a modern city of 3 million people. The stifling pall reaches such proportions that literally hundreds of people can be hospitalized for respiratory and cardiac problems on a bad day. American journalist Flora Lewis describes the view: "The ugly blanket of pollution over Athens is visible from the neighboring hills as a sharp line across the ardent blue sky."[1]

Along with Portugal, Greece is the poorest country in the EC, but unlike Portugal, which has bounded ahead in economic growth since joining the EC in 1986, Greece has actually lost ground. Its per capita income fell from 52 percent of the EC average in the mid-1980s to 48 percent by the end of the decade. Although Greece approved the Maastricht treaty for political and economic union, the country was among the furthest from attaining the treaty's mandated targets for government spending deficits and national debt. Moreover, the country has been so obstreperous, first in hindering EC relations with Turkey, and then, as Yugoslavia broke up, in blocking EC recognition of the Republic of Macedonia, that some EC countries regretted that the Community had no mechanism for expelling members, according to a report in *The Economist* in May 1992.[2]

The Macedonian imbroglio clearly illustrates the Balkan predicament. So petty to outsiders as to be risible, were it not for the threat that the bloody fighting in Croatia and Bosnia-Herzegovina could engulf Macedonia, too, the dispute encapsulates the central problems that plague the entire region: territorial claims dating back centuries or even millennia, grand delusions of regaining former borders and glory, dubious ethnic and cultural links to justify aggression.

Everyone knows that Aristotle and Alexander the Great were Greek, right? In fact, they were from that region extending northwest from the Aegean Sea that came to be known as Macedonia. Like the rest of ancient Greece, the province came under Roman and then Byzantine rule until Slavic people settled there in the sixth century. Successive Bulgarian and Serbian empires included the territory in their realms, until the Ottoman Empire gradually acquired it. The Ottomans kept it until 1912, when—history, history—the Serbs, Bulgarians, and Greeks banded together to repel the Turks, and then turned on one another in a second war to divide up the region. The Greeks had their claim to Alexander's homeland, while the Serbs and Bulgars both believed that the Slavs living in latter-day Macedonia were ethnically closer to their respective nations.

With Solomonic wisdom, Yugoslavian leader Marshal Tito in 1946 declared the people living in the part of Macedonia that Serbia had acquired to be Macedonians, the Slavic dialect they spoke to be the Macedonian language, and the Orthodox church they worshiped in to be the Macedonian church—all this to be included in the autonomous republic of Macedonia, a constitutive nation in the Yugoslav Federation. He hoped at a stroke to trim Serbian power by hiving off as a separate nation a region they saw as their own, and to defuse Bulgarian arguments for claiming it. As it was, Greece and Bulgaria both had their own parts of Macedonia, with Greece keeping the prosperous port city of Salonika, known as Thessaloniki in Greek.

This brings us to 1992. With Yugoslavia breaking up, the constitutive republic of Macedonia had little alternative but to join Slovenia, Croatia, and Bosnia-Herzegovina in declaring independence in 1991 if it wanted to avoid outright Serbian domination. When Germany pressed the EC to recognize the newly independent republics in early 1992, Macedonia was the only one that fulfilled all the EC's requirements for recognition, including specific constitutional provisions for minority rights. But it was the only one not to be recognized, because Greece objected vociferously to an independent republic called Macedonia. The name is part of Greek heritage, they argued. Moreover, any country called Macedonia sooner or later would try to make the case that all of historic Macedonia, including those parts in Greece and Bulgaria, should be "reunited" in that country.

In truth, the would-be Macedonia did not hesitate to provoke Greek sensibilities. Maps showing a Greater Macedonia were distributed in the former Yugoslav republic, and its proposed currency at first depicted the "White Tower," a symbol of Macedonia that happens to be situated in Salonika, Greece's second-largest city. The new country's flag featured the distinctive sixteen-pointed Star of Vergina, an ancient symbol of the Greek Macedonian dynasty.

And the nationalist party in Macedonia was intellectual heir to a nineteenth-century movement that sought political unification of Macedonia. But, countered officials of the breakaway republic, how could a landlocked country of 2 million people, with no army, no weapons, no currency reserves, and virtually no economy possibly challenge mighty Greece, with 10 million people and all the firepower of NATO and the EC behind it?

Greece's exasperated EC partners observed neutrally that most people were allowed to call themselves whatever name they chose to call themselves. In western Europe, Luxembourg managed to serve as the name not only of the sovereign Grand Duchy but of the neighboring Belgian province—both entities carved out of the historic Luxembourg duchy of the Holy Roman Empire. But Athens was adamant. The government replaced one foreign minister for speaking too bluntly, but did not back down on the name issue. When the Dutch foreign minister attacked the Greeks for their obstinacy, the country launched a boycott of Dutch goods.

For luckless Macedonia, recognition was a matter of life and death, so that it could develop its own trade and economy and secure some legitimation for resisting eventual Serbian incursions. Greece, for its part, should have had more important things to look after. The OECD, which issues annual economic reports on its members that usually veil criticism behind an impenetrable screen of jargon, warned in unusually blunt language that unless Greece acted immediately to reform wasteful practices, it would be left out of Europe's economic integration. Tax evasion and bureaucratic inefficiency were impeding economic development, the organization said.

Even aside from outright military rule from 1967 to 1974, Greece has had a spotty record on democratic freedom in the postwar period. The anti-American, anticapitalist government of the Panhellenic Social Movement under Andreas Papandreou, in power from 1981 to 1989, provided a welcome change of pace from right-wing repression, but did not encourage investment or economic development. Greece has, for instance, the largest merchant marine fleet in the world, even though two-thirds of the ships are under flags of convenience. In 1992, twenty-four Greek shippers had capacity topping a million tons, but hardly any of them lived in Greece or invested money in their home country. So this Greek industry par excellence has limited economic benefit for the country. None of the top 100 EC companies has its headquarters in Greece—even Portugal has at least one.

Greece does not like to be lumped together with "the Balkans," because of all the connotations of economic and social backwardness that term carries. But Greek customs and practices, as well as geography, have firmly anchored the country to the Balkan peninsula. Even though Greece has ancient historic ties to southern Italy, across the Ionian Sea in the west, the modern nation, centered on the Aegean Sea in the east, has much closer links to the central Balkan nations. Northern Greece, bordering on Albania, Macedonia, and Bulgaria, paced the southern half of the country in economic growth during the 1980s, averaging 2.3 percent a year, compared with 1.7 percent for the nation as a whole.

The port city of Salonika, in northern Greece, is the country's second-largest city, with nearly 1 million people. The breakup in Yugoslavia and the sluggish pace of change in Bulgaria diminished Salonika's initial enthusiasm about the potential economic benefits from communism's collapse in the Balkans. Nonetheless, Salonika embarked on a $150-million program to expand and improve port facilities for Balkan trade. Meanwhile, Greeks invested in more than two hundred joint ventures in Bulgaria in the first two years after the fall of dictatorship. Sofia, the Bulgarian capital, was three hours away from Salonika by car, compared to five hours for Athens. Greek exporters supplied pent-up Bulgarian demand for consumer goods like coffee, ice cream, jeans, and athletic shoes. Seven Greek towns obtained support from the EC's Interreg program for cross-border cooperation to promote commercial ties with four Bulgarian towns. In one southern Bulgarian village, residents were just glad for the chance once again to take their sheep down the mountain to graze across the Greek border, in an age-old tradition of transhumance.

A Broad Peninsula

The Balkan peninsula is not as much an "almost island"—the root meaning of the word peninsula—as some of the others in Europe, like the Italian or Iberian peninsulas. Although surrounded by water on three sides, the Balkan peninsula is joined to the mainland not by a narrow isthmus, but by a broad seam of mountains a good five hundred miles long. The mountains, in fact, isolate the peninsula much more effectively than the relatively narrow stretches of water. The Adriatic Sea, which forms the western boundary of the Balkan Peninsula, averages only 110 miles in width, and the Aegean Sea, on the eastern boundary of the Balkan Peninsula, is dotted with islands that have served as stepping stones since time immemorial for traffic plying the waters between mainland Greece and Asia Minor. Nevertheless, these seas serve conveniently as the eastern and western boundaries of the region, with the Mediterranean itself in the south. Two straits, the Dardanelles and the Bosporus, leading into and out of the small Sea of Marmara, and the Black Sea, at the other end of the Bosporus, extend the Peninsula's eastern border northward.

In the north, the superregion Balkan Peninsula shares a border with Danube Basin. This follows the Croatian border parallel to the Adriatic Coast northward through the Dinaric Alps, and then eastward along the Sava River, skirting the Bosnian mountains, past Belgrade, along the Danube, turning south to follow the border between Serbia and Bulgaria through the Balkan Mountains, turning east to pass through Sofia and then to follow the mountains due east to the Black Sea coast. Thus the Balkan Peninsula superregion includes Bosnia-Herzegovina, Serbia—with the former autonomous region Kosovo in the south, but not the other once autonomous region Vojvodina in the north—Montenegro, the former Yugoslav republic of Macedonia, the southern half of Bulgaria, all of Albania and Greece, and the small part of Turkey on the southeast corner of the peninsula. If the conflict in the former Yugoslavia leads to a partition of Bosnia-Herzegovina, the Croatian territory will join the rest of Croatia in Danube Basin, while Moslem and Serbian territories remain in Balkan Peninsula. Likewise, if Serbia permanently suppresses the autonomy of Vojvodina, that will then be drawn into Balkan Peninsula as well. One of Europe's smaller superregions in population, with about 43 million people, Balkan Peninsula is, with Slavic Federation, the poorest.

The problem in Balkan Peninsula, of course, is not determining the external borders of the region, but the internal borders separating the patchwork of populations that have coexisted there for centuries. The very word "Balkanization" means the "breaking up into small, mutually hostile political units, as the Balkans after World

War I," according to one dictionary. The Ottoman Empire, which controlled the entire region for four or five centuries, maintained stability by harsh political repression combined with a measure of cultural autonomy. The Turks also preserved the peasant agricultural society in the region as a further method of pacification, blocking any economic modernization.

In this century, too, the borders in the Balkans and the fate of the peoples within them has largely been determined by outside forces—the wartime powers who dictated the terms of settlement after the two world wars. Their decisions ranged from dilettantish to cavalier. American writer William Pfaff recounts that, at the end of World War I, for instance, U.S. president Woodrow Wilson assigned Walter Lippmann, then a journalist scarcely in his twenties, to head a five-man committee to redraw the borders of central and southeastern Europe along national and ethnic lines.[3] The group took maps and statistics and correlated concentrations of the various nations with secret treaties between the wartime allies to arrive at a "logical" set of new boundaries. But the dispersal of ethnic settlements throughout the territory foredoomed such efforts—all borders included more than one nationality, inevitably creating friction between a dominant nation in the majority and one or several vulnerable minorities.

The settlements after World War II largely restored 1920 borders, reversing Germany's wartime redrawing of the map, but cynically carved up the region into spheres of influence in the nascent Cold War between the Western allies and the Soviet Union. In a 1944 meeting with Stalin, British prime minister Winston Churchill scribbled his famous formula for partitioning the Balkans—Romania was to go 90 percent to "Russia," 10 percent to "the others"; Greece was proportioned 90/10 in favor of Britain and the U.S.; Bulgaria 75/25 in favor of the Soviet Union; Yugoslavia and Hungary were to be split up 50/50. Even Churchill considered this to be cavalier in view of the millions of lives affected, but he preferred to settle it at the negotiating table rather than let the Red Army determine divisions on the battlefield. In the end, of course, Stalin ignored the finer points of this accord just as he did the safeguards in the Yalta agreement designed to let eastern Europe's nations choose their postwar regimes. Only Greece, after several years of civil war, landed firmly in the Western camp. Still, some historians feel that the postwar development of the Balkan countries somehow reflected the proportional spheres of influence in their degree of Stalinization.

The Balkan War

The war that started in 1991 in Yugoslavia threatened to halt Europe's optimistic progress toward greater unity. The fighting between Serbia and the other constitutive nations that made up Yugoslavia during the seventy-four years of its existence deflated many hopes. Even if history had ended, as one bestseller had it, human brutality and aggression obviously had not. With the collapse of communism, gangsters masking as politicians had stopped exploiting Marxist ideology for their own personal aggrandizement, but now there were plenty of new thugs—or sometimes the same ones—cynically manipulating nationalist feeling for their own ends.

The fighting in the former Yugoslavia and the incapacity of any outside force to intervene and stop the bloodshed has made a mockery of the vaunted New World Order. The European Community—paralyzed politically by the opposition of France, traditionally allied to Serbia, and Germany, historically linked to Croatia—demonstrated its impotence in a pathetic manner, with the unhappy Lord Carrington limping from one illusory ceasefire to another. The panoply of institutions promising to guarantee security in Europe—the UN Security Council, the Western European Union, the Conference on Security and Cooperation in Europe, NATO—all found excuses not to act while Europeans slaughtered, maimed, tortured, and uprooted other Europeans with a savagery all too reminiscent of the continent's two earlier wars in this century. Worse, the pusillanimous political calculation of the major west European countries to avoid entanglement in the Balkan region reflected the narrow, selfish basis of their thinking, demonstrated already in their miserly response to the yawning economic need in eastern Europe after the fall of communism. This smug myopia keeps west European politicians from seeing that their peoples' own continued prosperity, which they so jealously guard from the unwelcome intrusions of their needy neighbors, is vitally threatened by the conflict in the Balkans.

The fighting among nationalist "militia" units—often only gangs of drunken bandits intent on robbery, rape, murder, and wanton destruction—backed by unscrupulous politicians and military men in Serbia and Croatia, devastated large areas of Croatia and then Bosnia-Herzegovina. Political analysts coolly predicted that once its territorial gains in Croatia and Bosnia were secured, Serbia would then instigate a "bloodbath" in Kosovo—a formerly autonomous region where ethnic Albanians make up more than four-fifths of the population—in order to drive out the Albanians and reclaim the historic homeland of Serbia's medieval empire.

It was in Kosovo, in 1389, that the expanding Ottoman Turks decisively defeated the Serbs, and subjugated them for the next five centuries. That date and place, so distant and obscure for the outside world, burns in the collective memory of Serbia. In June 1989, Serbian nationalist leader Slobodan Milosevic announced in a major speech in Kosovo, commemorating the six hundredth anniversary of that battle, that he wanted to make Kosovo a flourishing Serbian territory once again. Outright persecution of Albanians in Kosovo runs the risk of drawing Albania into an international conflict, weak and backward as that country is after decades of virtual isolation from the rest of the world. Extending the violence farther southward into Macedonia risks involving Greece and Bulgaria in the war. Bulgarian president Zhelyu Zhelev, urging the West late in 1992 to intervene militarily, warned that if fighting spread to Macedonia, Bulgaria might have to get involved: "We could not possibly stop the influx of refugees and this would provoke Bulgarians living on the border, most of whom have relatives in Macedonia, to take arms and go to the rescue."[4]

The central Balkan nations seem to require the iron hand of a repressive ruler—the Turks or the communists—to keep them from destroying one another. The violence in the 1990s mirrored that of the 1940s, when Croatian Ustashis and Serbian Chetniks already were fighting for "ethnic cleansing." But if French and Germans and Poles can reach a political accommodation after the horrors of World War II, so can Serbs and Croats. The pretence of many western politicians and media that the ethnic conflicts of the Balkans belong in some special category of intractable problems is a mendacious alibi with racist overtones.

Serbia and Yugoslavia

Before its disintegration, Yugoslavia was a country of 24 million people, the largest in Eastern Europe after Poland. Practicing its own version of communism, which featured worker control of companies rather than central planning, it enjoyed the highest standard of living in the East, with its per capita income nearly equal to that of EC member Portugal and only slightly behind that of democratic neighbor Greece.

But it was a nation in name only, created for the convenience of its neighbors rather than its own people. In a countdown similar to the Christmas carol about the partridge in a pear tree, Yugoslavia was said to have six republics, five nations, four languages, three religions, two alphabets, and one political party. Between the wars, the new country, established in 1918 with the dismemberment of the Austro-Hungarian and Ottoman empires, experienced widespread unrest, political assassination, and dictatorship before partition during the war and cruel mutual persecution by Serbs and Croats. Only the authoritarian rule of Marshal Tito, a communist partisan who won the support of the Allies during World War II, kept the country's inherent tensions under control during the postwar period. Even after Tito's death in 1980, the looming presence of the Soviet Red Army in the region subdued nationalist pressures. The waning of Soviet power heralded the end for a country that never really established an inner equilibrium.

Yugoslavia had a special membership in the Organization for Economic Cooperation and Development (OECD) the capitalist club par excellence. Its citizens could travel freely, its currency was partially convertible, its borders open to tourists. Tito, too big a personality for the modest-sized country, had founded the nonaligned movement to rally Third World countries caught between rival claims of the superpowers. But the anticapitalist organization tilted to the left—nonalignment, like Yugoslavia itself, was an illusion born of Tito's talent for acquiring power. By 1992, his accomplishments had proved as ephemeral as earlier "empires" in the region, like that of Stefan Dushan, the "czar of the Serbs and the Greeks" in the fourteenth century, or the one established by the Bulgarian czar Simeon in the tenth century.

Born of Croatian and Slovenian parents, Tito designed Yugoslavia to contain Serbia. He recognized Macedonia as a nationality, he fostered decentralization in the Yugoslavian economy, he strengthened the autonomy of the two Serbian provinces where other nationalities predominated—Vojvodina in the north and Kosovo in the south. The Serbs resented this. As the largest nationality in Yugoslavia, they felt they should enjoy primacy in a more tightly centralized Yugoslavia. Five years after Tito's death, the Serbian Academy of Sciences in 1985 produced a Memorandum that urged a reversal of what it saw as the "discrimination" against Serbia, and a return to the open Serb dominance of the royalist Yugoslavia that existed between the wars. Christopher Cviic, an anglicized Croat who covered Eastern Europe for *The Economist* for many years, describes this Memorandum as a modern version of the 1844 "Outline" for a "Greater Serbia," a nationalist manifesto calling for recreation of the fourteenth-century Serbian empire.[5]

The 1985 document, dismissed by other Yugoslav republics as Serbian propaganda, took on greater importance a year later with the rise of Slobodan Milosevic in the Serbian Communist Party. Milosevic exploited Serbian resentment and "reformed" the Communist Party along his nationalist lines. In 1989, he pushed through constitutional changes that virtually rescinded the autonomy of Vojvodina and Kosovo, and in 1990 a grateful Serbia elected him president.

Milosevic's nationalist policy thus put Serbia at odds with other Yugoslav republics, who wanted greater autonomy within the federation, not stronger centralization under Serbian control. One after the other, the other republics declared independence as an act of self-defense against Serbia's power play. Foiled in his attempt to "Serbianize" all of Yugoslavia, Milosevic set his sights on a smaller version of Greater Serbia, aiming to redraw the republic's borders to include all those areas in neighboring republics where Serbs lived. These territorial ambitions led to the conflicts in Croatia and Bosnia-Herzegovina and seemed to augur later violence in Kosovo, Vojvodina, and Macedonia.

While bringing death and devastation to neighboring republics, Milosevic's aggressive policies have wrought considerable hardship on Serbia, too. Condemnation of Serbian policy by the world community has humiliated the proud Serbian people, and international sanctions have worsened an economy already severely strained by the war and the influx of refugees. In the absence of any effective outside intervention, the growing Serbian resistance to continued adversity is the sole check to the expansionism of Milosevic and his military advisers. Whether popular resistance would be sufficient to force a political settlement of the Yugoslavian conflict is far from sure as Serbia continues its systematic conquest of Bosnian territory.

Archduke Franz Ferdinand once described Serbia as a land of "thieves and murderers and bandits and a few plum-trees." His judgment was facetious but prophetic. Western exasperation with Serbia in the early 1990s, unable to transform itself into an effective form of intervention, has been insufficient to stop a dangerous escalation of the violence.

Bosnia's Moslem Identity

Caught between Catholic Croats and Orthodox Serbs, Bosnia throughout its history was ready to embrace any new religion to differentiate the territory from its neighbors. The region served as refuge in the thirteenth and fourteenth centuries for the Christian Bogomile heresy, which originated in Bulgaria but was suppressed there. The Turks conquered Bosnia in the fifteenth century; the southern sector held out a couple of decades longer under its duke, who was titled *herceg,* giving Bosnia its double name. A great portion of the territory's population converted to Islam, to preserve a distinct identity and autonomy for Bosnia.

Following a peasant revolt, Austria-Hungary occupied Bosnia-Herzegovina in 1878 and in 1908 annexed it outright. The Habsburgs saw Bosnia as a foil against Serbian ambitions—a fateful policy, for it was a Serbian-backed assassin who killed the Austrian heir on in 1914, in Sarajevo, to protest Habsburg rule. This nationalist action unleashed World War I and led to the dissolution of the Austro-Hungarian Empire. The tragic destruction of Sarajevo in 1992–93 marked the sequel to that conflict, as Serbia and Croatia once again tried to carve out their respective portions of Bosnia-Herzegovina at the expense of the Moslem population that dominated the republic.

In the face of bloodshed in Bosnia-Herzegovina, the political leaders in western Europe in 1992–93 proved themselves worthy heirs of the men whose shortsightedness and timidity in 1914 and 1938 allowed regional aggression to embroil the entire continent in a destructive war. It is no wonder that they want the United States to take over command. Although the Clinton administration has hesitated to intervene militarily in Bosnia without European support, Washington seems determined to keep the conflict from spreading throughout the peninsula.

Albania's Dismal Destiny

Geography fated Albania to the isolation it has experienced up till now. Surrounded on three sides by rugged mountains and deep gorges, its swampy and unhealthy lowlands face the Adriatic Sea on the west coast. An indigent people descended from the Illyrians, a group of Indo-European tribes who settled the region two millennia before Christ, the Albanians call themselves *Shqiptare,* "the sons of eagles"—and eagles are the ones who can most easily get in and out of the country. Greeks and Romans colonized the coast but never settled inland. The Ottoman Turks gained control of the region when they defeated Serbia in the fourteenth century, and kept it until 1912. But they, too, failed to develop the country. Herding dominated agricultural activity and manufacturing was restricted to handcrafts. After gaining independence, Albania fell into anarchy during World War I. It became a satellite of fascist Italy between the wars, under King Zog I. After the war, Albania, like neighboring Yugoslavia, came under Moscow's sway. When the Soviet Union and China split the communist world into two camps, Albania, under its longtime leader Enver Hoxha, followed the militant Chinese leadership.

The outcome of this dismal political destiny is backwardness—economic, social, and cultural, as well as political. Illiteracy was still at 80 percent between the wars, and 85 percent of the population in 1950 were engaged in primary industries of farming and forestry. Under the communists, industrial employment rose to 33 percent, but Albanian industry cannot compete on world markets. Civil rebellion forced liberalization in 1991, but by that time Albania had the living standards and economic structure of a Third World country. With one of the highest birthrates in Europe, it has a young population—about half of the 3.2 million people were under the age of twenty-six in 1990, and one-third under fifteen. A report from the World Health Organization in 1989 found that two-fifths of Albania's children were undernourished. A German reporter visiting Albania at the beginning of 1992 rode in a train where the outer surface of the cars was rusted through, the windows were broken out, letting in freezing winds, and the seats had been removed. He described the desolation: "All of Albania is made up of scrap-metal and is ruled by chaos and anarchy."[6] The director of a home for handicapped children in a northern Albanian city begged the West *not* to send any more aid, because the food and blankets they had received were only an invitation to bandits to raid the home and rob it.

Elections in March 1992 brought an opposition Democratic Party to power and things started to improve somewhat. Cars, buses, and bananas, mostly unknown under the communists, began to fill the cities. Foreign aid workers from such hardship posts as Chad and Bangladesh arrived to apply their skills to Albania's problems. Foreign investors made tentative approaches to exploit Albania's mineral resources, particularly oil and chromium. Emigration also eased the pressure. Although Italy only allowed 25,000 Albanian refugees to get off boats that crossed the Adriatic, as many as 200,000 crossed the mountains into Greece in the first two years of freedom, most of them illegally. In addition to Albania's own rapidly growing population, an estimated 2 million ethnic Albanians live in Kosovo, the erstwhile autonomous province in Serbia, on the northeast Albanian border. These Albanians, although fearful of the future under Serbia, are understandably cautious about linking their fate to backward Albania. A further 400,000 Albanians live in Macedonia, to the east of Albania, where they make up about one-fifth of the population. A nascent movement in Albania envisaged the old dream of uniting the entire region inhabited by Albanians into a single country, but most Albanians would be content if they could have free and easy interchange across existing national borders.

"Century of the Turks"

The fall of communism in eastern Europe and the Soviet Union has not robbed Turkey of its strategic importance. The country bridging Europe and Asia, key to NATO strategy during the Cold War, found its geographic position just as vital in the war against Iraq, when the United States relied on Turkish air bases. A secular Moslem state with a rapidly growing capitalist economy, Turkey found much to talk about with the former Soviet republics in central Asia—Kazakhstan, Uzbekistan, Turkmenistan, Tadzhikistan, Kirghizia—whose exotic names reflect the common Turkic origin of the languages in most of the region. Turkey suggested setting up a free-trade zone with these newly independent countries to help them make the transition to a market economy. Turkey also led formation of a Black Sea economic zone together with the former Soviet republics Russia, Ukraine, Moldava, and Georgia, and the Balkan countries Bulgaria and Romania, all of which border the Black Sea directly, and some of their neighbors—Greece, Albania, Armenia, and Azerbaijan. Small wonder that Turkish president Turgut Ozal could say in November 1992, "If we take advantage of the historic opportunity and avoid mistakes, the twenty-first century can turn into the Century of the Turks."[7]

Many of Turkey's European neighbors feel that the Turks have had enough centuries already, after the long dominance of the Ottoman Empire in southeastern Europe—centuries marked by political repression and economic stagnation. Modern industrial Turkey, though, is simply too big and too dynamic to ignore. Its 1990 population of 57 million put it on a par with France or Britain, while its projected growth to 66 million by the year 2000 far outstripped the forecasts for stable west European populations. Istanbul recorded a population of 3 million in 1980, which had mushroomed to 6.7 million by 1990 and reached well over 8 million by 1993, making it the largest city in Europe after London, Paris, and Moscow.

Yes, in Europe. Even though a portion of Istanbul spills across the Bosporus, and so technically is in Asia, the site occupied by Turkey's largest city lies geographically in Europe and has played a major role throughout European history. From its beginnings as Byzantium in the seventh century B.C., to its designation as capital of the Eastern Roman Empire with the name Constantinople in the fourth century A.D., to its role as seat of government of the Ottoman Empire, the Sublime Porte, from the fifteenth to the twentieth centuries, Istanbul stood at the crossroads of Mediterranean civilization. At its zenith in late antiquity, Constantinople was the largest and most splendid city in the world. When it fell to the Turks in 1453, it became the capital of Christendom's "evil empire," the nemesis of all that Europe held to be holy, the heathen enemy to be fought and resisted even as the armies of Suleiman the Magnificent pushed northward in the sixteenth century to the gates of Vienna.

Decades of decay and disintegration in the Ottoman Empire preceded its final defeat in World War I. The victorious allies occupied Constantinople for five years, deposing the last sultan in 1922. In 1923, nationalists proclaimed the new Turkish republic with its capital in Ankara, in central Anatolia, the region corresponding to the peninsula of Asia Minor. The first president, Mustafa Kemal Ataturk, secularized the state, adopted the Latin alphabet, and in general modernized the new republic. Constantinople officially became Istanbul in 1930. Turkey remained neutral in World War II, making Istanbul a rendezvous for spying and intrigue. The country joined NATO in 1951.

When Turkey restored democratic elections in 1987, after seven years of military control, the country officially applied to become a member of the EC. Turkey has had an association agreement since 1963 and has been trying for most of the time since then to talk the EC into accepting full Turkish membership. In the 1980s, Turkey's economy grew 75 percent in real terms, much faster than that of the EC, which rose 25 percent. Despite this rapid growth, however, Turkey continued to have a much lower standard of living than even the poorest EC members, not least because of the high birthrate. The country also has a poor image regarding human rights, not only because of the recent military dictatorship, but because of its persecution of the Kurdish minority in southeastern Turkey. The Armenian genocides at the end of the nineteenth century and during World War I, which together claimed the lives of an estimated 1.3 million Armenians living in Turkey, also darken the country's image.

Turgut Ozal claimed that the EC rejects Turkish membership because it is overwhelmingly Moslem—98 percent of the population. Turkey does pose a problem of cultural identity for Europe. The moderate, secular Moslem faith of Turkey is not in such sharp contrast to European society as the fundamental Islamism of Iran or Saudi Arabia, however. Long before the EC was founded, Ataturk westernized the country, abolishing Islam as the state religion, adopting Western clothes, and even designating Sunday as the day of rest just as in Christian countries. In June 1993, Tansu Ciller, forty-seven, became the country's first woman prime minister. The former economics minister and academic is well known in Turkey for having forced her husband to take her maiden name.

Most of Turkey's territory lies in Asia; the geographic argument for making the Bosporus a frontier is hardly compelling. The narrow strait has never been a political frontier and did not exclude Asia Minor from European events. While the Turkish tribes were still roaming the steppes of central Asia, like so many other peoples who later settled in Europe, Greek tribes colonized much of the western coast of Asia Minor. The Aegean Sea, interspersed with so many islands, was a well-traveled highway between the two parts of "Greece." Asia Minor, like the rest of the Mediterranean coast, was an integral part of the Roman Empire and a center of the Hellenic subculture that continued to flourish under the Romans. The Ottoman Turks, who controlled most of the territory around the eastern Mediterranean, have left an indelible imprint on the cultures of southeastern Europe, particularly in the Balkan peninsula.

French historian Pierre Behar marshals several illustrious French geographers to testify to the European character of Asia Minor. They note that the Aegean always was the center of the Hellenic world, that Anatolia "looks" toward Europe, that it "tilts" its inhabitants toward Europe. Behar says of Asia Minor: "Geographically, it is closer to Europe than to Asia. And so, humanly as well. . . . The Aegean islands forever link Greece and Anatolia, which should be considered as the first peninsula of Europe, its mother-peninsula."[8] There is in fact a school of thought in archeology that regards Anatolia as the cradle of early European culture. Advocates of this notion trace a trail of ancient artifacts from Asia Minor up the Danube valley to demonstrate the migration of tools, implements, and perhaps people themselves.

The EC shelved Turkey's 1987 application for membership, postponing action indefinitely, but offered to consider a customs union for 1996. Now that the collapse of communist rule in the region opens up new opportunities for Turkish political and economic influence, however, the country has adopted a more noncommital attitude toward EC membership. Emerging democracies in southeastern Europe, getting the same chilly reception in Brussels as Turkey did, are gravitating toward Istanbul. Not only is Turkey's blend of capitalism and government intervention an economic model for the Balkan countries, but Istanbul is a marketplace geared to their more modest needs and accomplishments.

Large-scale displacements of Greeks and Turks in this century mean that many businessmen in each country speak the other's language. Bulgaria has a large ethnic Turkish minority in the south, anywhere from half a million to a million. In the final stages of Bulgaria's communist dictatorship, in 1989, Sofia drove as many as 300,000 Turks out of the country in a heavy-handed attempt to impose Bulgarian language and institutions on them. About half of those returned when communism fell, but economic distress forced more emigrations afterward. Nonetheless, the support of the Turkish nationalist party in Bulgaria was the key to forming the first democratic government. One Turkish leader in Bulgaria declared that "Bulgaria's path to Europe leads over the Bosporus."[9] The 1.6 million Moslems in Bosnia-Herzegovina, two-fifths of the population, are descendants of Slavs converted to Islam during the Ottoman rule. In the 1992-93 conflict with Serbia, they received encouragement from their Turkish coreligionists, spurred on by an estimated 2 million Turkish citizens descended from Bosnians who emigrated to Istanbul when Austria-Hungary gained control of Bosnia in the nineteenth century.

The question of Cyprus continues to poison relations between Greece and Turkey, which in turn complicates Turkey's dealings with Brussels. Cyprus is a bit of the Balkans planted in the eastern Mediterranean. Controlled by the British from 1878 until it was granted independence in 1960, Cyprus currently has a population of three-quarters of a million people, four-fifths of whom are ethnic Greek and the rest Turkish. In 1974, the Turkish army invaded Cyprus to counter what it saw as discrimination by the Greek majority against the Turkish minority. The Turks occupied the northern two-fifths of the island, including part of the capital, Nicosia, and established a Turkish republic there that was recognized by no one except Ankara.

Cyprus, a dynamic small country that likes to cast itself as a "dragon" of the Mediterranean similar to the Southeast Asian dragons like Taiwan, Hong Kong, and Singapore, applied for EC membership in 1990. Brussels would prefer that the Greek Cypriot republic reach a settlement with the Turks, but the Greeks argue that their membership should not depend on Turkish whims. Cyprus has been averaging 6 to 7 percent economic growth a year, except in 1991, when the Gulf war depressed activity. It successfully wooed much of the regional financial activity forced to flee Beirut in the 1970s and 1980s. Its offshore company register masks the usual gamut of illegal activities—for instance, Serbia was able to evade many of the U.N. economic sanctions by using front companies registered in Cyprus.

At the June 1992 summit meeting in Istanbul to formalize creation of the Black Sea zone of economic cooperation, Greek and Turkish prime ministers nonetheless shook hands and discussed wider-ranging cooperation. In the midst of their dispute about the former Soviet fleet based in the Black Sea, Russian president Boris Yeltsin and Ukrainian president Leonid Kravchuk also attended. Most tellingly, the new presidents of Armenia and Azerbaijan, countries locked in the bloody conflict over Nagorno-Karabakh, the Armenian enclave in Azerbaijan, both attended the meeting. Economic prosperity in the region remains a distant and long-term goal, but in view of the impassioned ethnic rivalries, Turkey achieved a significant political victory simply getting everyone into the same room.

Balkan Aspirations

In early 1993, the halting progress of the U.N.-sponsored peace talks in Bosnia-Herzegovina, bolstered by support from the Clinton administration, made it difficult to foresee whether peace could be achieved or how long it would last. It seemed unthinkable that Europe could let the war go on, but then it seemed unthinkable two years earlier that Europe would let the war go as far as it did. The Serbian propaganda machine remained effective in forestalling foreign intervention because, like those in Nazi Germany and apartheid South Africa, it let people off the hook. The merciless television coverage put the lie to the dissimulations of politicians and pundits, but public opinion was slow to demand sterner measures.

A first, important step in achieving some solution in the Yugoslavian war would be to debunk the mystique of ethnic intractability in the conflict. By portraying the war as a continuation of mysterious, Balkan blood vendettas that westerners could not hope to comprehend or cope with, Serbia disguised its naked aggression with a voodoo mask that frightened away timid diplomats. A British journalist, Mark Thompson, decries Western collusion in accepting this mummery. He dismisses the excuses proffered for European Community reticence in intervening.

Another lie underpins these arguments. This is the claim, repeated daily by a thousand journalists, that this is an *ethnic war*. . . . It is a misnomer, because the Serb, Croat and Muslim nations are ethnically indistinguishable. . . . And it is pernicious, because it disguises a consequence as a cause and mystifies the conflict as an orgiastic free-for-all, far removed from political calculation: a spontaneous Balkan combustion—an outbreak of Balkan violence, endemic and insensate, that must be left to burn itself out.[10]

There are, of course, genuine ethnic differences in the Balkan peninsula, between the South Slavs and Albanians, or Greeks, for instance (but even here one has to be cautious after centuries of ethnic mingling). But the differences among the national groupings in the former Yugoslavia are cultural and historic, not ethnic. There was nothing more mysterious about these cultural aspirations than those of the Catalonians or Flemish. Although he remains skeptical himself, Thompson reports that many in the region share the idealism of Europe, citing as typical the remarks of Slobodan Lang, a Croatian cabinet minister under the old regime.

It was poignant to see how his [Lang's] perspicacity became clouded with idealism as soon as I asked about Europe's role in the crisis. He shares with so many of his compatriots an unnerving zeal for the concept and potential of Europe. "Nobody in Yugoslavia desires a state in the nineteenth-century sense," he exhorted, not quite convincingly given the Croatian government's posturing. "What these countries are fighting for is to be a European region in which their own cultural dignity can be preserved." With the Cold War over, "for the first time ever, all the regions and nations and cultures of Europe can be recognized at the same time. The rainbow of Europe can be realized."[11]

CHAPTER TWELVE

SLAVIC FEDERATION: THE ENDLESS EAST

Moscow, for decades a drearily monotonous place, has become a city of outrageous contrasts. The streets leading to Red Square resemble an oriental bazaar, with people selling everything from the family samovar to a bar of soap. At the same time, queues of well-heeled Muscovites form outside the hard-currency stores that have moved into the historic GUM shopping mall just off the square. The lines to buy bread and meat are still long, but McDonald's, Pizza Hut, and Taco Bell are setting up fast-food outlets as quickly as they can.

Pensioners suffer from a 1,300 percent annual inflation rate, while an upstart "entrepreneurial" class sports wads of hard currency and flaunts its new wealth in flashy cars. The collapse of the ruble on foreign exchange markets has so skewed currency relationships as to cleave society into two different worlds. Those with hard currency resources are building suburban villas for $200,000 while skilled factory workers earn the ruble equivalent of $30 a month.

In the wake of the failed coup in August 1991, the world has watched anxiously as the former Soviet Union struggles to find some sort of political and economic stability after communism foundered. The successor states have entered into an unprecedented and painful transformation that entails radical changes in the government, the economy, and the society.

The rest of the world, too, has had to adjust. We have had to change our view of the globe. Gone is the bipolar world of two superpowers confronting each other across a field where European countries appear as so many pawns. The Soviet Union has gone from this dominant global position to being just another world power on the eastern end of Europe. It would be a mistake to underestimate the residual strength of this erstwhile superpower, or its potential for the not-so-distant future. For now, though, Russia and the other successor states to the Soviet Union are groping toward their proper relationship to their neighbors in Europe and Asia, as well as to their former superpower rival and the rest of the world. The process brings anguish and opportunity, for those in the ex-Soviet republics and for many others.

Clichés about Russians' willingness to suffer, their historic need for autocratic rule—after all, they had known only czars and communists—their putative inability to cope with either democracy or capitalism, have been proffered as eventual excuses for the failure of the transition even as the struggle is going on. It has been largely overlooked that it was the Russian people who overthrew communism in the three days of the 1991 coup attempt and its aftermath.

The easy clichés about Russian autocracy ignore the country's authentic, albeit faint, tradition of democracy, beginning with the case of Novgorod. Up until the fifteenth century, Novgorod was one of the principal Russian cities, growing in importance as the Vikings receded and Baltic trade was organized by the German-dominated Hanseatic League. Novgorod became the eastern terminal of the Hanseatic trade routes, a prosperous commercial city, ruled by an oligarchy of merchant families answerable to the town assembly—much like Venice and other Italian city-states.

The city was one of the first victims of Muscovy's rising might. On the pretext that Novgorod was seeking an alliance with Russia's enemy Lithuania, Moscow's grand prince Ivan III in 1478 abolished the city's assembly, deported its leading citizens, and divided up its property among his servitors—a fateful turning point for the history of Russia. As Robin Milner-Gulland, a British expert on Russia, writes:

Novgorod represented "the possible other case," an authentic part of Russia that shared the same . . . antecedents as its rivals Muscovy and Lithuania, yet grew into a society more attractive than either to modern minds: it commanded the loyalty rather than the fear of its citizens, was freedom-loving, relatively democratic, famously resourceful and hardworking, tolerant in its law code and penal practice, artistically prolific.[1]

Czarist autocracy went on to provoke many uprisings in Russian history. Long before the 1917 revolutions, Russia offered a rich field for anarchists—Bakunin is the most famous—and terrorists, who exerted constant pressure to liberalize the regime. One of the most idealistic and impractical of the movements was that of the Decembrists, so called because their civilized attempt at a coup d'etat took place in December 1825. Czarist regiments fired on the passive rebel troops and quickly crushed the uprising, but the Decembrists remained a rallying point for liberal resistance to tyranny. Large-scale revolts in 1905 forced the last czar to adopt a constitution and a parliament. The February revolution of 1917 forced him to abdicate in favor of a parliamentary government, until the October revolution, when the Bolsheviks hijacked the country and subjugated it to seven decades of ruthless state terror and police control.

As the Soviet Union crumbled, the former communist apparatchiks who seized positions of power showed little connection to this alternative democratic tradition in Russian history. It was far from certain that democratic forces would prevail in the chaos that followed the dissolution of the Soviet empire. Reactionary nationalists, resurgent communists, a politicized military—all posed a dangerous threat to the fragile democratic structures that rose from the wreckage. Helene Carrere d'Encausse, a French expert on the Soviet Union who correctly predicted its breakup, identified several major streams of Russian nationalism in the post-Soviet turmoil, including some that were liberal, moderate, and Western-oriented, drawing on intellectual resources from the beginning of this century, as well as some that were not so liberal.[2]

Which of these forces would gain the ascendancy was impossible to foresee. Whatever his faults, Boris Yeltsin seems to have a strong political instinct that enables him to read the feelings of his constituency and to move the country through its wrenching transition toward a democratic, capitalistic system. His vote of confidence in the April 1993 referendum and his successful launch of Russia's privatization program offered some hope that he can continue on the path of reform.

Russia's Borders

The Slavic Federation consists essentially of the European territories of the former Soviet Union. It embraces the new states of Belarus, variously known as Byelorussia and White Russia in history, and Ukraine. It also takes in most of European Russia, known as Rodina, "the motherland"—a territory bigger than India by itself, but only one-fourth of the entire Russian Federation, which spans the continent of Asia and reaches to the Pacific Ocean. This European part of Russia contains five-sixths of the country's population. Although the border of Europe, and so of the superregion, is at the Urals, the Asian territories, especially mineral-rich western Siberia, will remain part of Russia, making Slavic Federation virtually endless in the east.

The western border of Russia, historically including Belarus and Ukraine, has moved often through the centuries, in tandem with the eastern border of its great rival, Poland. Inevitably, the one's gain was the other's loss. The original Russian state, Kievan Rus, reached as far west as the Bug River, the current border between Poland and ex-Soviet territories. But Poland, during its zenith in dynastic union with a powerful Lithuania in the fifteenth and sixteenth centuries, extended as far east as the Dnieper River, including virtually all of today's Belarus and much of Ukraine. Through the partition of Poland in the eighteenth century by Prussia, Russia, and Austria, Russia pushed back its border to the Bug again. This boundary was reinforced after World War I, when the British official Lord Curzon ruled that Poland's eastern border should run along the Bug River, where, after jockeying until 1945, it is today.

The border between the Mitteleuropa and Slavic Federation superregions is a bit farther west. It follows the Vistula River from Torun in the north to Cracow in the south, reflecting the double orientation of Poland to Germany in the west and the former Soviet republics in the east. The border runs through Warsaw, which faces in both directions. In the north, Slavic Federation shares the border with Baltic League, running east and north along the borders of the

Baltic republics, paralleling the coastline through St. Petersburg north to the Kanin Peninsula and the Barents Sea. In the south, it shares the Danube Basin border from Cracow, along the Carpathian Mountains, following the Dniester River to the Black Sea. The sea itself continues the southern border to its eastern shore, where the Caucasus Mountains, the border between Europe and Asia, run between the Black and Caspian seas. The border follows the shore of the Caspian Sea north and east to the Ural River, then northeast up the Ural River to the Ural Mountains, following the range north into the Arctic tundra and the Barents Sea. The area contains about 175 million people, making the Slavic Federation the most populous superregion, as well as the largest in area.

Russia's geography is so monumental and primordial that it defines many basic concepts. Terms like *steppe, tundra,* and *taiga* come from the Russian. They describe some of the bands of vegetation that stretch east and west across the country's vast territory. Steppes are the flat, grassy plains in southern Ukraine and southern Russia that reach eastward deep into Asia. Tundra refers to the level, treeless plains in the arctic regions. Taiga is the broad swathe of coniferous forest south of the tundra that spans the Eurasian continent from the Gulf of Finland in the west to the Kamchatka Peninsula on the Bering Sea in the east. Historically, development of the land was concentrated in two narrow strips between the steppe and the taiga, a band of mixed forest in the north and of wooded steppe in the south.

"Russia," comments the 1989 *Atlas of Russia and the Soviet Union,* "is astonishingly far north."[3] Kiev, the southernmost large city with nearly 3 million inhabitants, lies at the same latitude as the southern tip of Hudson Bay in Canada, well to the north of Toronto or Montreal. St. Petersburg is even with the Shetland Islands, north of Scotland in the Atlantic Ocean. In fact, half of Russian territory lies north of that 60 degree latitude—that is, on a level with Alaska. Hostile Russian winters, credited with defeating invaders like Napoleon and Hitler, last half the year.

Russia's geography predestined it to empire. After the fall of Constantinople to the Turks in the fifteenth century, Moscow saw itself as the "third Rome." Residence of the head of the Russian Orthodox Church, it became the home of a new Caesar and capital of a new empire. That empire eventually extended west as far as Warsaw and Finland, and east not only to the Pacific Ocean, but across the Bering Strait into North America, taking in a territory called Russian America, which is known today as Alaska. For some years in the first half of the nineteenth century, Russia had a settlement as far south as northern California, at Fort Ross, sixty miles north of San Francisco in today's Sonoma County, near the Russian River.

After World War II, the establishment of communist governments in eastern Europe made these countries satellites of the Soviet Union and extended Soviet rule even farther west, creating the dangerous confrontation between the superpowers along the ideological barrier that came to be known as the Iron Curtain.

Mission: Impossible

When the former head of Germany's cartel office went to Moscow in the summer of 1992 to work as an economic consultant for the Russian Federation, a leading official there told him it would be two hundred years before Russia completed the transition to a market economy. The German adviser, Wolfgang Kartte, replied that, in that case, he may as well return home. "No, no," answered the Russian, "if you stay, it will only take one hundred years." Kartte found this half-serious forecast excessive, and even the estimate of fifty years from former German chancellor Helmut Schmidt was not convincing to him. For Kartte, "The decisive moment is when a perspective emerges for the people, when they can see it is going upward."[4] That perspective could come within just five years, Kartte says, if proper conditions were established, even if it then took much longer to actually achieve the transformation.

The German expert, who was advising on ways to develop small businesses in Russia, was one of a train of Western specialists called in by Moscow to help make the momentous transition from seventy-four years of central planning to a market economy. These ranged from Paul Volcker, the prestigious former chairman of the Federal Reserve Board in the United States, who advised Boris Yeltsin's government on economic and banking reform, to Jeffrey Sachs, the young Harvard economist who brought his gospel of shock therapy ("you don't leap a chasm in several steps") to Russia after testing it in smaller cases like Bolivia and Poland.

Yeltsin had already installed a government of home-grown experts, led by the young economist Yegor Gaidar, born in 1956, to ride herd on the economic stampede. Quickly labeled the "kamikaze government" because its measures would be suicidal in a normal political situation, Gaidar's government freed most prices to find their own level, creating enormous hardships for working people, and attempted to hold down government spending. Yeltsin himself bore the full brunt of the criticism from parliament and industrialists, the military, and even the conspirators from the failed coup, who weighed in with their comments from prison. It was a gamble without historic parallel. Gaidar's kamikazes were in the end shot down, even though a weakened Yeltsin, bolstered by new support from the Clinton administration, is maintaining the economic reforms.

Primitive capitalism is not a pretty thing, and the thrusting entrepreneurialism that overtook Russia and the other former republics of the Soviet Union often resembled not-so-organized crime more than modern business. Nimble operators, often former members of the Communist Party or even the secret police, have been using their old networks to cash in on black market and smuggling activities amid the general breakdown of the old Soviet system, before new laws and structures can catch up with capitalist practices. The most serious abuse is the illegal export of Russia's oil and mineral resources, which has netted smugglers billions of dollars in profits that are sorely missed by the national economy.

To justify their actions, budding entrepreneurs in Russia cite America's "robber barons"—those capitalists who made fortunes in the hurly-burly of the United States' industrial revolution in ways considered immoral by many at the time, but now forgotten in the shining prestige of their corporate descendants.

At the same time, the Soviet industrial conglomerates are trying to maintain production and even exports. The Soviet automaker Lada managed to lift its sales in Germany by 50 percent in 1991, due to continued strong demand by loyal customers in the former East Germany. Lada built a new technical facility in Hamburg, where the imported cars—built in Moscow and Togliatti, a factory town on the Volga, transported by rail to Riga, the Latvian port, and shipped across the Baltic to Hamburg—were outfitted with catalytic converters and other special equipment for the German market.

Such adaptability is rare, though. The collapse of the Russian economy was due in great part to the inability of industry under the Soviet system to innovate and change. From the 1970s on, the

Soviet economy had started to slow because of the malfunctions, low productivity, and inefficient resource allocation that was inherent in central planning, according to a 1991 survey of the Soviet economy published by the leading development organizations. As a summary of the report said: "An economy such as that of the Soviet Union, protected from competition and burdened with all kinds of rigidities, was incapable of perceiving that change was necessary, and even less capable of effecting it."[5]

An infusion of capital and expertise from abroad would certainly improve the situation. Foreign investment into Russia, however, has remained sparse—scarcely $1 billion in 1992. Political uncertainty but also monetary chaos made potential investors cautious. As a *Financial Times* survey of Russia summed it up in May 1993: "Foreign investment is negligible and foreign confidence dropping because of a largely bad experience with joint ventures and with direct investment."[6] Many American multinationals who have invested—Procter & Gamble, Philip Morris, RJR Reynolds, Gillette—preferred to go to the more sympathetic St. Petersburg rather than to chaotic Moscow or elsewhere inland. Peter the Great's capital, like Novgorod before it, was imperial Russia's "window on the West," and seems ready to take on that role again.

Russia has managed to derive some benefit from its decades as a superpower. It stormed into the satellite launching business, undercutting the market leader, Europe's Ariane consortium, by nearly half to land a contract from a Western mobile telephone consortium. With the resources and experience of the Soviet Union's space program behind it, Russia's bid for a share of the $2 billion-a-year business poses a greater threat to U.S. and European launchers than China's tentative efforts or even Japan's planned entry into the field. U.S. vice presidential candidate Al Gore accused nonmarket economies of "predatory pricing" in their launch bids. In Russia's case, at least, the charge would hardly stick if the country's ruble costs were factored in at market rates, following the massive devaluation of the Russian currency. The existence of a First World technology in a country that had a bankrupt, Third World economy is simply another consequence of the unprecedented situation in Russia.

Many other high-technology endeavors that had a privileged claim on resources in the Soviet Union have found Western partners eager to profit from the low-priced expertise on offer. Chemical multinationals like Du Pont of the U.S., Hoffmann-La Roche of Switzerland, and BASF of Germany have contracted for cardiological research in Moscow. Union Carbide and Monsanto have invested in biochemical research. AT&T finally found in Russia a team for advanced optic fiber research, after a long and fruitless search elsewhere. The Western contracts to existing Russian research centers have helped slow down the country's brain drain; many other highly trained scientists have accepted lucrative Western offers to emigrate.

But any good news has been engulfed by the daunting monstrosity of the task to reform legal, social, and economic structures of an erstwhile superpower. Runaway inflation, shortages in food, heat, and consumer goods, inequities, and insecurity threaten a conservative backlash that could be exploited by nationalists or former communists to install a new dictatorship in Moscow. Old Soviet industrial managers joined together with other conservative forces to oppose Boris Yeltsin and his program for rapid economic restructuring, including the scheme launched late in 1992 to privatize the bulk of Russian industry. Yeltsin received moral support from Western leaders—phone calls from U.S. president George Bush, lunch with the Queen of England and a speech before the combined houses of Parliament in London, and the summit with president Bill Clinton in Vancouver—but the political and economic situation remains volatile.

At the same time, while trying to put its relations with other large republics on a new footing, Russia has had to contend with ethnic warfare in the Caucasus, and separatist movements among the score of autonomous republics included in the Russian Federation itself. Foreign advisers urged Moscow to push for decentralization and increased autonomy, while domestic political opponents campaigned for stronger central power, and some openly called for a restoration of the Soviet Union. The risk that the centrifugal force which burst apart the Soviet Union would do the same to the Russian Federation remained quite real.

Whatever the political frictions, the region has to restore economic cooperation, to stop the decline in living standards, and to catch up with the rest of Europe. While Russia's former rival, the United States, will be a major partner in the economic turnaround, Europe, and particularly Mitteleuropa, will play an important role. Thousands of industrial managers in the former East Germany speak

Russian. Even with the radical transformation on both sides, important vestiges of former trade ties are likely to survive. In the long term, as Russia recovers and the other successor states develop, the Slavic Federation should be able to counterbalance Mitteleuropa economically and eventually become an engine of growth for the entire continent.

In the meantime, the Moscow subway continues to run, and people still ride it to work, although every family needs a grandmother or child to take the time to stand in line for food and other necessities, and many without other work can spend the day bartering whatever luxury they have—a bottle of shampoo, a box of chocolates—in the spontaneous flea markets that have sprung up everywhere. The frustration and dread uncertainty are palpable there as in other ex-Soviet republics. Still potentially one of the richest regions in the world, Russia and its neighbors stand poised precariously between their past and their future.

Ukraine

One of the most amazing consequences of the August 1991 coup attempt in the Soviet Union was the emergence of a full-blown independent country equivalent in area and population to France. Within hours of the coup's failure, Ukraine declared its independence. When Ukrainian voters overwhelmingly confirmed the declaration in a December 1 referendum, they ended any hopes of preserving the Soviet Union intact. The so-called Commonwealth of Independent States was founded a week later as a kind of bankruptcy administrator to oversee the disposal of Soviet assets. In that December vote, Ukrainians elected Leonid Kravchuk as president, perhaps the most disarmingly cynical turncoat among former communist leaders. A longtime apparatchik, Kravchuk rallied to the nationalist cause and won the support of opposition forces, who felt it was more important to secure independence than to worry about his democratic credentials.

Literally overnight, Europe found itself with a new nation of 52 million people, one-fifth of the Soviet Union's total population, that accounted for one-fourth of the Soviet Union's gross national product and one-fifth of its agricultural production. A country with a thousand-year-old tradition gained sovereignty for the first time,

except for a brief period of nominal independence during the civil war from 1917 to 1920.

From the formation of the first Russian state in Kiev in the ninth century, Ukraine has always been part of either Russia or Poland. The homeland of the eastern branch of the Slavic peoples—at least the first one that historians have been able to find—was probably in the area of central Europe around the Vistula River, in present-day Poland. The first Russian state emerged in the ninth century, when the Vikings—the same Nordic warriors who settled in Normandy, Britain, and Ireland in western Europe—sailed their ships down the lakes and rivers of Russia, establishing trading posts in the local Slavic settlements. The very name Russia goes back to *Rus,* the name of this first state, which may be derived from the Finnish word for Sweden. It was the Vikings who established a dynasty to organize the territory politically, at Kiev, on the Dnieper River, the main waterway between the Baltic and the Black Sea. Kievan Rus was one of the largest states in medieval Europe—its trade and culture were oriented toward the West.

It was the Kievan prince Vladimir I who in the tenth century deliberately chose Christianity in its Eastern Orthodox version as the religion for his people. In the meticulous "beauty contest" he conducted to make the choice, legend has it, he rejected Islam because it forbade its adherents to drink alcohol—too strict a requirement even then for the Russians. Vladimir II moved the capital to a new town bearing his name, northeast of present-day Moscow, to mark a shift in trade toward the Volga and the Caspian Sea.

Kievan control over the state was lost forever. The Mongol hordes swept into Russia in the thirteenth century and retained control of most of the territory for two and a half centuries. At the end of the Khan's rule, Muscovy, with its capital in Moscow, emerged as the main principality. It was the autocratic rulers of Muscovy who consolidated the Russian principalities to form the Russian Empire.

The notion of a distinct nationality for Ukraine came only in the nineteenth century, as it did for many other eastern European nations, when nationalist Ukrainian intellectuals in Galicia, which enjoyed the relatively liberal regime of the Habsburgs at that time, codified the language, conjured up some national myths, and claimed to be the exclusive heirs of Kievan Rus and the Cossack territories.

For all the passion of anti-Soviet and anti-Russian feeling in the 1991 declaration of sovereignty, it was actually Soviet rule that enabled Ukrainian nationalism to come to fruition. Anxious to consolidate communist control in the newly conquered territory in 1920, Moscow made Ukraine a constitutive republic of the Soviet Union, drew generous boundaries for it, and promoted Ukrainian language and culture. Stalin later reversed this liberal attitude. He imposed Russification with a heavy hand, and exacted a horrific toll in human life in his Great Terror of the mid-1930s, including the massacre of *millions* of peasants, largely through enforced starvation. But during and after World War II, Ukraine acquired even more territory, at the expense of Poland, Romania, and Czechoslovakia, and gained its own seat in the United Nations. In 1954, the three hundredth anniversary of the treaty that affiliated Ukraine's Cossack territories to Russia, Soviet leader Nikita Khrushchev, himself a Ukrainian, attached the Crimea, the Black Sea peninsula, to Ukraine—a whimsical gesture much regretted by Moscow after Ukraine's declaration of independence in 1991.

With his recidivist authoritarianism, Kravchuk quickly disappointed potential Western investors who thought that Ukraine, because of its proximity to western Europe and its smaller size, might be a more manageable proposition than Russia itself. Kravchuk kept tight state control on mass media, suppressed criticism, centralized political power in his office, and procrastinated on reforms to move the economy from centralized planning to market structures.

Kravchuk devised a disastrous monetary policy. To escape the Soviet ruble, he printed coupons as a form of transition domestic money. Because the paper had no backing, it plummeted in value, making the crumbling ruble look like a hard currency by comparison. He further sabotaged internal monetary mechanisms by providing unlimited credit to state-owned companies. All this, predictably, brought hyperinflation.

The Ukrainian leader's opportunism produced some good policy, too, however. Hoping to win hard currency aid from Germany, Kravchuk offered new homes for up to half a million ethnic Germans, out of the 2 million descended from the "Volga Germans" Stalin forcibly resettled in the Central Asian republic of Kazakhstan. These settlers had originally been invited to Russia in the eighteenth century by German-born Catherine the Great to help develop the uncultivated steppes. Lenin made the Volga Germans a self-governing territory, but Stalin suppressed it after Germany attacked the Soviet Union in 1941, and transferred the Germans to Central Asia.

Once Kazakhstan became independent in 1991, heightened nationalism and Islamic fundamentalism made life uncomfortable for the Germans there, so many of them wanted to go somewhere else. Germany has a keen interest in supporting Ukraine's project because its constitution provides for an ethnic citizenship. All of Russia's 2 million ethnic Germans could go to Germany and claim citizenship there—a daunting prospect for Germany, already overrun by refugees from the ex-Yugoslavia and other countries.

A veteran of Communist Party infighting, Kravchuk also secured a large share of Soviet military capability for Ukraine. Authoritative Western statistics published in late 1992 showed that Ukraine had 1,100 combat aircraft—more than any other European country except for Russia. In tanks and armored vehicles, Ukraine ranked third in Europe, after Russia and Germany. Ukraine was one of the four ex-Soviet republics—along with Russia, Belarus, and Kazakhstan—to emerge from the breakup as a nuclear power, and showed signs that it might want to remain one, unlike Belarus, which was eager to hand over its nuclear weapons to Russia.

Ukraine also laid claim to the Soviet Union's Black Sea fleet, based in Sevastopol. Russia's acquisition of the Crimea in the eighteenth century had enabled it to gain a foothold on the Black Sea and to play an active role in Balkan politics. As with its advance to the Baltic at the beginning of the century, this push to the Black Sea permitted Russia to build a new port, and Odessa, now a city of 1.2 million, became the southern counterpart of St. Petersburg.

In the postputsch collapse of the Soviet Union, both Odessa and the Crimea came under the control of newly independent Ukraine. The loss of such historic achievements accounts for much of the shock in Russia caused by the split with Ukraine. The dispute between Ukraine and Russia over how to divide up the fleet has further complicated the future of the Crimea. Yeltsin and Kravchuk agreed to postpone resolution of the problem while they attended to the urgent economic crises in their republics.

As with most other former Soviet republics, the long decades of economic symbiosis between Ukraine and Russia mean that an independent Ukraine is scarcely viable on its own. Yet Ukraine, like the other successor states, has resisted cooperation with Russia. They fear, no doubt with some justification, that Russia will wield economic pressure in the same way it did political and military force to subordinate its neighboring territories.

Like it or not, though, the former Soviet republics are condemned to cooperation. The communist system, giving absolute authority to central planners to direct the economy, meant that Moscow could mandate manufacture of components in the Baltic republics for products assembled on the Volga. This "trade" between republics as goods and parts were shuttled across the Soviet Union accounted for one-fifth of Russia's gross national product. For the smaller republics, the proportion was much higher—from two-fifths (Ukraine) to four-fifths (Lithuania).

Yet this inter-republic trade plummeted by 50 percent in the wake of independence, paralyzing much production and causing declines of 30 to 50 percent in the GNP of the individual successor states. As the European Bank for Reconstruction and Development noted in its Annual Economic Review for 1992, the challenge facing the former Soviet republics was much greater than for other ex-communist countries. When trade in the former bloc declined in the wake of the transition, Poland and Hungary simply had to adapt their products to new markets in the West. For the ex-Soviet republics, it meant they no longer had the wherewithal to produce anything for any market, at home or abroad.[7]

Ukraine and other republics skeptical of Moscow's intentions had kept the Commonwealth of Independent States from becoming a real association. But by spring 1993, nine of the ten members, including Ukraine, signed a declaration of intent to form an economic union. Their plans included twenty-five measures to make the union a reality. The most important of these were the creation of a customs union and the establishment of a settlements bank to handle payments between the members.

All the Russias

For most of their history, no one made much distinction among Russians. When the bulk of Kievan Rus, the medieval Russian state, fell under the control of the Tatars in the thirteenth century, the westernmost territories remained free a while longer. Lithuania, a major force in the region at that time, wasted little time, though, in taking over the exposed region. It went on to push back the Tatars, and by the fourteenth century controlled today's Belarus and western Ukraine.

Lithuania entered into a dynastic union with Poland in the fourteenth century, and when that dynasty died out, the two nations created a full-fledged dual state in the sixteenth century. Poland-Lithuania kept control of the western Russian territories until the eighteenth century. It was this long period separated from Muscovite Russia that enabled Belorussians and Ukrainians to differentiate themselves in language and culture. The Treaty of Lublin in 1569, which joined the states of Poland and Lithuania, fixed the border between the two that corresponds to today's border between Belarus, in the Lithuanian half of the dual state, and Ukraine, in the Polish half. Thus, as French expert Andre Sellier puts it, "one can define the Belorussians as those eastern Slavs who have spent about half their history in the company of Lithuanians."[8]

No one seems to know the origin of the designation "White Russians," the English equivalent of Belorussians. The Ukrainians, who came under Polish dominion with the Lublin treaty, derived their name from the Russian word for "borderland," although Russians had referred to them condescendingly as "Little Russians," in distinction to "Great Russians" in the Muscovite territories.

Belarus, or Byelorussia as it was normally known, did not experience the same growth of nationalist feeling as Ukraine. It is much smaller, with only one-fifth the population. Minsk, the capital, never as charming as Kiev, was largely destroyed in World War II, and rebuilt in the shabby, boxy style distinctive of Soviet architecture. The war devastated Belarus's territory, and as many as 4 million persons perished there during the conflict. The Chernobyl nuclear reactor accident in 1986, which took place in northern Ukraine, did most of its damage in Belarus, leaving one-fifth to one-third of its territory contaminated. But Belarus had one of the highest labor productivity rates in the old Soviet Union, and the country, like Ukraine, stands to profit from its location between Germany and Russia.

But not for a while. The former communist nomenklatura kept a tight grip on the new country, which only reluctantly declared independence. It was slow to initiate any reforms and let it be known that it was ready for an economic and military union with Russia. The full emergence of Belarus as an independent democratic state will probably come only with a clear stabilization in Russia.

"Shadows of Borders"

The historic ties between western Ukraine and eastern Poland have smoothed relations in that end of the Slavic Federation super-region. The case of Lviv—called Lvov in Russian and Lemberg in German—is typical. The city has both gained and lost from its location in a region with no natural borders, and various powers have cast a net over it to draw it toward them. Eastern Galicia, where Lviv is located, is now part of western Ukraine, while western Galicia, always distinct because of its largely Polish and Catholic population, lies in Poland. As a result of this mixed past, Lviv has as much affinity to eastern Poland as it does to eastern Ukraine. German writer Karl Schlogel has high hopes that Lviv can again play a bridging role in contemporary Europe: "Europe is finding its voice again at the end of a long postwar period. This Europe has need of cities that emerge from the shadows of borders and desolate East-West provincialism. Europe needs new border cities, cities where borders are blotted out."[9]

The Polish-Ukrainian border, while not quite blotted out, is becoming fainter in the wake of political changes. A *New York Times* reporter visiting Przemysl, sixty miles west of Lviv and ten miles across the border, found in fall 1991 that Polish employers were hiring Ukrainians and Russians for everything from construction work to playing violin in the local orchestra. The former Soviets worked harder than their Polish counterparts, for half the pay.[10]

Przemysl was founded sometime before the tenth century and was part of the Kievan Rus principality of Galich, which gave its name to the Austro-Hungarian crownland Galicia. Apart from this Russian origin, though, the city has been Polish or Austrian most of its history. Ukrainians come into Poland, when they can, to buy higher quality consumer goods, particularly clothes. Poles cross into Ukraine to buy gas, which is practically free when paid for in devalued rubles.

Set on the border between Mitteleuropa and Slavic Federation, Warsaw, the capital of Poland, has enjoyed a boom in commercial real estate. In early 1992, rents ranged from $38 to $56 per square foot—compared to $25 to $35 in New York's depressed market. The thirty-seven-story Palace of Culture and Science, the Stalinist high rise which dominates the Warsaw skyline, housed everything from Coca-Cola to the newly arrived Goethe Institute, the German cultural agency. When Polish prime minister Hanna Suchocka visited Bonn in late 1992, she extracted a pledge from German chancellor Helmut Kohl to help Poland get into the European Community as soon as possible, with a long transition period like the one Greece had before rules were fully applied. The two leaders wanted to ease problems along the German-Polish border, caused by the disparities in wage and price levels. Poland was positioned to become an economic buffer between the high living standards of western Europe and the much lower standards in the east.

This western edge of Slavic Federation is its anchor in Europe. The old debate about whether Russia belongs to Europe still has proponents on both sides. Poland and Ukraine, which clearly are in Europe, can tip the balance for the region. By the same token, Russia, so interlinked with Ukraine in the west and extending so far into Asia in the east, can be the bridge between the two continents.

Slavic Struggles

The European dilemma that pits central authority against local control burst apart the Soviet empire, too. Only Stalinist terror, even in the institutionalized and atrophied form of the Brezhnev regime, could hold together the diverse nationalities of the Soviet Union and its satellite states. The striving for independence and autonomy continued to roil under the surface of Soviet control, even when Stalin's control was at its height. In 1939, just before the outbreak of war, a contemporary French account tells us, the Soviet empire was fraying at its edges.

> . . . [W]e are seeing a series of *national* revolutions in the peripheral territories of the empire—Finland, Latvia, Estonia, Lithuania, Poland, Ukraine, Armenia, etc. For the inhabitants of these regions, the revolution means an end to the czarist yoke and a return to the traditions preceding the seizure by Moscow. In these lands, the people are not struggling for the extension of Marxism or the triumph of world revolution; they are combatting to recover their lost independence, and with it, the right to speak their own language, to govern themselves, and to develop in accord with their own particular genius.[11]

A Ukrainian poet addressed a plea for freedom to Czar Alexander III in the nineteenth century that still speaks for all subjects of the czars and the Soviet regime that followed them—including the Russians themselves. "Leave us our prairies; leave us our steppes! Whose are they if not ours? Do their flowers recognize you? They'll never recognize you. Just seeing you from afar makes them wither. Here the stars are more brilliant, the sky deeper and bluer than anywhere else. The steppe is limitless, but not our patience: beware the wrath that gathers together under so much blue."[12]

In the successor republics to the Soviet Union, there is a historic struggle to establish democracy and a more liberal economic system. Reactionary forces readily exploit the immediate need for food, shelter, and energy to slow down this transition. But the centrifugal forces unleashed by the collapse of Stalin's system of dictatorship brook no backlash. More profoundly than in western Europe, these eastern European and Asian territories are caught between forces of decomposition and consolidation that are bound to create torment and anguish, but also hope and opportunity, for many years.

CHAPTER THIRTEEN

SUPERREGIONS OR SUPERPOWER?

Today's Europe is a pell-mell, a jumble of overlapping jurisdictions and networks. The European Community, driven in nearly equal proportions by the continent's need for economic integration and its peoples' fear of political centralization, lurches along as the vehicle of consolidation. The rest of Europe jumps on as it can or runs along behind.

Cities and regions network into superregions, and these large territories interact with each other. Other networks span the continent, plying their contacts, exchanging experience. Together, apart—the countervailing forces of integration and disintegration ripple through the continent, as they have so often in the past. This has its good side and its bad side. "We are entering into a new Middle Ages," says Pierre Hassner, a Romanian-born scholar who teaches in Paris, "which is the bearer, for some, of universality and flexibility, of a fecund multiplicity of types of belonging and allegiance, and so of openness and tolerance; for others, of religious wars, of armed bands, of beggars and pirates, in short, of anarchy and permanent conflict."[1] Contemporary Europe has examples of both.

The epochal change occurring in Europe now is the latest version of the disruption and progress that has characterized its entire history. It is a renaissance—literally, a rebirth—as though the continent is finally recovering from the exhaustion of the two world wars. For those willing to take the long view, it is an extension of what economic historian Eric Lionel Jones calls "the European miracle." During the earlier Renaissance, a tendency to political decentralization did not hinder economic development on a continental scale, or a cultural flowering of European dimension. "This picture of a Europe which shared in salient respects a common culture, or series of overlapped lifestyles, and formed something of a single market demonstrates that political decentralization did not mean a fatal loss of economies of scale in production and distribution,"[2] Jones writes of the late Middle Ages in words that could easily describe Europe in the late twentieth century.

This very diversity, fostering competition rather than regimentation, was the secret of Europe's ascendancy, Jones argues. The "miraculous preservation" of a balance of power in a politically decentralized Europe at once impeded the rise of repressive monolithic empires and mitigated some of the consequences of war. "The pith of the European miracle lies somewhere here, in politics rather than economics," Jones concludes.[3]

The superregions continue that tradition. A forum for political cooperation and a terrain of economic development, they supply the new balance of integration and diversity needed for contemporary Europe to continue its "miraculous" progress. Just as nation-states arose to accommodate the growth of capitalism, superregions are emerging now in response to the development of the global economy. As Jones writes, "What the rise of the nation-state does seem to account for is the establishment of the stable conditions necessary for expanding development and growth, for the diffusion of best practices in technology and commerce. . . ."[4] This is the role falling to the superregions today, in the context of an integrated Europe.

This view of Europe exposes the notion of a United States of Europe as something of a red herring. Europe's contribution to global civilization was and is something different than the contribution of the United States of America. Europe's future lies more in following its own tradition of diversity and balance, integration and decentralization, than in copying the federal formula of the United States. Europe's postnational political organization, like its prenational system of principalities, bishoprics, kingdoms, and empires, will be something original, essentially European, rather than a second United States, with Congress, Senate, and District of Columbia.

Trying to form a United States of Europe means forcing three dozen Quebecs into a straitjacket of centralization. It is hardly possible to keep just one Quebec in Canada, which is much less centralized than the United States. The European Union envisaged in the Treaty of Maastricht remains well below even Canada's level of federation, grouping twelve nations in search of a common policy on an ad hoc basis. Even if the treaty is ratified and implemented, "Europe," as an entity in its own right, would still have no political basis, as long as the directly elected parliament has no voice and the real executive and legislative power remains vested in leaders who have only a national mandate. Because the constituencies remain national, it is not surprising that the European Community cannot wring out a common policy on any politically sensitive issue except under duress. Even a crisis, as the breakup of Yugoslavia demonstrated, is not always sufficient to force unity. No wonder Brussels is not eager to enlarge the Community and intensify the cacophony.

Why fight it? A united Europe, yes, but united on its own terms and in a way derived from its own traditions. A Europe that remains polyphonic, that does not necessarily speak with a single voice. Not a superpower on the model of the United States or the Soviet Union, not an empire like Napoleon's or Hitler's, but the creative, productive interplay of diverse forces that it has always been, outfitted with a flexible political and economic structure adapted to the circumstances of the twenty-first century.

Europe should seek its models in Renaissance Burgundy, Kievan Rus, the Holy Roman Empire, the Hanseatic League. These loosely knit entities with weak central authorities succumbed eventually, it is true, to stronger forces. But they lasted longer than the "strong" empires established by Charlemagne, Napoleon, Bismarck, or Lenin, and provided the basis for economic prosperity and cultural creativity for long periods of time.

The Malleability of Superregions

The superregions of Europe are just beginning to form. Even though I have tried to describe their borders with some precision, these frontiers are hardly fixed. They will most likely shift as time goes on; they may even have moved by the time this book appears. Perhaps Vilnius, nearly two hundred miles from the Baltic coast, will orient Lithuania again in the direction of its historic partners and rivals, Poland and Russia, and the bulk of that country will become part of Slavic Federation rather than Baltic League. Perhaps Austria will definitively turn its back on eastern Europe in favor of integration into the EC and be absorbed into Mitteleuropa, leaving Slovakia, Hungary, Croatia, and Romania to subside into the conflicts of Balkan Peninsula.

Another possibility is that the negative backlash to the Maastricht ratification process will attenuate the gains of the Single Market, slowing down economic integration and the emergence of the superregions in favor of a return to strictly national priorities. But any return to nation-state thinking in Europe would be a high-risk adventure, because inevitably Germany would emerge as a hegemonic power, with all the potential dangers that entails. Rather, it seems likely that Europe will continue to progress in the directions described here, with all the fits and starts that characterize its moves forward. As that happens, the contours of the superregions should become clearer, and their inner cohesion stronger.

It is even possible that superregions may develop a political structure in their own right. Perhaps talk of a "Danubian Confederation" or even a "Balkan Confederation" will crystallize into some formal organization. Maybe the Commonwealth of Independent States, or something like it, will become a genuine supranational structure for the Slavic Federation. In the west, perhaps a "core Europe" of France, Germany, and the Benelux countries—Mitteleuropa—will push ahead with their own monetary union and joint central bank, and let the rest of Europe continue at a slower speed.

In time, patterns of interaction between the superregions should also become visible. The most distinctive feature, of course, is the role of Mitteleuropa at the core of the European economy. Prosperity and growth in the periphery depend on the activity in this heartland. Latin Crescent and Atlantic Coast, and eventually Slavic Federation, are big enough to have their own economic dynamic, but the role of Mitteleuropa remains so strong even for these big regions that in the long run they depend on Mitteleuropa's lead.

In addition to the interchange between the core and the periphery, though, the peripheral regions will have their own economic exchange. Chances are they will form two huge arcs: a Northern Arc connecting Atlantic Coast via Baltic League to Slavic Federation, and a Southern Arc linking Atlantic Coast to Slavic Federation by way of Latin Crescent and Danube Basin—although the latter is a weak link for the time being. The Northern Arc revives the trade routes of the Hanseatic League, while the Southern Arc, to a lesser extent, inherits the role of the Venetian empire.

The phenomenon of superregions need not be confined to Europe, even though it fits European traditions particularly well. The Maghreb countries in North Africa form a natural superregion. The Black Sea economic zone may develop into a superregion, too. If the North American Free Trade Agreement is ratified and implemented, it could reinforce the superregions identified by Joel Garreau in his landmark book, *The Nine Nations of North America*. These included a "Mexamerica" taking in Mexico, the southwest United States, and southern California, and an "Empty Quarter" comprising the thinly populated, mineral-rich territory in the western United States and western and northern Canada, including most of Alaska.[5] Trade groups like the Association of South East Asian Nations in the Pacific and the Andean Pact in South America could be precursors of superregions. It would not be hard to imagine a southern African superregion if the racial conflict in South Africa were peacefully resolved.

Fortress Europe?

As the European Community launched its Single Market at the beginning of 1993, the rest of the world began to worry about Europe turning into an economic fortress. The fear is that Europe will raze its interior barriers to trade and build up its exterior walls as a sort of compensation. Unification of such a large space, it is implied, will inevitably tempt Europe to autarky, an economic self-sufficiency that excludes the rest of the world.

The dependence of Europe itself on world trade is not sufficient to dispel such fears. Merchandise trade with non-EC partners, imports and exports together, represents nearly one-fourth of the EC's gross domestic product. But the EC restricts certain imports—of autos, farm goods, steel, and others—to protect its own industries, and increasing integration promises to put it in a stronger position to keep out unwanted products.

Economists and pundits have painted a picture of global trading blocs—large, increasingly fortified territories practicing free trade within their walls and less free trade with other blocs. Europe is one such bloc; the proposed North American free trade zone embracing the U.S., Canada, and Mexico is another, eventually extending to South America; Japan, vaguely lumped together with Southeast Asia, constitutes a Pacific bloc. An alternative vision, offered by French scholar and writer Jacques Attali among others, is a two-bloc system: a Pacific bloc *joining* Japan and the U.S. (the latter, in Attali's profoundly anti-American view, being the junior partner); and a Eurasian bloc, linking the EC and the (ex-)Soviet bloc.[6] French historian Pierre Behar also favors the Eurasian option, extending Europe in the northeast via Russia to secure the strategic mineral wealth of Siberia, and in the southeast via Turkey to coopt and secularize the emerging Islamic republics in Central Asia.[7]

But economic exchange does not always follow such neat lines. Judging by early events in the former Soviet Union, for example, former fellow superpower United States of America seems to be the most suitable economic partner for Russia as it tries to get its economy sorted out. From high-technology industries like space and biochemistry, to primary extractive industries like oil and minerals, to mass consumer services like fast food and soft drinks, the American economy best matches Russia's needs. The erstwhile superpower rivals speak the same "language," think in the same dimensions, and share a certain respect for each other. Besides, given its human and natural resources, Russia still has the potential to be a ranking world power and an important partner, or rival, for the United States.

Also, blocs overlap. Trade across the Atlantic between the EC and the U.S. totaled $200 billion in 1990, a sizable enough amount to speak of an Atlantic bloc, overlapping the American bloc and the European bloc. Britain and Germany were among the European countries who thought a formal accord between NAFTA and the EC might be desirable. The U.S., of course, also sees itself as a major factor in the Pacific bloc. Upon his appointment as assistant secretary of state for East Asian and Pacific Affairs in the Clinton administration, veteran diplomat Winston Lord called for the U.S. to help build a New Pacific Community.

Because of the crippling effect of the debt crisis on Third World countries in the 1980s, much of the bloc talk leaves out the threshold countries of the south, from Brazil to Nigeria to Indonesia, but they will become important sooner or later. The leverage of the Organization of Petroleum Exporting Countries may have declined with the price of oil, but EC trade with OPEC countries, in both directions, adds up to half of that with the United States. Nor should we ignore the risk that a politicized Islamic bloc, stretching from the northern half of Africa across the Middle East into southern and southeastern Asia, could emerge as an economic force in the foreseeable future. Not last and not least is China, growing rapidly under the economic reforms of a regime that retains some of the worst aspects of communism's political repression but is abandoning its economic tenets.

Free trade, far from being inevitable, is hardly achievable. The complex structure of bilateral conventions, multilateral product agreements, voluntary restraint accords, and the voluminous rules of the General Agreement on Tariffs and Trade that together regulate world commerce today scarcely fits the description "free trade." But free trade as a reference, an ideal, a goal, however distant, still seems to be preferred as a basis for negotiation. Given the high level of interpenetration in the world economy, there is no compelling reason why this should not continue to be the case even if macro-regional trading blocs do in fact emerge.

Multinational enterprises, according to conventional wisdom, have been busy in recent years establishing a foothold in each potential bloc, in order to be on the inside, so to speak, when the protectionist walls are built and the moat bridges are drawn up. No doubt that resistance to Japanese imports in the U.S. and Europe has encouraged Japanese makers of automobiles and home electronics equipment to set up manufacturing facilities in those markets. The EC, for instance, subjects Japan to 150 import quotas and launches an average of forty antidumping investigations against Japanese imports each year.

But sidestepping import restraints is one tactical consideration in an overall global strategy, part of the "de-materialization" of world business that is described so aptly by Robert Reich.[8] Multinational companies are becoming pools of management and technological expertise and investment capital with a global network of research and production facilities. The existence or threat of trade barriers may reinforce the desire for geographic diversification, but these companies have many other reasons for seeking it anyway, to take advantage of a variety of factor mixes. Nissan or Sony may find it advantageous to build cars and color TV sets in Britain for the European market rather than shipping them halfway around the world, even without the EC's imposing trade restrictions. Nissan, for instance, has become *Britain's* fourteenth largest exporter, selling 90 percent of its British vehicle production abroad. More than half of Japanese-owned television factories in Europe are in Britain, enabling that country to register a trade surplus of nearly $1 billion in color TV sets in 1991. Better technology and better management from the Japanese companies made these industries competitive in Britain once again, after the failure of domestic companies in the 1970s and 1980s.

There will continue to be political pressures to protect domestic jobs, everywhere, but most politicians, certainly in Europe, realize by now that these are stopgap measures to buy time for the adjustment process. The experiences of the 1970s and 1980s have been too painful for them to forget so soon.

The Sometime-Maybe Superpower

The crisis in former Yugoslavia undoubtedly did the most to deflate Europe's superpower ambitions. But it was only the most dramatic example of how Europe remained incapable of surmounting short-term, nationalistic goals not only to maintain peace and stability on behalf of the world community, but to secure its own prosperity in the long term. Other examples abounded—the irresoluteness of most European countries in coping with the threat posed by Iraq's invasion of Kuwait; the ungenerous welcome the EC and most of its members prepared for the emerging democracies in eastern Europe, from trade concessions to financial aid, to absorption of refugees; the narrowly averted collapse of the Uruguay round of trade talks over the issue of increased subsidies for European oilseeds; and so on.

The foreign affairs analyst of London's *Financial Times,* Edward Mortimer, in November 1992 attested to the European Community's quick fall from grace:

The EC is once again famous mainly for its internal divisions and its consequent inability to do anything constructive in relations with the rest of the world. . . . To outsiders, western Europe presents a remarkably unattractive spectacle as 1992, supposedly its year of glory, draws to a close. We look like selfish children squabbling among ourselves, ignoring the problems of neighbors who, for the most part, are much worse off than us.[9]

That same month, William Pfaff, in his syndicated column, concluded that it would fall to the new Clinton administration to provide the leadership Europe was unable to, most urgently in former Yugoslavia: "[I]t is evident today that if the United States does not lead, no one does. The Europeans ruefully, even bitterly, admit this."[10]

There is certainly much to be disappointed about in Europe's performance, and many justified recriminations. But it is also true that Europe and the rest of the world had inflated expectations too high. The leaders who brought the EC as far as the Single Market had already achieved quite a bit; they probably overreached themselves with the ambitions of the Maastricht treaty. But a new generation of European politicians will probably continue the work, perhaps at a slower pace. Let us hope that this new generation will be able to grow into the more statesmanlike role the world expects from Europe.

The political order of half a century cannot be swept away or replaced in a couple of years. The United States will naturally have the leadership role in managing the transition into the post–Cold War world, and it will need to work closely with Russia, which, despite its parlous postcommunist economy, is still a world power. Europe may in time grow into a true superpower, relatively speaking, if it develops its own political and economic institutions that reflect the strength of its diversity.

In the meantime, and probably for some time to come, the superregions are likely to be a prominent feature of the European landscape. They seem to offer the proper terrain for the economic and social innovation Europe needs in its efforts to grow together. In this way superregions can help generate the stability and prosperity that will enable Europe to make its contribution to world peace and development.

ENDNOTES

INTRODUCTION

1. Jeno Szucs, *Les Trois Europes,* translated from the Hungarian by Veronique Charaire, Gabon Klahiczay, and Philippe Thureau-Dangin (Paris: Editions L'Harmattan [Domaines danubiens], 1985), p. 16.

CHAPTER ONE. EUROPE'S NEW SUPERREGIONS

1. Pascal Privat et al., "Redrawing the Map," *Newsweek* (International Edition), Nov. 26, 1990, p. 22.
2. Charles Lambroschini, "La nouvelle Europe des nationalités," *Le Figaro,* Dec. 29–30, 1990.
3. Ibid.
4. Commission of the European Communities, Directorate-General for Regional Policy, *Europe 2000: Outlook for the Development of the Community's Territory,* Brussels-Luxembourg, 1991, p. 22.
5. Immanuel Wallerstein, *Geopolitics and Geoculture: Essays on the Changing World-System* (Cambridge and Paris: Cambridge University Press, Editions de la Maison des Sciences de l'Homme, 1991), p. 185.
6. Eric J. Hobsbawm, *Nations and Nationalism Since 1780: Programme, Myth, Reality* (Cambridge: Cambridge University Press, 1990), p. 3.

7. Ernest Gellner, *Nations and Nationalism* (Oxford: Basil Blackwell, 1983), p. 49.
8. Quoted in Hobsbawm, *Nations and Nationalism,* p. 12.
9. Suzanne Citron, *Le mythe national: L'histoire de France en question* (Paris: Les Editions ouvrieres et Etudes et Documentations internationales, 1989), p. 30.
10. Jean-Baptiste Duroselle, *L'Europe: Histoire de ses peuples* (Paris: Librairie academique Perrin, 1990), p. 49.
11. Flora Lewis, *Europe: A Tapestry of Nations* (New York: Simon & Schuster, 1987; Touchstone Books, 1988), p. 126.
12. Edward James, *The Franks* (Oxford: Basil Blackwell, 1988), p. 5.
13. Ibid., p. 9.
14. Robert Lafont, *Nous, peuple europeen* (Paris: Editions Kimé, 1991), p. 12.
15. Wallerstein, *Geopolitics and Geoculture,* p. 187.
16. Robert Kuttner, *The End of Laissez-Faire: National Purpose and the Global Economy After the Cold War* (New York: Alfred A. Knopf, 1991).
17. David Thomson, *Europe Since Napoleon* (London: Longmans, 1957; Penguin Books [revised], 1966, 1975), p. 295.
18. Hobsbawm, *Nations and Nationalism,* p. 30.
19. Dennis Mack Smith, *Il risorgimento italiano: Storia e testi* (Rome-Bari: Editori Laterza, 1987), p. 422.
20. Ralf Dahrendorf, "Europa der Regionen?", *Merkur: Deutsche Zeitschrift fur Europaisches Denken,* August 1991, p. 705.
21. Gyorgy Konrad, "Die Melancholie der Wiedergeburt," translated from the Hungarian by Hans-Henning Paetzke, *Kursbuch,* December 1990, p. 42.
22. Bertrand Le Gendre, "Un entretien avec Joel Roman," *Le Monde,* Sept. 15, 1992.
23. Lewis, *Europe,* p. 83.
24. Ibid., p. 84.
25. Charles Millon, "L'effet Europe," *Le Monde,* Aug. 1, 1992.

CHAPTER TWO. COMMON EUROPEAN HOUSE

1. Duroselle, *L'Europe,* p. 19.
2. Detailed in Denis de Rougemont, *Vingt-huit siècles d'Europe: La conscience européenne à travers les textes, d'Hésiode à nos jours* (Paris: Payot, 1961; Christian de Bartillat, 1990), pp. 253–57.
3. Nico Colchester, "The European Community," *The Economist,* July 11, 1992, p. 9.
4. See for example the leader "Dutch Treat," *The Economist,* Dec. 14, 1991, p. 13.

5. Clive Archer, *Organizing Western Europe* (London: Hodder & Stoughton [Edward Arnold], 1990, reprinted 1991), p. 51.
6. Pierre Servent and Daniel Vernet, "Un entretien avec Mme. Lalumiere," *Le Monde,* Nov. 26, 1991.

CHAPTER THREE. CITIES AND THE WEALTH OF REGIONS

1. Krzysztof Pomian, *Europa und seine Nationen,* translated from the French by Matthias Wolf (Berlin: Verlag Klaus Wagenbach, 1990), p. 26.
2. John Ardagh, *A Tale of Five Cities: Life in Europe Today* (New York: Harper & Row, 1979), pp. 2-3.
3. Massimo d'Azeglio, quoted in Hobsbawm, *Nations and Nationalism,* p. 44.
4. Andrzej Szczypiorski, "Der verwandelte Staat: Die deutsche Kultur und das Problem der Vereinigung Deutschlands," translated from the Polish by Klaus Staemmler, *Frankfurter Allgemeine Zeitung,* Aug. 10, 1991.
5. Henri de Bresson, "Allemagne: un entretien avec le president du SPD," *Le Monde,* Nov. 13, 1991.
6. Jan Patocka, *L'idee de l'Europe en Boheme,* translated from German and Czech by Erika Abrams (Grenoble: Editions Jerome Millon, 1991), pp. 19-20.
7. Eurostat, "Regions: Nomenclature of Territorial Units for Statistics (NUTS)," Luxembourg, November 1991. The units are modified as deemed necessary.
8. Ash Asmin, David R. Charles, and Jeremy Howells, "Corporate Restructuring and the Potential for Regional Cohesion in the New Europe," Centre for Urban and Regional Development Studies, University of Newcastle upon Tyne, 1991, p. 5.
9. Reported in *Frankfurter Allgemeine Zeitung,* Oct. 21, 1992.
10. Jane Jacobs, *Cities and the Wealth of Nations: Principles of Economic Life* (New York: Random House, 1984), p. 32.
11. Ibid., p. 39.
12. Robert Koll, " 'Europa der Regionen': Politisches Programm, beileibe noch nicht Realität," *ifo-Schnelldienst,* No. 17-18, June 17, 1992, p. 9.
13. Robert B. Reich, *The Work of Nations: Preparing Ourselves for 21st-Century Capitalism* (New York: Alfred A. Knopf, 1991).
14. Ibid., p. 264.
15. Commission of the European Communities, *Europe 2000,* p. 136.
16. Jean Labasse, *L'Europe des regions* (Paris: Flammarion [Geographes], 1991), p. 30.
17. Ibid., p. 36.

18. Szucs, *Les Trois Europes*, p. 26.
19. *The Economist*, "Britain Stands Alone," Aug. 8, 1992, p. 27.
20. Giles Merritt, "Preparing a Europe of the Regions," *International Herald Tribune*, Nov. 17, 1990.

CHAPTER FOUR. LATIN CRESCENT: EUROPE'S SUNBELT

1. Olivier Balabanian et al., *Les Etats méditerranéens de la CEE: Espagne, Grèce, Italie, Portugal* (Paris: Masson, 1991), pp. 100–101.
2. Alain Berger et al., *La revanche du Sud* (Paris: Editions L'Harmattan, 1988), p. 55.
3. Commission of the European Communities, *Europe 2000*, p. 15.
4. Josette Alia, "Le trésor de la banane bleu," *Le Nouvel Observateur*, May 18–24, 1989, p. 75.
5. Commission of the European Communities, *Europe 2000*, p. 51.
6. Balabanian, *Les Etats méditerranéens*, p. 110.
7. Henri Pirenne, *Mahomet et Charlemagne*, Paris: Presses Universitaires de France, 1970, Quadrige, 1992.
8. James, *The Franks*, p. 9.
9. Mario Rivosecchi, "Economie et équité," in *Civilisation latine*, ed. Georges Duby (Paris: Olivier Orban, 1986), pp. 255–62.
10. Birth rates and demographic projections in Centre d'Economie et de Finances Internationales (CEFI), *La Méditerranée économique: Premier rapport général sur la situation des riverains au debut des années 90* (Paris: Economica, 1992), pp. 31–32.
11. Ardagh, *A Tale of Five Cities*, p. 287.
12. Tom Burns, "A Fruit and Veg Bonanza," *Financial Times*, Dec. 12, 1991.
13. Paul Betts, "Realising the Reality of a 20-Year Dream," *Financial Times*, Oct. 14, 1991.
14. Georges Benko, *Géographie des technopoles* (Paris: Masson, 1991), p. 174.
15. John Hooper, *The Spaniards: A Portrait of the New Spain* (New York: Viking, 1986; Penguin, 1987), p. 15.
16. Pirenne, *Mahomet et Charlemagne*, p. 120.
17. Fernand Braudel, *The Mediterranean and the Mediterranean World in the Age of Philip II*, vol. 1, trans. Sian Reynolds (French edition, 1949; second revised edition, 1966; London: William Collins Sons, 1972; Fontana: 1975, 1990), p. 118.
18. Gilles Martinet, "Faut-il avoir peur de l'Allemagne," *Le Monde*, Jan. 15, 1992.
19. Henri Regnault, "La Méditerranée dans la division internationale du

travail," in Xavier Gizard, *La Méditerranée inquiète* (Paris: Datar/Editions de l'Aube, 1993), p. 52.

20. Pascale Amaudric, "Peur de l'Allemagne unie? Moi, jamais! (Interview with Alain Minc), *Journal de Dimanche,* July 29, 1990.
21. CEFI, *La Méditerannée économique,* p. 125.
22. Alexander Stille, "Letter from Palermo: The Mafia's Biggest Mistake," *The New Yorker,* Mar. 1, 1993, pp. 60-73.
23. Ibid., p. 61.

CHAPTER FIVE. BALTIC LEAGUE: TRADING PLACES

1. Olof Ruin, "Conflict and Cooperation: Historical Patterns Around the Baltic," *Framtider International,* 1991, p. 8.
2. Olof Ruin, quoted in Alain Debove, "Retrouvailles autour de la Baltique," *Le Monde,* Dec. 17, 1991.
3. As reported in *Der Tagesspiegel* (Berlin), Apr. 13, 1992.
4. As reported in Christian Schmidt-Häuer, "Die Krise im Baltikum: Kälteschock der Freiheit," *Die Zeit,* Feb. 7, 1992.
5. Kristian Gerner, "Overcoming the Past: Towards a New Modus Vivendi in the Baltic," *Framtider International,* 1991, p. 13.
6. Statement in "North European Club: North European Cooperation Within Trade, Business, Science and Art," brochure distributed by North European Club, 1992.
7. As recounted in Michael Englebrecht, "Interview mit Björn Engholm: 'Ich fühle mich in Skandinavien zu Hause,' " *Nordeuropa Forum,* No. 4, 1991, p. 27.
8. Björn Engholm, "Ars Baltica: Towards a New Understanding," *Framtider International,* 1991, p. 5.
9. Speech reprinted in *Report from the Conference of the Baltic Cities,* Gdansk, Sept. 19-20, 1991.
10. Engelbrecht, "Interview mit Björn Engholm," p. 27.
11. Raoul Blanchard and Raymond E. Crist, *A Geography of Europe* (New York: Henry Holt and Co., 1935), p. 213.
12. Gillian Tett, "Kaliningrad Flings Open Its Doors," *Financial Times,* Nov. 26, 1991.
13. Advertising Section, "The Oresund Region: Investment in Northern Europe," *International Herald Tribune,* Apr. 22, 1992.
14. Quoted in Hilary Barnes, "All Dressed Up for the EC," *Financial Times,* Nov. 19, 1991.
15. Yevgeny Yevtushenko, "The City with Three Faces," in *Insight City Guides: St. Petersburg* (Hong Kong: APA Publications, 1992), p. 26.
16. Johannes Salminen, "Viborg: Alexandria of the Baltic," *Framtider International,* 1991, p. 15.

17. *The Need for Renewal of the Transport Infrastructure in the Baltic Sea Region,* Background Report to the Second Parliamentary Conference on Cooperation in the Baltic Sea Area, Oslo, April 22–24, 1992 (Stockholm: The Nordic Council, 1992), p. 1.
18. Pertti Joenniemi and Ole Waever, *Reorganiztion Around the Baltic Rim: Notions on Baltic Sea Politics,* Background Report to the Second Parliamentary Conference on Cooperation in the Baltic Sea Area, Oslo, April 22–24, 1992 (Stockholm: The Nordic Council, 1992), p. 1.
19. Ibid., p. 32.
20. Ibid., p. 34.

CHAPTER SIX. ATLANTIC COAST: EUROPE'S EDGE

1. Claude Lacour, professor at the University of Bordeaux I, is director of l'Institut d'Economie Regionale du Sud-Ouest and a consultant for the French regional planning authority. He has presented his ideas in several forums. See, for example, "Les reseaux du Futur: Villes— Régions," a paper presented at the Fourth Interregional Conference Southern Europe Atlantic in Oporto, Portugal, Jan. 14–15, 1992.
2. Hugh Kearney, *The British Isles: A History of Four Nations* (Cambridge: Cambridge University Press, 1989), p. 59.
3. A. Alvarez, *Offshore: A North Sea Journey* (London: Hodder & Stoughton, 1986; Sceptre Edition, 1987), p. 15.
4. *The Key to Scotland* (Glasgow: Scottish Development Agency, 1992), p. 9.
5. Gordon Donaldson, *A Northern Commonwealth: Scotland and Norway* (Edinburgh: Saltire Society, 1990), p. 13.
6. Michael Middleton, *Cities in Transition: The Regeneration of Britain's Inner Cities* (London: Michael Joseph, 1991), p. 185.
7. Keith Wheatley, "Raising the Stakes for the Games of 2000," *Financial Times,* Aug. 6, 1992.
8. Benko, *Géographie des Technopoles,* p. 113.
9. Michael Cassell, "United Kingdom: Question Mark Over Popularity," *Financial Times,* Oct. 21, 1992.
10. John Osmond, *The Divided Kingdom* (London: Constable [A Channel Four Book], 1988), p. 168.
11. Ibid., pp. 181–83.
12. Company endorsement quoted in *Scotland: Europe's Centre of Electronics Excellence* (Glasgow: Locate in Scotland, 1991), p. 3.
13. Quoted in Jean-Pierre Péroncel-Hugoz, "Bordeaux, sang chaud, tête froide," *Le Monde,* Apr. 25, 1992.
14. Alexis Lichine, *Lichine's Encyclopedia of Wines and Spirits* (London: Cassell, 1967; fourth edition, revised and updated, 1979), p. 372.

15. Commission Arc Atlantique, *Europe to the Fore* (Nantes, 1991), p. 3.
16. Hooper, *The Spaniards,* p. 246.
17. Gordon Neil Minshull, *The New Europe: Into the 1990s* (London: Hodder & Stoughton, 1978; fourth edition, 1990), p. 294.
18. Jacques Beauchard, "Introduction Repères," in Jacques Beauchard, ed., *Destins atlantiques: Entre mémoire et mobilité* (Paris: Datar/ Editions de l'Aube, 1993), p. 15.
19. Loeiz Laurent, "De nouvelles organisations territoriales," in Beauchard, *Destins atlantiques,* p. 175.

CHAPTER SEVEN. MITTELEUROPA: EUROPE'S HEARTLAND

1. Heleno Sana, *Das vierte Reich: Deutschlands später Sieg* (Hamburg: Rasch and Röhring Verlag, 1990), p. 108.
2. Pierre Béhar, *Du Ier au IVe Reich: Permanence d'une nation, renaissances d'un Etat* (Paris: Editions Desjonqueres, 1990), p. 163.
3. Described in Hans-Dietrich Schultz, "Deutschlands 'natürliche' Grenzen," in Alexander Demandt, ed., *Deutschlands Grenzen in der Geschichte* (Munich: Verlag C.H. Beck, 1990), pp. 33–89.
4. Karl Schlögel, *Die Mitte liegt ostwärts: Die Deutschen, der verlorene Osten und Mitteleuropa* (Berlin: Siedler, 1986), pp. 16–17.
5. Ibid., pp. 96–97.
6. As described in Schulze, *Die Wiederkehr Europas,* p. 22.
7. Ibid., pp. 22–23.
8. Alain Minc, *La Grande Illusion* (Paris: Bernard Grasset, 1989), p. 48.
9. Blanchard and Crist, *A Geography of Europe,* p. 216.
10. Pierre Béhar, *Une géopolitique pour l'Europe* (Paris: Editions Desjonqueres, 1992), p. 33.
11. Sana, *Das vierte Reich,* p. 109.
12. Cited in Sana, *Das vierte Reich,* p. 110. (Source given in note, p. 282: Victor Hugo, "Le Rhin. Lettres a un ami," in *Oeuvres politiques completes. Oeuvres diverses,* Paris, 1964, p. 862.)
13. Michael M. White, *Opportunity in Crisis: Money and Power in World Politics, 1986–88* (London: Firethorn Press, 1985), p. 3.
14. Ibid., p. 235.
15. Ibid., p. 306.
16. Minshull, *The New Europe,* p. 191.
17. Christopher Parkes, "Dying Heart Still Beats," *Financial Times,* Dec. 6, 1991.
18. Ibid.
19. Norman J.G. Pounds, *An Historical Geography of Europe* (Cambridge: Cambridge University Press, 1990), p. 129.

20. Frédéric Bobin, "La foi européenne de Sélestat," *Le Monde,* June 9, 1992.

21. Quoted in David Marsh, " 'For Us There Is No France, No Germany,' " *Financial Times,* Dec. 7, 1991.

22. Franco Cardini, *Europe 1492: Portrait of a Continent Five Hundred Years Ago* (New York-Oxford: Facts on File, 1989), p. 18.

23. Michel Albert, *Capitalisme contre capitalisme* (Paris: Editions du Seuil, 1991).

24. Ibid., p. 137. Lester C. Thurow describes the distinction in similar terms in *Head to Head: The Coming Economic Battle Among Japan, Europe and America* (New York: William and Morrow, 1992; London: Nicholas Brealey Publishing, 1993), p. 32. Thurow attributes the distinction between the two types of capitalism to George C. Lodge in *Perestroika for America* (Boston: Harvard University Business Press, 1991).

25. Quoted in Stefan Engel, *Europa auf dem Weg zur Supermacht: Im grossdeutschen Fadenkreuz* (Essen: Neuer Weg Verlag, 1990), p. 54.

26. Quoted in E.S. Browning, "Neighborly Ways: Businesses in France Begin to Seek Lessons from Across the Rhine," *The Wall Street Journal Europe,* July 23, 1991.

27. Roger Brunet et al., *Vers des réseaux transeuropéens* (Montpellier: GIP Reclus, 1991), p. 10.

28. Béhar, *Du Ier au IVe Reich,* p. 163.

29. Kurt Biedenkopf, "Westeuropa-Osteuropa: Haben wir eine gemeinsame Zukunft?", *TU Berlin intern,* June 1992, p. 9.

30. " 'Das Glas ist halbvoll': Interview mit Kurt Biedenkopf," *Capital,* June 1993, p. 187.

31. Franz Rudolf Brüggemann, quoted in Catherine Monroy, "Le complexe allemand de la Tchécoslovaquie," *Le Monde,* Mar. 29–30, 1992.

32. Alexander Loesch, "Angst vor dem mächtigen deutschen Nachbarn nimmt zu," *Der Tagesspiegel* (Berlin), Dec. 17, 1991.

33. Quoted in Edith Heller, "Keine Furcht vor deutschen Divisionen, doch Angst vor der DM," *Der Tagesspiegel* (Berlin), Jan. 25, 1992.

34. Quoted in Edith Heller, "Zu deutschfreundlich: Misstrauen gegen Kattowitzer Regionalismus," *Der Tagesspiegel* (Berlin), Nov. 14, 1992.

35. Golo Mann, *The History of Germany Since 1789,* trans. Marian Jackson (London: Chatto and Windus, 1968; Penguin, 1974, 1988), p. 129.

36. Ibid., pp. 129–30.

37. Sana, *Das vierte Reich,* p. 273.

CHAPTER EIGHT. THE SPECIAL DISTRICTS: MONEY AND POWER

1. Mark Girouard, *Cities and People: A Social and Architectural History* (New Haven and London: Yale University Press, 1985), p. 171.

2. Jean-Pierre Faye, "Le grand dessein d'Henri IV," *Le Monde,* Sept. 19, 1992.
3. Jane Kramer, "Letter from Europe," *The New Yorker,* July 29, 1991, p. 72.
4. Luigi Barzini, *The Europeans* (New York: Simon and Schuster, 1983; London: Penguin, 1984), p. 117.
5. Philip Crawford, "Paris Downturn Tied to Prolonged Boom," *International Herald Tribune,* Nov. 2-3, 1991.
6. James, *The Franks,* pp. 83, 88.
7. See map in Commission of the European Communities, *Europe 2000,* p. 23.
8. Axel Krause, *Inside the New Europe* (New York: HarperCollins Publishers [Cornelia & Michael Bessie Books], 1991). See Chapter One, pp. 1-33.
9. Paul Kennedy, *The Rise and Fall of the Great Powers* (New York: Random House, 1987; Vintage Books, 1989), p. 79.
10. Quoted in Hamish McRae and Frances Cairncross, *Capital City: London as a Financial Centre* (revised edition, London: Methuen, 1991), p. 7.
11. Ibid., p. 1.
12. Jimmy Burns, "Man with a plan tries to make sense of London," *Financial Times,* June 5-6, 1993.

CHAPTER NINE. ALPINE ARC: THE MICROCLIMATE

1. Bruce Marshall, ed., *The Real World: Understanding the Modern World Through the New Geography* (Boston: Houghton Mifflin, 1991).
2. Ibid., p. 9.
3. D.H. Lawrence, *Twilight in Italy* (London: Duckworth, 1916; Penguin, 1977), pp. 134-36.
4. Albert, *Capitalisme contre capitalisme,* p. 101.
5. Ibid., p. 102.
6. Jean-Paul Laurencin, *L'Europe, l'avenir de Rhone-Alpes* (Grenoble: Presses Universitaires de Grenoble, 1992), p. 36.
7. Jane Kramer, "Letter from Europe," *The New Yorker,* Sept. 21, 1992, p. 110.
8. Ibid., p. 122.
9. Jean Ziegler, *La Suisse lave plus blanc* (Paris: Editions du Seuil, 1990), p. 13.
10. Ibid., p. 180.
11. Ibid., p. 167.
12. Quoted in Maya Jurt, "Hätschelkinder der Nation," *Bilanz,* March 1993, p. 29.

CHAPTER TEN. DANUBE BASIN: THE EMPIRE STRIKES BACK

1. Bill Bryson, "Main-Danube Canal Links Europe's Waterways," *National Geographic,* August 1992, p. 31.
2. Pierre Béhar, *L'Autriche-Hongrie, idée d'avenir: Permanences géopolitques de l'Europe centrale et balkanique* (Paris: Editions Desjonqueres, 1991), p. 173. See also the author's *Du Ier au IVeme Reich* and *Une géopolitique pour l'Europe.*
3. Quoted in Robin Okey, *Eastern Europe, 1740-1985: Feudalism to Communism* (London: HarperCollins Academic, 1982; second edition, 1986), pp. 113-14.
4. Ibid., pp. 121-22.
5. Claudio Magris, *Danube: A Sentimental Journey from the Source to the Black Sea,* trans. Patrick Creagh (London: Collins Harville, 1989, 1990), pp. 80-81.
6. Dietmar Steiner, "Das Grossstadtmuseum am Rande des Balkans," *Frankfurter Allgemeine Zeitung,* Sept. 1, 1992.
7. André Sellier et Jean Sellier, *Atlas des peuples d'Europe centrale* (Paris: Editions La Découverte, 1991), p. 132.
8. Deputy Prime Minister Ilko Eskenazy, quoted in Klaus W. Bender, "Sofia über die Haltung von EG und Efta ernüchtert," *Frankfurter Allgemeine Zeitung,* Oct. 29, 1992.
9. Quoted in Blaine Harden, "Bulgaria's Capitalist Revolution Rolls On, However Slowly," *International Herald Tribune,* Mar. 7-8, 1992.
10. Okey, *Eastern Europe,* p. 11.
11. Magris, *Danube,* p. 279.
12. Ibid.
13. Quoted in Waltraud Baryli, "L'Autriche dopée par l'Est," *Le Monde,* Nov. 24, 1992.

CHAPTER ELEVEN. BALKAN PENINSULA: THE BACKWATER

1. Lewis, *Europe,* p. 178.
2. In "Greece: The Sick Man of Europe," *The Economist,* May 9, 1992.
3. William Pfaff, "Reflections: The Absence of Empire," *The New Yorker,* Aug. 10, 1992, p. 68.
4. Quoted in Virginia Marsh and Theodor Troev, "Balkans War Alarms Bulgaria," *Financial Times,* Nov. 5, 1992.
5. Christopher Cviic, *Remaking the Balkans* (London: Pinter Publishers-The Royal Institute of International Affairs, 1991), pp. 65-66.
6. Dirk Kurbjuweit, "Klinisch tot: Albanien—das ärmste Land in Europa ist am Ende," *Die Zeit,* Jan. 31, 1992, p. 33.
7. Quoted in "Worte der Woche," *Die Zeit,* Nov. 6, 1992, p. 2.
8. Pierre Béhar, *Une géopolitique pour l'Europe,* p. 38.

9. Ahmed Dogan, quoted in Rüdiger Wischenbart, " 'Auch die Osmanen hatten ihr Reich auf den Balkan hin ausgerichtet,' " *Der Tagesspiegel* (Berlin), Aug. 9, 1992.

10. Mark Thompson, *A Paper House: The Ending of Yugoslavia* (New York: Pantheon Books, 1992), p. 326.

11. Ibid., p. 285.

CHAPTER TWELVE. SLAVIC FEDERATION: THE ENDLESS EAST

1. Robin Milner-Gulland and Nikolai Dejevsky, *Atlas of Russia and the Soviet Union* (Oxford: Phaidon Press, 1989), p. 61.

2. Hélène Carrère d'Encausse, *La gloire des nations, ou la fin de l'Empire soviétique* (Paris: Librairie Arthème Fayard, 1990), pp. 312–20.

3. Milner-Gulland, *Atlas of Russia,* p. 16.

4. Quoted in "Interview mit Wolfgang Kartte: Russen brauchen bald eine Perspektive," *Berliner Morgenpost,* Sept. 6, 1992.

5. "Radical Reform for the Soviet Union: A joint study by the IMF, the World Bank, the OECD, and the EBRD," *The OECD Observer,* April/May 1991, p. 11.

6. John Lloyd, "Pressing ahead on the long road to reform," *Financial Times,* May 27, 1993.

7. European Bank for Reconstruction and Development, *Annual Economic Review 1992* (London, 1993), p. 22.

8. Sellier, *Atlas des peuples d'Europe centrale,* p. 67.

9. Karl Schlögel, *Das Wunder von Nishnij, oder Die Rückkehr der Städte* (Frankfurt am Main: Eichborn Verlag, 1991), p. 79.

10. Stephen Engelberg, "Polish Bosses Find Their Best Men Speak Russian," *International Herald Tribune,* Oct. 7, 1991.

11. Jacques Benoist-Méchin, *Ukraine: Le fantome de l'Europe* (Paris, 1939; Editions du Rocher/Valmonde, 1991), p. 72.

12. Ibid., p. 111.

CHAPTER THIRTEEN. SUPERREGIONS OR SUPERPOWER?

1. Quoted in Bertrand Le Gendre, "Un entretien avec Pierre Hassner: 'Nous entrons dans un nouveau Moyen Age,' " *Le Monde,* Oct. 27, 1992.

2. Eric Lionel Jones, *The European Miracle: Environments, Economies and Geopolitics in the History of Europe and Asia* (Cambridge: Cambridge University Press, 1981; second edition, 1987), p. 117.

3. Ibid., p. 125.

4. Ibid., p. 149.

5. Joel Garreau, *The Nine Nations of North America* (Boston: Houghton Mifflin, 1981; New York: Avon, 1982).

6. See Jacques Attali, *Lignes d'Horizon* (Paris: Librairie Arthème Fayard, 1990).

7. See Béhar, *Une géopolitique pour l'Europe.*

8. See Reich, *Work of Nations.*

9. Edward Mortimer, "Wake up, Europe," *Financial Times,* Nov. 18, 1992.

10. William Pfaff, "Europe Awaits Clinton, Who Has Other Problems," *International Herald Tribune,* Nov. 21, 1992.

ACKNOWLEDGMENTS
AND NOTE ON SOURCES

First of all, I'd like to acknowledge my debt to *The Nine Nations of North America* by Joel Garreau. Published in 1981, this book first opened my eyes to superregions. In Europe, superregions are somewhat different from those in North America—greatly determined by geography, they have deep roots in history as well. I'm grateful to Stuart Krichevsky of Sterling Lord Literistic and Rachel Klayman, Matthew Carnicelli, and John Paine at Dutton: Their interest, encouragement, and support enabled a book to emerge from that original idea.

Many people in the cities, regions, universities, companies, and other organizations that I visited were receptive and helpful; they are too numerous to name here, but I want to express my gratitude to them and to the many others who supplied supplementary information by phone, fax, and mail. I'm also grateful to several colleagues and friends who commented on my project and made useful suggestions for research and for refining the superregion borders. My deepest thanks go to my wife, Veronika Hass, who put aside her own work for several months to accompany me on the thousands of miles of travel to all corners of Europe—a rewarding but often strenuous venture. She also contributed much to my research and suggested many improvements in the text.

Webster's New Geographical Dictionary, from Merriam-Webster, was an indispensable reference. I also consulted many contemporary and historical atlases; among the most useful were *The Times Atlas of World History, The Economist Atlas of the New Europe, The Atlas of Russia and the Soviet Union,* and a French publication that proved an invaluable guide to the complex ethnic geography of Central Europe, *Atlas des peuples de l'Europe centrale.*

Most of the statistics came from these sources and the latest compilations available from the EC Statistical Office, as well as some national sources. Magazine articles, conference papers, studies, surveys, and information brochures from numerous sources throughout Europe, many of which are cited in the text, helped shape the outline of the superregions and fill in the content. The reporting of some of the best newspapers in the world—*International Herald Tribune, Financial Times, Frankfurter Allgemeine Zeitung, Le Monde, The Wall Street Journal Europe*—supplied a steady stream of evidence and examples for the changes in Europe described here.

Many of the books cited in the text are not available in English. The "Suggested Reading" includes many of the English titles mentioned, as well as some others that will enable those interested to delve further into the subject matter.

SUGGESTED READING

Joel Garreau's pioneering work, *The Nine Nations of North America* (Boston: Houghton Mifflin, 1981), looks at superregions in North America. David Rieff's two books, *Going to Miami: Exiles, Tourists, and Refugees in the New America* (New York: Little Brown, 1987) and *Los Angeles: Capital of the Third World* (New York: Simon and Schuster, 1991), also break new ground in discussing how the history and geography of a place shape the lives of the people who live there—an objective of this book as well.

For a general discussion of Europe, Flora Lewis's *Europe: A Tapestry of Nations* (New York: Simon and Schuster, 1987; new edition 1992) is one of the most informed and intelligent. Although the author takes a country by country approach, she pays a good deal of attention to history and regional differences. Axel Krause's *Inside the New Europe* (New York: HarperCollins [Cornelia and Michael Bessie Books], 1991) focuses exclusively on the European Community, with many details and anecdotes. William Pfaff's *Barbarian Sentiments: How the American Century Ends* (New York: Hill and Wang, 1989) devotes considerable attention to Europe's role in the world today. Likewise, Michael M. White's *Opportunity in Crisis: Money and Power in World Politics, 1986-88* (London: Firethorn

Press, 1985) discusses Europe in a global context. *The European Miracle: Environments, Economies and Geopolitics in the History of Europe and Asia* by Eric Lionel Jones (Cambridge and New York: Cambridge University Press, 1981; second edition, 1987) takes a long-term historical view of Europe. Lester C. Thurow's *Head to Head: The Coming Economic Battle Among Japan, Europe and America* (New York: William Morrow, 1992) has Europe winning the economic race.

On the development and role of nation-states, I'd suggest *Nations and Nationalism* by Ernest Gellner (Oxford: Basil Blackwell, 1983), *Nations and Nationalism Since 1780: Programme, Myth, Reality* by E. J. Hobsbawm (Cambridge and New York: Cambridge University Press, 1990), and *Geopolitics and Geoculture: Essays on the Changing World-System* by Immanuel Wallerstein (Cambridge and Paris: Cambridge University Press/Editions de la Maison des Sciences de l'Homme, 1991).

For an understanding of economic growth and development in the late twentieth century, I'd recommend *Cities and the Wealth of Nations: Principles of Economic Life* by Jane Jacobs (New York: Random House, 1984), *The Work of Nations: Preparing Ourselves for 21st-Century Capitalism* by Robert B. Reich (New York: Alfred A. Knopf, 1991), and *The End of Laissez-Faire: National Purpose and the Global Economy After the Cold War* by Robert Kuttner (New York: Alfred A. Knopf, 1991).

European history is, of course, a vast field, with many marvelous writers and works. Among those I found most useful for understanding the historical roots of the superregions were *The Franks* by Edward James (Oxford: Basil Blackwell, 1988), *The British Isles: A History of Four Nations* by Hugh Kearney (Cambridge and New York: Cambridge University Press, 1989), *The Habsburg Monarchy, 1809–1918* by A.J.P. Taylor (London: Hamish Hamilton, 1948; Penguin, 1990), and *Eastern Europe, 1740–1985: Feudalism to Communism* by Robin Okey (London: HarperCollins Academic, 1982; second edition, 1986).

There are many good portraits of individual European countries, often written by foreign correspondents. By a curious convention, these usually name the people in the title, rather than the country, so that you can hardly lose by going into a library or bookstore and looking for the nationals you are most interested in (*The French, The Germans, The Italians, The Russians*, and so on). Two recent books that pay particular attention to regional roots and history are *The Spaniards: A Portrait of the New Spain* by John Hooper (New York: Viking, 1986; Penguin, 1987) and *Germany and the Germans* by John Ardagh (London: Hamish Hamilton, 1987; Penguin, 1988).

While a growing number of books in Europe are taking a regional or superregional approach, few of them have made their way into English so far. Among those in English that are cited in the text are *The Divided Kingdom* by John Osmond (London: A Channel Four Book/Constable, 1988), *Capital City: London as a Financial Centre* by Hamish McRae and Frances Cairncross (London: Methuen, 1973; new edition, 1991), *Danube* by Claudio Magris (Milan: Garzanti, 1986; New York: Farrar, Straus and Giroux, 1989), and *Remaking the Balkans* by Christopher Cviic (London: Royal Institute of International Affairs, 1991).

INDEX